Ancient History of India

Ancient History of India

— Manusmṛti Revisited —

Dr Charles J. Naegele, JD, LLM, SJD

D.K. Printworld (P) Ltd.
Publishers of Indian Traditions

Cataloging in Publication Data — DK
[Courtesy: D.K. Agencies (P) Ltd. <docinfo@dkagencies.com>]

Naegele, Charles J. (Charles Joseph)

Ancient history of India : Manusmṛti revisited / Charles J. Naegele. — Rev. ed.

p. cm.

Includes bibliographical references (p.) and index.

ISBN 13: 9788124605813

1. Manu (Lawgiver). Mānavadharmaśāstra. 2. Hindu law. I. Title.

DDC 294.5926 22

First published by C. Naegele Press, USA in 2009
Revised edition published in India in 2011

ISBN 13: 978-81-246-0581-3 (HB) ISBN 10: 81-246-0581-5

Published and printed by:
D.K. Printworld (P) Ltd.
Regd. Office: 'Srikunj', F-52, Bali Nagar
Ramesh Nagar Metro Station
New Delhi-110 015
Phones: (011) 2545 3975; 2546 6019; *Fax*: (011) 2546 5926
E-mail: indology@dkprintworld.com
Website: www.dkprintworld.com

Introduction

Old Theory: Young Law Code, Limited Influence

THE current legal-historical majority view regarding the Law Code of Manu (*Manusmṛti*) of ancient India is that it was probably formulated by one man (maybe a king, or sage) about 2100 years ago (100 BCE) and its influence remained confined mostly to India and some parts of South-East Asia; this view has not yet been revised, in spite of relatively recent scientific and archaeological research findings that appear to shed light upon a possible rethinking of this view.

New Theory: Old Law Code, Wider Influence

This book explores a new theory that a possible ancient version of the *Manusmṛti* was formulated and revised by more than one person, or many people over several thousands of years, up to 5000 years ago (from about 3000 to 500 BCE) and its influence possibly spread outside of India to Egypt, Mesopotamia and Sumaria. This theory will be examined in the light of the history and archaeology of ancient India, including the relationship of the *Manusmṛti* to the *Ṛgveda*, and the possible relationship to the Indus/Haṛappan Civilisation and its trading partners, as well as other ancient legal codes.

chronology of the Hindus. William Jones wrote that government in India was first established and [illegible] [illegible] [illegible] [illegible]

[illegible]

[illegible] of the *Manusmṛti* [illegible] Müller (1859) [illegible] (1902) [illegible] and [illegible] individually [illegible]

[illegible] the *Manusmṛti* [illegible] different [illegible] the [illegible] "Manu" [illegible] intelligent. "Manu" [illegible] generally [illegible] "the Man *par excellence*" or the representative [illegible] father of the human race. The name "Manu" is also [illegible] being or a mythical progenitor of the [illegible]

[illegible] translation of the *Manusmṛti* [illegible]

[illegible] English Dictionary by Monier-Williams

Acknowledgement

THE author first became fascinated with India in 1970, at his undergraduate *alma mater*, the University of California, Berkeley, and wishes to thank all those friends that he has met in the US and in India that have influenced his life and this book.

Next, the author wishes to thank all of his family, friends and professional colleagues who gave support and encouragement towards the research and completion of this work.

Special thanks in the United States go to Golden Gate University, San Francisco, Professor Sompong Sucharikul and Professor Chris N. Okeke, in addition to the helpful students and staff. The University of California, Berkeley library was invaluable in providing unparalleled research assistance.

In India, special thanks go to the National Museum in New Delhi (deemed University), D.P. Sharma, the Archaeological Survey of India (ASI), R.S. Bisht and B.B. Lal.

Contents

1

Overview

1.1 Law Code of Manu (Manusmṛti) "Discovered" in late 1700s / William Jones

WESTERNERS "discovered" the Law Code of Manu (*Manusmṛti*) at approximately the same time as the United States was adopting its Constitution, in the late 1700s, through the publication of the first English translation by a British judge in India, William Jones.[1]

In order to make the administration of justice more efficient in India, William Jones, who was already fluent in Latin, Greek and Persian, learned the ancient Indian language of Sanskrit. Jones supervised the collection of all the existing laws of India and their translation into English. He found that the oldest law composition in India was the Law Code of Manu (*Manusmṛti* or *Mānava-Dharmaśāstra*). He also found that there existed different versions, written and oral (mostly in blank verse) of this body of law, including mistranslations of a "law-digest" in the Persian language. Even though learned men of the day in India told him that the *Manusmṛti* was many thousands of years old, he believed that it could not be much more than about 3000 years old.[2] He translated the *Manusmṛti* and upon publication, said that it was 3200 years old (he assigned a date of 1500 BCE to the translation). In another essay, "On the

1. See William Jones, *The Works of Sir William Jones* (*The Institutes of Hindu Law or The Ordinances of Manu*), G.G. and J. Robinson, 1794.
2. See Garland Cannon, ed., *The Letters of Sir William Jones*, vol. II, 794-800, 821, Oxford, 1970.

Chronology of the Hindus," William Jones wrote that government in India was first established and laws enacted 3,800 years ago[3] (which roughly corresponds to this book's theory regarding the possible contemporaneousness of the *Manusmṛti* and the Indus/Haṛappan Civilisation of 4000 to 5000 years ago).

Other translations of the *Manusmṛti* followed. The ones that will be used in this book are that first translation by William Jones himself (1794), Dutt[4] (1895), Buehler[5] (1896), Jha[6] (1920), Doniger and Smith[7] (1991), and Olivelle[8] (2005).

The word "Manu," as in the *Manusmṛti*, has many different meanings depending on the context. "Manu" can mean "thinking, wise or intelligent." "Manu" can also generally mean man or mankind, or "the Man *par excellence*" or the representative man and father of the human race. The name "Manu" is also used to describe a divine being or a mythical progenitor of the earth.[9]

In the examination of the *Manusmṛti*, a brief mention regarding the sophistication of the Sanskrit language follows.

1.2 Sanskrit-English Dictionary by Monier-Williams

Translations of other Sanskrit works from India were very popular in the West over the next 90 years following the Law

3. See Garland Cannon, *Oriental Jones*, 169, Asia Publishing House, 1964.
4. See M.N. Dutt, *Manusmṛti*, Chaukhamba Sanskrit Pratishthan, 1998.
5. See G. Buehler, *Laws of Manu*, Oxford (Sacred Books of the East, v. XXV), 1896.
6. See Ganganath Jha, *Manusmṛti with the Manubhāṣya of Medhātithi*, Motilal Banarsidass (1st edn. 1920-39; 2nd 1999).
7. See Wendy Doniger and Brian K. Smith, *The Laws of Manu*, Penguin Classics (1991).
8. See Patrick Olivelle, *Manu's Code of Law, A Critical Edition and Translation of the Mānava-Dharmaśāstra*, South Asia Research (2005).
9. See Monier-Williams, *A Sanskrit-English Dictionary*, Oxford (1899).

Code of Manu (*Manusmṛti* or *Mānava-Dharmaśāstra*) translation by William Jones. In the year 1886, the process of translating Sanskrit to English was made easier by the publication by Monier-Williams (a British philologist) of his detailed *Sanskrit to English*[10] and *English to Sanskrit*[11] dictionaries. These are the dictionaries which will be used in this book.[12]

1.3 Sanskrit, the "Mother" of Many Languages

William Jones "discovered" that Sanskrit was similar to many other European languages and he virtually "founded" the field of comparative linguistics. In 1786, in his famous address to the Asiatic Society of Bengal, he said:

> The Sanskrit language, whatever be its antiquity, is a wonderful structure, more perfect than the Greek, more copious than the Latin and more exquisitely refined than either; yet bearing to both of them a stronger affinity, both in roots of verbs, and in the forms of grammar, than could possibly have been produced by accident.[13]

Until its translation into English, the *Manusmṛti* was apparently composed and preserved in the Sanskrit language. Most individuals who study the Sanskrit language in depth consider Sanskrit to be one of the most complex and precise of all human languages yet discovered.

1.4 Transliteration of Sanskrit to English: Harvard-Kyoto Convention

Although the author can read the "Devanāgarī" script of modern Hindi and Sanskrit, he has written the American version of this

---

10. See Monier-Williams, *A Sanskrit-English Dictionary*, Oxford (1899).
11. See Ibid.
12. Some of the analysis that follows will include Sanskrit words, their translations and definitions, in order to gain greater insight into the words used in the *Manusmṛti* and other works.
13. See Devendra Handa, "Vedic *vis-à-vis* Harappan Culture", in Agrawal (ed.), *In Search of Vedic-Haṛappan Relationship*, Aryan Books International (2005), p. 75.

book with the following "Devanāgarī" script representation, so as to make the correct Sanskrit pronunciation available to "non-Devanāgarī" readers. The transliteration of Sanskrit to English in the American version of this book is based on the Harvard-Kyoto (HK) Convention of representing Sanskrit sounds as follows:

Vowels

	a	A	i	I	u	U
	R	RR	lR	lRR		
	e	ai	o	au	M	H

Consonants:					
Guttural:	k	kh	g	gh	G
Palatal:	c	ch	j	jh	J
Cerebral:	T	Th	D	Dh	N (cerebral capitalised)
Dental:	t	th	d	dh	n (dental not capitalised)
Labial:	p	ph	b	bh	m
Semi-Vowels:	y	r	l	v	
Sibilants:	z	S	s		
Aspirant:	h				

(*Note*: Sanskrit words will appear first in their current common English spelling, followed by the word in parenthesis, underlined, using the above "Harvard-Kyoto" Convention, for those readers who are searching for the correct pronunciation of Sanskrit words used here. For example, take the word, "Sanskrit": the Harvard-Kyoto Convention transliteration is: (*saṁskṛta*), which has the definition: "constructed well or completely formed, perfected.")

1.5 Ṛgveda Translated into English

In the 1800s, after the *Manusmṛti* was discovered by the Westerners, the most ancient work of Indian philosophy and spirituality that pre-dates the *Manusmṛti*, the *Ṛgveda*, was also translated into English.[14] The *Manusmṛti* and the *Ṛgveda*, as well as many other ancient works, gave modern readers much insight into the minds of the people of Ancient India.

1.6 Oral Preservation of Ṛgveda and Manusmṛti

Both the *Ṛgveda* and the *Manusmṛti*[15] appear to have been passed down by oral tradition for thousands of years before being first written down. All philosophical, spiritual and other compositions of ancient India appear not to have been reduced to writing, or such writing was done on paper or wood or some other medium, none of which survived the bugs and heat of

---

14. See Ralph T.H. Griffith, *Hymns of the Ṛgveda* (1889), Munshiram Manoharlal (1999).

15. For the readers who missed the passage on transliteration above, it is repeated here. The transliteration of Sanskrit to English in the American version of this book is based on the Harvard-Kyoto (HK) Convention of representing Sanskrit sounds as follows:

Vowels:

a	A	i	I	u	U
R	RR	lR	lRR		
e	ai	o	au	M	H

Consonants:

Guttural:	k	kh	g	gh	G
Palatal:	c	ch	j	jh	J
Cerebral:	T	Th	D	Dh	N (cerebral capitalised)
Dental:	t	th	d	dh	n (dental not capitalised)
Labial:	p	ph	b	bh	m
Semi-Vowels:	y	r	l	v	
Sibilants:	z	S	s	Aspirant: h	

(*Note*: Sanskrit words will appear first in their current common English spelling, followed by the word in parenthesis, underlined, using the above "Harvard-Kyoto" Convention, for those readers who are searching for the correct pronunciation of Sanskrit words used here. For example, take the word, "Sanskrit": the Harvard-Kyoto Convention transliteration is: (*saṁskṛta*), which has the definition: "constructed well or completely formed, perfected.")

tropical India. If any such writing was done on wood, for example, it probably went the way of wooden boats. Many wooden boats were constructed by the people living in ancient India. None of these wooden boats have survived in India. At least no wooden boats have been as yet excavated by archaeologists studying the remains of the cities and towns of ancient India. The author has seen 5,000 year old boats in Egypt that might fit in this theory.

1.7 Memorisation of Long "Hymns" through Life

Other theories are that the people of ancient India either knew that paper would be lost or that they wanted to control the flow of information for political or religious reasons. Whatever the case may have been, it is clear that a different method of preserving knowledge was discovered or invented. That method was the method of precise memorisation. It required the lifelong dedication of certain individuals to commit long passages of information to memory, which had been rendered into a form that was easier to memorise and recite: a type of "poetry" or "hymn" that was chanted to a particular rhythm or beat.

Such hymns or poems were not only memorised and chanted daily, but also taught to the next generation and thus, preserved. How many generations kept up with this is not known. Even today, with the advent of pencils, pens, paper, typewriters, printing and computers, there are some individuals in India who continue to memorise many of these hymns or poems, especially those hymns from the *R̥gveda*, recite them everyday and teach them to the next generation. This does not appear to be the case with the *Manusmr̥ti*, which probably went through many alterations and additions and survives apparently only by written text and translations, although the author has met Indians who knew *Manusmr̥ti* "reciters" up until the 1980s in India.

These hymns or poems of the *Manusmr̥ti* or *R̥gveda* have not been "dated" in the modern Western conventional sense. Some parts of the *R̥gveda* are especially difficult to understand and it is difficult to determine what is factual and what is not factual. Other parts of Ṛgveda seem beyond current human comprehension, relating apparently, that the world, or world populations, have been created many times, stretching over a period of thousands and thousands of years.

1.8 Aryan "Invasion" Theory Examined for "Time-Line" Purposes

There has been a theory advanced by Westerners for the last 200 plus years, of "foreigners" invading India 3500 years ago (in 1500 BCE) and composing the *Ṛgveda* in their "non-Indian" Sanskrit language 3200 years ago (about 1200 BCE). This theory will be examined to see whether or not it holds weight.

Perhaps in response to the assertion of William Jones that the Sanskrit language was more perfect than Greek, some Western colonialists advanced a theory that the native people of India did not come up with the sophisticated language of Sanskrit and they did not compose the sophisticated *Ṛgveda*, but that all of the above came from a civilisation outside India by people called "Aryans" (perhaps originating in northern Europe) and that the unsophisticated native population of India was forced to submit to these sophisticated, super-intelligent invaders, intermarry and gradually accept the invading army's thoughts, words and philosophy.

In part, the Westerners did not have far to look to find some support for their theories because in the *Ṛgveda* itself, there are many references to battles between different forces, especially "the *Ārya* versus the *Dasyu*" (sometimes referred to as *light* versus *dark*). Although nowadays some scholars are wondering whether or not these battles are references to a never-ending fight between good and evil, and not a battle between real, living, human beings.

The Sanskrit language shows such linguistic sophistication that modern scholars say it must have taken many thousands of years to develop. This "Aryan Invasion Theory" said that almost no other type of sophistication was seen in ancient India prior to the coming of Alexander the Great with his army 2300 years ago (about 326 BCE). Now, in the light of scientific discoveries over the last century, most scholars are asking the question whether the Aryan Invasion Theory is a myth.

1.9 Is "Aryan Invasion Theory" a Myth?

It is difficult now for many scholars to believe that mighty warriors who had travelled for thousands of miles and conquered India would suddenly turn their swords into ploughshares and switch from war to spirituality. It is difficult for those same scholars to believe that these supposedly "linguistically-super-sophisticated warriors" would never mention in their compositions such as the *Ṛgveda* where they came from prior to their sudden invasion of India. And also there is no mention of how quickly and easily they developed the complicated and sophisticated Sanskrit language, especially since it has not "survived" outside of India. Also there is no mention as to how the foreigners convinced the native population to quickly give up their native language, learn the complicated Sanskrit language and recruit large numbers of unsophisticated native people to become educated and sophisticated and dedicate their lives to learning, memorising, reciting and teaching this new and difficult "foreign" Sanskrit language.

The invaders, according to this theory, were called Aryan and their native enemies *Dāsa* or *Dasyu*. *Ṛgveda* had some references to "Aryan" being light or white and *Dāsa* or *Dasyu* being dark. This worked well for those Westerners seeking to economically profit from India, who reasoned that if the enemies of the Aryans were "dark" or "dark skinned," that could naturally refer to the majority of the native population of India, most of whom had a darker colour of skin than Westerners. Some Westerners who wanted an economic advantage in India claimed to be more directly related to the "sophisticated Aryan invaders".

But sometimes the Ṛgvedic references to some battles between Aryan and *Dāsa* were confusing. For instance, the enemies of the Vedic king, Sudās, were described in the *Ṛgveda* as being both Aryans and *Dāsa*s. Additionally, *Dāsa*s were sometimes described as dark-skinned.

1.10 Does "Arya" mean "White-Skin" or "Clean Soul"?

Some scholars are now questioning whether the *Ṛgveda* really referred to skin colour, that is, did the *Dāsa*s or *Dasyu* have dark skin and the Arya light or white skin, or was the *Ṛgveda* speaking of a symbolic battle between light and dark; good and bad?[16]

The word, Arya is defined by Monier-Williams in his *Sanskrit to English Dictionary* as: a respectable or honourable or faithful man, an inhabitant of Āryāvartta; one who is faithful to the religion of his country; Name of the race which immigrated from Central Asia into Āryāvartta; opposed to (an-Arya), (*dasyu*), (*dāsa*), . . . a man highly esteemed, a respectable, honourable man . . . a master, an owner; a friend . . . of a good family; excellent; wise . . . [see Old German (era); Mod(ern) Germ(an) (Ehre); Irish (Erin)].[17] It seems that even Monier-Williams, as a writer of a dictionary, had to document the "politically-correct" theory of his day (the "Aryan Migration" theory).

The *Sanskrit-English Dictionary* of Monier-Williams is excellent in providing a root definition of each Sanskrit letter, since each Sanskrit letter actually is a root sound that makes up simple words and the roots of more complicated words. In the case of the Sanskrit word "Arya," it apparently comes from the following Sanskrit letters (note that there are two possibilities for spellings using one of two different "R" sounds):

16. See K.D. Sethna, *The Problem of Aryan Origins*, S&S Publishers, 1980, p. 104.

17. See Monier-Williams, *A Sanskrit-English Dictionary*, Oxford, 1899.

A--a . . . prefix of verbs, near, near to, towards

R-- . . . in heaven, to go, move, rise, tend upwards (or)

ra-- . . . acquiring . . . giving . . . fire, heat, love, brightness, splendour

ya-- . . . joining, restraining . . . attaining

Putting all this together, the roots seem to indicate: "one who is near towards acquiring and joining splendour or is rising upwards to attain heaven," which, one might suppose, could mean some type of special or "heaven-oriented" people, but it is difficult to see how those root letters could add up to mean white foreign warriors.

The additional evidence of lack of an Aryan invasion includes some of the following observations. The composers of *Ṛgveda*, sometimes called "poets" or "hymn makers" (since the *Ṛgveda* is primarily "sung" or "chanted" daily still throughout some parts of India) often referred to themselves as "Aryan." The Westerners translated the word "Aryan" as being "white-skinned," even though there is no firm basis for such a translation, and in part due to the fact the enemies of the Aryans were sometimes described as "dark" in *Ṛgveda*. As described above, the names of the "dark" enemies of the "Aryans" were *Dāsa*s or *Dasyu*s.

After Second World War, Western scholars began to give more credibility to scholars from India, like Sri Aurobindo, who believed that *Dāsa*s were not human beings at all, but "dark" spirits *versus* spirits of light; even (the British scholars) MacDonnell and Keith said that the word *dasyu* is clearly applied to "superhuman enemies" and that the word *dāsa* sometimes denotes enemies of a demoniac character in the *Ṛgveda*.[18] In *Ṛgveda*, the god of fire, "Agni," is often portrayed as the Bringer of Light, one who killed the *Dasyu*s, the dark (spirits).[19] *Ṛgveda*,

18. See K.D. Sethna, *The Problem of Aryan Origins*, S&S Publishers, 1980, p. 104.

19. Ibid., p. 109.

book V, chapter 14, verse 4, says: "Agni (the god of fire) shone bright when born, with light killing the *Dasyus* and the dark."[20]

Max Müller, the German-born scholar, who was a professor in England and one of the translators of the *Ṛgveda* into English, suggested in 1881 that the term "Arya" may have evolved from the term "*irā*," earth; in historical times it was regularly used in the sense that "sir" is used in English.[21] For example, one character from the *Ṛgveda*, Trasadasyu, was dark skinned (*śyāva*), even though he was an Aryan.[22] Monier-Williams also defines the word used in the *Ṛgveda*, *śyāva*, to be "brown, dark-coloured, dark."[23]

In *Ṛgveda* I.96.3, the term *aria* is used, not *arya*, it is *viza Arīrāhutam*, even though it is translated in English as "Aryan": "Praise him, ye Aryan folk"; the correct word should be *aindra*, which means "belonging to or sacred to Indra (the Vedic god), coming or proceeding from Indra."[24] Monier-Williams defines *ari* as "attached to faithful; a faithful or devoted or pious man" and *arī* as "to pour, let drop, to trickle or flow upon; to flow over." This seems very different from "light-skinned" or "white-skinned" invaders called Aryans.

Some scholars who have studied the word "Aryan" have come to the conclusion that it might mean "those speaking the same language" and does not necessarily mean those that belong to the same racial or ethnic stock; many scholars now believe that the word "Aryan" might refer to a Proto-Indo-European language rather than a single race.[25] This seems to be more in

---

20. See Griffith, Ralph, *Hymns of the Ṛgveda* (1889).
21. See Bhagwan Singh, *The Vedic Harappans*, Aditya Prakashan, 1996, pp. 27-29.
22. See M.K. Dhavalikar, *The Aryans: Myth and Archaeology*, Munshiram Manoharlal, 2007, p. 46.
23. See Monier-Williams, *A Sanskrit-English Dictionary*, Oxford, 1899.
24. See Malati Shendge, *The Aryas: Facts Without Fancy and Fiction*, Abhinav Publications, 1996, p. 26.
25. See R.S. Sharma, *Looking for the Aryans*, Orient Longman, 1995, p. 1.

conformity with the findings. Those scholars further believe that the division between "Arya" and *Dasyu* is a mythological one, a spiritual one or a linguistic one. In any case, there is no direct evidence of a recorded Aryan invasion of India. This "Aryan Invasion Theory" is not recorded in any written document and cannot be traced archaeologically.[26]

1.11 How Can "Warrior Aryans" be "Peace-Loving Spiritualists"?

There are also possible new arguments that can be made from an examination of the text of the *Manusmṛti* regarding the duties of the Aryans. The new arguments also do not support the idea of an Aryan invasion. These so-called "Aryans," at least the ones referred to in the Law Code of Manu, seem to be non-material, extremely spiritually-oriented individuals. They do not sound like the fierce foreign fighters.

To quote the *Manusmṛti*, chapter 2, verse 108:

> Let an Aryan who has been initiated, (daily) offer fuel in the sacred fire, beg food, sleep on the ground and do what is beneficial to his teacher, until (he performs the ceremony of) *samāvartana* (on returning home).

Manusmṛti, chapter 2, verse 165:

> An Aryan must study the whole Veda together with the *rahasyas*, performing at the same time various kinds of austerities and the vows prescribed by the rules (of the Veda).[27]

1.12 "Aryan Invasion" Countered by "Discovery" of Cities of Mohenjo-Dāṛo and Haṛappā in 1920s

In the 1920s, two extremely old archaeological sites were "discovered" (i.e. "recognised" by the British and published in

26. Ibid.

27. See G. Buehler, *Laws of Manu*, Oxford (Sacred Books of the East, v. XXV), 1896.

England) and excavated near the Indus River in the then north-west India (today Pakistan), the ancient cities of Moheñjo-Dāṛo and Haṛappā. The civilisation was called the Indus or Haṛappan Civilisation or Indus/Haṛappan Civilisation and was dated to about 4,500 years ago (2500 BCE). More recently, modern scientists have "carbon-14" dated Indus/Haṛappan Civilisation artefacts to more than 5,000 years ago (3000 BCE).

At first this was a setback for the proponents of the Aryan Invasion Theory. It could no longer be claimed that the native population of India was unsophisticated 4,500 years ago. Here was conclusive proof of sophisticated and carefully planned cities with streets and roads that ran according to cardinal directions, (north-south and east-west), with bathrooms in every house and the most sophisticated waterways and drainage system in the then-known world. Such advanced drainage systems did not come again for another 2,000 years until the time of Roman engineers and urban planners.

After the cities of Moheñjo-Dāṛo and Haṛappā were "discovered," the theory of Aryan invasion was changed to say that these cities were constructed by some other prior invaders who magically built the cities, lived in them for hundreds of years and then either left or were defeated by outsiders.

Now, after careful study for almost 100 years, there appears to be no clear evidence of the Aryan invasion or any other such invasion. Probably the Indus/Haṛappan Civilisation died out from overuse of the land, earthquakes which dried up the large river next to the Indus River, the river Sarasvatī, and a drop in foreign trade.[28]

1.13 Satellite Photos of 1970 Show "River Sarasvatī" Dried up in 1900 BCE

Two things happened in the 1970s that completely changed

28. See B.B. Lal, in Agrawal (editor), *In Search of Vedic-Harappan Relationship*, Aryan Books International (2005), p. 3.

modern analysis of the history of India. First, space satellite pictures were taken of the earth (including India), which showed the dried-up path of an ancient river, matching a river described in *Ṛgveda*, the river Sarasvatī, which flowed, according to *Ṛgveda*, from the "mountains to the sea." This river, possibly the river Sarasvatī, was completely dried up about 3,900 years ago (by about 1900 BCE), apparently due to earthquakes. Many scholars now believe that this dried-up river was the river Sarasvatī and was structurally controlled by en échelon faults; for this reason, they say, even relatively minor tectonic movements caused big changes in the configuration of the palaeo-channels.[29]

Prior to the excavations of the 1920s of the ancient cities of Moheṅjo-Dāṛo and Haṛappā, most Western scholars believed that India had no civilisation prior to 2,300 years ago (326 BCE) when Alexander (the Great) invaded India.[30] However, after that discovery and those excavations, the theory of "no-prior-civilisation" had to change.

1.14 Mehrgaṛh Discovered in 1974

The discovery in 1974 and excavation of the even-more-ancient city of Mehrgaṛh made this change even more pronounced. Archaeologists discovered the city of Mehrgaṛh, which was located not too far from the city of Moheṅjo-Dāṛo in the ancient Indian Indus/Haṛappan Civilisation area (in present-day Pakistan), and dated Mehrgaṛh to about 7000 BCE (about 9000 years before present). The discovery of Mehrgaṛh changed the idea of what type of ancient civilisations existed in the Indian subcontinent. Mehrgaṛh was now seriously competing for the title, "Cradle of civilisation."

1.15 World's First "Dental Drilling" in Mehrgaṛh Discovered in 2001

Within the past ten years, in 2001, evidence of the world's first

29. See B.B. Lal, *The Sarasvatī Flows On*, Aryan, 2002, p. 14.

30. Ibid., p. 25.

dental drilling of tooth decay (with hand drills) (approximately 7,000 to 9,000 years ago) has been found in Mehrgaṛh.[31] Also remains indicating the first use of cotton fibre (sixth millennium BCE) were found.[32] In addition to farming, as will be discussed below, Mehrgaṛh was found to have artefacts that were sophisticated and there is ample evidence of long-distance trading.

1.16 Civilisation Prior to Drying up of River Sarasvatī 3,900 Years Ago

Prior to the discovery and excavation of Mehrgaṛh in 1974 and prior to the picture from space of the path of what many scholars believe to be the dried-up river Sarasvatī in 1970, the proponents of the Aryan Invasion Theory did not know what to do with references to the sister-river of the Indus River, the river Sarasvatī, sometimes spelled "Saraswatī." Since the *R̥gveda* refers to the Sarasvatī River as a "great and mighty river" in the present tense (not in the past), and the Law Code of Manu refers to the Sarasvatī River also as a large river boundary in the present tense (not in the past), this would seem to indicate that the composers of both the *R̥gveda* and the *Manusmr̥ti* experienced the river Sarasvatī as is described in *R̥gveda*, that "flowed from the mountains to the sea." If this dried-up river bed is indeed the river Sarasvatī, then this seems to indicate that both the *R̥gveda* and the Law Code of Manu were composed before the Sarasvatī River dried up 3,900 years ago (in 1900 BCE). The idea that the *Manusmr̥ti* was composed prior to 3,900 years ago (in 1900 BCE) would support the theory that it is one of the oldest law codes in the world.

---

31. See A. Coppa et al., *Early Neolithic Tradition of Dentistry, Nature*, pp. 775-756, 2006.

32. See Moulherat, Tengberg, Haquet, Mille, *Journal of Archaeological Science*, "First Evidence of Cotton at Neolithic Mehrgaṛh, Pakistan"; Analysis of Mineralised Fibres from a Copper Bead, pp. 1393-1401, 2002.

Additionally, the term "cradle of civilisation" in Western scholarly circles, has come to mean the first location and time in human history when nomadic hunter-gatherers switched to farming and produced sufficient crops to allow some members of the society to work on developing a culture, a civilisation. Historians and archaeologists conjecture that the hunter-gatherers noticed wild grains growing without human help, usually on the fertile land of a large river that regularly overflowed, depositing a soil rich in nutrients for wild grains, near the river. The seeds of wild grains were deposited on this rich and fertile soil by birds picking up the seeds in their beaks, flying to the fertile ground and dropping the seeds to be planted without human intervention to grow "naturally." The wind also performed this task, thus enabling the wild grains to sprout in the fertile land and grow. At several places throughout the world, at different times, the switch to farming came next, when people gradually stopped hunting-gathering and started picking the wild grains and planting them in the fertile soil. After some period of time, whether hundreds or thousands of years, there was sufficient excess food crops to allow some of the members of the farming community to turn their attention to other pursuits, such as trading excess food crops of one kind or variety for another from another farming community located at increasingly far distances from the original farming community. This was followed by the development of towns and cities, the division of labour, the beginning of simple technology and the beginning of "civilisation."

1.17 River Sarasvatī "Fertile Crescent"

The phrase "fertile crescent" is the name given by some Western researchers to the crescent-moon-shaped area in the Middle East that incorporated ancient Mesopotamia (much in modern-day Iraq), the Levant, and, in some cases, ancient Egypt. However, there existed other large rivers in the world that regularly had overflowed and had a type of crescent shape, so one could say that more than one "fertile crescent" or evidence of a "past fertile crescent" has been found. These were the sites of ancient farming communities, some of which later became towns, cities and later civilisations, in China and India, perhaps simultaneously with the "cradle of civilisation" in the Middle East. The fertile crescent that is of interest to us in this book is the one prior to 3,900 years ago (pre-1900 BCE) surrounding the river Sarasvatī in north-west India that has been found to have been home to many cities and towns of the Indus/Haṛappan Civilisation. The river called "Sarasvatī" in India can also be used as a kind of historical marker. As described above, the river was mentioned many times in the most ancient compositions from India, the *Ṛgveda*. It was also mentioned in the *Manusmṛti*. In the *Ṛgveda*, the river Sarasvatī is often mentioned as being a "mighty and wide river" that flows from the "mountains to the ocean."

In the seventh chapter or seventh *maṇḍala* (since chapters are called *maṇḍala*s or "circles"), of *Ṛgveda*, hymn 95, verses 1 and 2, the river Sarasvatī is spoken of as "surpassing . . . all other waters . . . pure in her course from mountains to the ocean. . . ."[33]

1.18 India International Trade more than 4000 Years Ago Gives Clues

Archaeological evidence points to the fact that international trade and investment began in India more than 4,000 years ago and yields clues relating to the age of *Ṛgveda* and the *Manusmṛti*. Foreign objects from the Indus/Haṛappan Civilisation have been found in Bahrain, Egypt and Iraq. The latest archaeological research shows the city referred to above, Mehrgaṛh, which was in existence 9,000 years ago (from at least 7000 BCE) and which shows evidence of being a large city of about 30,000 persons.

---

33. (1) This stream of Sarasvatī with fostering current comes forth, our sure defence, our fort of iron. As on a car, the flood flows on, surpassing in majesty and might all other waters.

(2) Pure in her course from mountains to the ocean, alone of streams Sarasvatī hath listened.

Foreign objects have been found in Mehrgaṛh that are dated prior to the Indus/Haṛappan Civilisation of 4,300–3,200 years ago. There exist ceramic similarities (clay pots and other vessels) in Mehrgaṛh and the Indus/Haṛappan Civilisation with southern Turkmenistan and northern Iran, which suggest considerable mobility and trade. There are other indications that the river Sarasvatī mentioned in the *Ṛgveda* and the *Manusmṛti* was an often-used transportation route for shipping Indus/Haṛappan Civilisation goods internationally to Egypt and Mesopotamia.

Archaeologists have found the remains of stone anchors from shipwrecks that relate to ancient India (Indus/Haṛappan Civilisation) in the Gulf States, such as in Bahrain. One type of stone-anchor is the "ring-stone" anchor, which is a large stone shaped like a doughnut. These anchors have also been found off the coast of India and in the twin cities ("discovered" in 1920) Haṛappā and Moheṅjo-Dāṛo.[34]

Ancient India (Indus/Haṛappan Civilisation) was famous for its boats and international trade. One boat was called the *dhow*. The *dhow* was a popular boat of ancient India. The *dhow* was originally built in India, with the wood used for the making of the boat cultivated and grown in India. Later on, some of the wood grown in India was exported to Mesopotamia and Egypt and the boats were made there. The *dhow* was actually a "sewn boat," that is, the planks of wood were actually sewn or lashed together, not nailed, even though nails were available at that time. After the river Sarasvatī dried up 3,900 years ago (in 1900 BCE), international trade originating in India also fell off for more than 1,500 years. The *dhow* then became associated with Arab traders, and continued to be used for many centuries after that. Procopius, a Greek historian writing somewhat later, in the sixth century CE, recorded that ships used in the Indian seas were not

34. See Himanshu Prabha Ray, *The Archaeology of Seafaring in Ancient South Asia*, pp. 80-81, Cambridge University Press, 2003.

covered with pitch or any substance, and the planks were fastened together, not with nails but with cords. Sewn boats seem totally unusual to us in our modern times with steel ships and their ultra-modern engines. That is also true when we compare sewn boats with jet airplanes. It is amazing to think about how ancient sailors and merchants transported themselves and their goods.

1.19 "Weights and Measures" from Indus/ Haṛappan Civilisation Give Clues

Other indications of international trade by ancient India (Indus/ Haṛappan Civilisation) involve "weights and measures" which yield clues relating to the age of *Ṛgveda* and the *Manusmṛti*. Weights and measures of ancient India (Indus/Haṛappan Civilisation) were clearly either derived from other parts of the then-known world or given to other parts of the then-known world and were a direct product of international trade of India. Two different sets of weights have been found at some Indus/Haṛappan Civilisation sites, one set for trade within the Indus/Haṛappan Civilisation and one set for international trade, outside the Indus/Haṛappan Civilisation. These differences will be described more fully below. Some of the weights and measures that were preserved for posterity in the text of the *Manusmṛti* will also be examined below. It appears that the weights described in the *Manusmṛti* were very similar to the weights from the Indus/ Haṛappan Civilisation.

Historians believe that the now dried-up river Sarasvatī ran into the sea in the southern part of the Indus/Haṛappan Civilisation, in the current Indian state of Gujarat.

One of the ancient places, an important port city of the Indus/Haṛappan Civilisation called Lothal was found in Gujarat. The author has the opportunity of personally visiting Lothal and verifying the archaeological findings. Lothal is located several hours' drive south of the modern city of Ahmedabad. In addition to the site itself, Lothal has a good museum. In the museum in Lothal, there are Indus/Haṛappan Civilisation stone cubes of standard weights. Lothal was one of the Indus/Haṛappan Civilisation sites that had another series of weights conforming to the heavy Assyrian standard for international trade. This appears to be clear evidence that the ancient Indus/Haṛappan Civilisation conducted trade of an international nature. William Jones was of the opinion that the Hindus must have been navigators (international shippers at sea) in the age of the composition of the *Manusmṛti*, because the *Manusmṛti* mentions bottomry (the lending of money for marine insurance).

1.20 "Aryan Invasion Theory": No Findings in Support in Indus/Haṛappan Civilisation

The Aryan Invasion Theory continues on the path of being disproved, especially since the time that the two important archaeological sites of Mohenjo-Dāṛo and Haṛappā were "discovered" in north-west India (now Pakistan) and serious archaeological excavations were begun. It is also of interest to note that even though those sites had been "found" by other Western explorers previously, it was less than 100 years ago, in the 1920s when the first real excavations were begun. When Alexander (the Great) invaded India 2,300 years ago (in 326 BCE), he took along historians who documented his campaigns in writing. Since those particular writings were the writings that most Western scholars relied upon, it is of no surprise that most Western scholars believed that India had no civilisation prior to the campaign of Alexander.[35]

After the beginning of the discovery of the two sites of Mohenjo-Dāṛo and Haṛappā and the excavations of the 1920s, there came to be a realisation and acceptance that those sites of Mohenjo-Dāṛo and Haṛappā were ancient cities. Different levels of digging in Mohenjo-Dāṛo and Haṛappā yielded dates of at

35. See B.B. Lal, *The Sarasvatī Flows On*, Aryan, 2002, p. 25.

least 5,000 years ago (3000 BCE) and new names were thought up for the area and the civilisation that had been discovered to be contemporaneous with the civilisation of ancient Egypt and Mesopotamia. Many scholars now believe that the "Indus/ Haṛappan Civilisation" has made substantial contributions to the progress of man in the material and (perhaps) spiritual fields.[36] Even though we now have the archaeological remains of the "Indus/Haṛappan Civilisation," the sparse written script of that civilisation is not yet deciphered. Therefore, there is, as yet, no consensus as to the "contemporaneousness" of other culture, such as the *R̥gveda* culture.

1.21 Vedic Culture Described

When William Jones translated the Law Code of Manu, followed by the translation of the older work, the *R̥gveda*, a term was coined by Western scholars to describe the R̥gvedic Civilisation: "Vedic culture." One commentator summed it up:

> At first, the Vedic culture was praised by many British and Europeans who postulated that India was the original home of the entire human race and the cradle of civilisation; then other scholars advanced the Aryan Invasion Theory, which became popular; now that Aryan Invasion Theory has become discredited.[37]

Some other scholars still hold that the Aryan invasion of India happened 3,500 years ago (1500 BCE) and that the people of India "forgot" about this after about 200 years and that the *R̥gveda* was composed 3,200 years ago (1200 BCE). This seems improbable in the light of the fact that other groups coming to India, for instance, the Parsis from Iran, remember coming to India after nearly 1,300 years.[38]

36. See S.R. Rao, *New Frontiers of Archaeology*, Popular Prakashan, 1994, p. 2.
37. See Shivaji Singh, "Vedic Culture and Its Continuity: Paradigm and Dimensions", in Sita Ram Dube (ed.), *Vedic Culture and Its Continuity*, Pratibha Prakashan, 2006, pp. 22-23.
38. See K.D. Sethna, *Karpasa in Prehistoric India*, Biblia Impex (1981), p. 9.

The *Ṛgveda*, the oldest composition from India, was handed down by oral memorisation and recitation and was made popular in the West by a translation in English by Max Müller, the German-born, Cambridge Professor in the 1800s. Max Müller at first made a guess that the age of *Ṛgveda* was around 3,200 years ago (1200 BCE). This was due in part to the Aryan Invasion Theory and in part to the discovery by Western scholars that Gautama Buddha was born approximately around 2,600 years ago (600 BCE). Soon after, many people in India became Buddhists and therefore, the *Ṛgveda* must have been written before that time. Max Müller and other Western scholars did not know of the discovery of the Indus/Haṛappan Civilisation, since the excavations did not begin until the 1920s, when that "discovery" was published in England. Max Müller died in the year 1900. Towards the end of his life, he admitted that no one knew if the *Ṛgveda* or other Vedic hymns were composed 3,000, 4,000 or 5,000 years ago (1000, 2000 or 3000 BCE).[39] Little did he know, nor suspect, that less than 25 years after his death, the Indus/Haṛappan Civilisation would be "discovered" and would add a great piece of missing information to the puzzle that Max Müller was trying to put together. Even after the Indus/Haṛappan Civilisation cities of Mohen̐jo-Dāṛo and Haṛappā were "discovered" and excavated, the theory of Aryan superiority was "re-invented" in Germany prior to Second World War and modified for its political use. The theory of "Aryan superiority" was discredited following the defeat of Germany in Second World War.

After Second World War, a more careful study was begun and the majority consensus now is that there appears to be no evidence of an Aryan invasion. Most scholars now agree that probably the Indus/Haṛappan Civilisation died out from overuse of the land, the earthquakes which dried up the river Sarasvatī and a corresponding drop in foreign trade.[40]

39. See B.B. Lal, "Search for Vedic-Harappan Relationship", in Agrawal (ed.), *In Search of Vedic-Haṛappan Relationship*, Aryan Books International, 2005, p. 1.

40. Ibid., p. 3.

1.22 Where are "Horses" Referred to in Ṛgveda for Time-Line Purposes

In the *Ṛgveda*, horses are prominent in many of the hymns, although the most often-mentioned animals are cattle. During the initial archaeological excavations at Mohenjo-Dāṛo or Haṛappā, no horse bones were found. This led some scholars to immediately conclude that the Indus/Haṛappan Civilisation came and went before the Vedic culture began and that therefore the *Ṛgveda* was composed after the decline of the Indus/ Haṛappan Civilisation. If that were the case, the original "guess" of Max Müller that the *Ṛgveda* was composed about 3,200 years ago (1200 BCE) might have been correct. Later evidence seems to indicate otherwise.

Additionally, thousands of soapstone or steatite "seals" of various sizes were carved in the Indus/Haṛappan Civilisation, the majority with pictures of male bulls and Indus/Haṛappan Civilisation written "characters" also carved on them. No seals have yet been found with the carving of a horse, although there are carvings of magical or mystical horses, some that are "unicorns" with one horn. Since the plain horse was never pictured in the Indus/Haṛappan Civilisation seals, this same school of scholars believed that was another indication of no horse belonging to or known to the Indus/Haṛappan Civilisation and therefore no possibility of *Ṛgveda* coming before or being composed during the Indus/Haṛappan Civilisation period.

However, after additional excavations of many more Indus/ Haṛappan Civilisation sites, horse bones were found and dated to at least 4,000 years ago (2000 BCE). Since then, other horse bones have been discovered. Also small figures of horses made from terracotta clay have been found.

1.23 European Horse or "Shetland Pony" with 34 Ribs mentioned in the Ṛgveda

Many questions remain unanswered about the Indus/

Haṛappan Civilisation horses and how they compare and contrast with the horses mentioned in the *Ṛgveda*. In *Ṛgveda*, the horses mentioned were horses with 34 ribs instead of the European horse with 36 ribs. Were the Ṛgvedic "horses" really closer to the so-called "pony" version of the horse, like the Shetland pony or the North American mustang? Moreover, if there was a relationship or perhaps an intimate relationship between the Indus/Haṛappan Civilisation and *Ṛgveda*, why was the horse never depicted on the thousands of Indus/Haṛappan Civilisation seals? But one could also ask a counter-question: even though other animals were known, why were the majority of the seals of (male) humped bulls, and why cows, in particular, were never represented? It is impossible to believe that there were no cows.[41]

We do not know yet why there were no horses on the seals, although, as described above, there occurred frequently a representation of another type of horse. It was a magical horse, a unicorn. And its body was not the usual body of a common horse. Sometimes it was a combination of a horse body with a bull body and then had the unicorn-type single horn.

Other clues are available to us linguistically. The Sanskrit word for "horse," as used in the *Ṛgveda* is *aśva*, which many scholars say also meant the cousin to the horse, the "ass." In *Ṛgveda*, as was pointed out above, the horse or we should say *aśva* is mentioned often. As noted above, the *Ṛgveda* says the horse had 17 ribs (1.162.18), just like a Shetland pony and the wild mustang herds of the American West.[42]

Even though there has been a disagreement among scholars about the presence of horses in ancient India, especially at the

41. See K.D. Sethna, *Karpasa in Prehistoric India*, Biblia Impex, 1981, p. 14.

42. See B.B. Lal, *The Homeland of the Aryans: Evidence of Ṛgvedic Flora and Fauna and Archaeology*, Aryan Books International, 2005, pp. 99-100 ("The Horse. . . The four-and-thirty ribs of the Swift Charger, kin to the Gods. . .").

time of the Indus/Haṛappan Civilisation, such disagreement is rapidly disappearing. This is due to not only the terracotta horse figurines that have been discovered, but also the horse bones themselves, with the aforementioned 34 ribs.

The Sanskrit word for horse (*aśva*) in addition to the translation of "horse" also means "the fast animal." There exist other "fast animals other than the Shetland pony with 34 ribs; some scholars believe that *Ṛgveda* suggests that the word *aśva* applied to both the horse and the ass, or to the wild-ass that was native to India.[43]

The details of the horse bone findings of the Indus/Haṛappan Civilisation are thus: horse bones have been found in Surkoṭaḍā, an Indus/Haṛappan Civilisation site about 100 miles north-east of Bhuj, in the district of Kutch, Gujarat; hence, this refutes the notion that the Haṛappans did not know about the horse.[44] The excavations of 1965-68 under J.P. Joshi at Haṛappan Surkoṭaḍā in the Kutch show not only the remains of the ass (*Equus onager indicus*), but also the horse (*Equus caballus* Linn.). The possession of horses by the Gandhāra grave culture does not distinguish the people as Aryan invaders; they could possibly have been Indian borderlanders on the move.[45]

One piece of the puzzle that is unknown is why horses were not carved on to Indus/Haṛappan Civilisation seals by themselves. Perhaps when one wanted to carve a horse it was considered luckier to carve the apparently magical horse-bull unicorn. Or that to foreign traders, one symbol of the Indus/Haṛappan Civilisation was a bull and this was an easily recognised "picture of origin."

One thing is certain: that there is still much to learn from

43. See Bhagwan Singh, *The Vedic Harappans*, Aditya Prakashan, 1996, p. 57.

44. See K.D. Sethna, *The Problem of Aryan Origins*, S&S Publishers, 1980, p. 36.

45. Ibid., p. 9.

these ancient artefacts, ancient bones and ancient texts. In speaking about the words in the *Ṛgveda*, Colin Renfrew in 1987 quoted the scholar A.B. Keith that, "taking the linguistic evidence too literally, one would conclude that the original (Sanskrit) Indo-European speakers knew butter but not milk, snow and feet, but not rain and hands."[46]

1.24 "Aśvattha" Tree meaning "Horses Stand under This Tree"

There is a tree in India, in Sanskrit called *aśvattha*, which comes from the Sanskrit word, *aśva* meaning "horse." The end of the word, the *tha* can mean "a location" and the *aśvattha* tree is translated as the tree "under which horses stand."[47]

The *aśvattha* tree is also known in India today as the holy fig tree (*Fiscus religiosa*), or *pippala* tree (commonly called *pīpala*). It has heart-shaped leaves and its fruit is purple when ripe. Apparently, the fruit is good for the heart and liver. Some people believe this tree to be the Buddha's banyan or bodhi tree. The *aśvattha* tree (*pippala* or *pīpala*) was first depicted on a seal discovered at Moheñjo-Dāṛo, dated to about 5,000 years ago (3000 BCE). The leaf of this tree, *aśvattha* was the most popular leaf in the entire Indus/Haṛappan Civilisation, at least pictorially and in character-writing form. The leaf appears on pottery and on signposts, as well as on many seals and sealings. The importance of this leaf has survived over time. Even today in India, spiritual figures are often pictured with a leaf from the *aśvattha* tree as a background.

Although the Indus/Haṛappan Civilisation script is not yet deciphered, it may be that the language of the script is a type of ancient Sanskrit. If this is true, then there must have been horses in the Indus/Haṛappan Civilisation, since the people of the

46. See M.K. Dhavalikar, *The Aryans: Myth and Archaeology*, Munshiram Manoharlal, 2007, p. 9.

47. See Monier-Williams, *A Sanskrit-English Dictionary*, Oxford, 1899.

Indus/Haṛappan Civilisation were so enchanted by the leaves of the *aśvattha* tree so as to paint them and inscribe on them frequently. Even if the language of the Indus/Haṛappan Civilisation is not ancient Sanskrit, many of the practices of the Indus/Haṛappan Civilisation have survived in India and Pakistan. The survival of painted leaves of the *aśvattha* tree (in India especially) may have some link to Indus/Haṛappan Civilisation horses.

The name of this tree is very similar to the name of another important tree in India, which needs to be clarified. The *aśvattha* tree (*pippala* or *pīpala*) is not to be confused with the *pippalī* tree (also called *pippilī*), which is Indian long pepper (*Piper longum*).

Dr Vasant D. Lad is a well-known author (in English language) of books on the subject of the health care that comes from ancient India, namely, Āyurveda. In Lad's book, that he co-wrote with Dr David Frawley on herbs, it is said that according to Āyurveda, the herb, *pippalī* (*pippilī*), is good for breathing difficulties and asthma.[48]

It is not clear why the *aśvattha* tree was named the tree "under which horses stand"[49] or why the tree was so popular in the Indus/Haṛappan Civilisation.

1.25 Ṛgveda Lists "Tropical" Trees, Including "Pippala" Tree

Previously, some Western scholars mistakenly believed that ancient books of India referred to non-tropical Indo-European words for trees such as birch, Scotch pine, linden, alder and oak. This view is apparently incorrect. In *Ṛgveda* there are many mentions of the the *aśvattha* tree (*pippala* or *pīpala*) and other trees that one would expect to grow only in the tropical climate of

48. See David Frawley, and Vasant Lad, *The Yoga of Herbs*, Lotus Press, 1986, pp. 180-81.

49. See Monier-Williams, *A Sanskrit-English Dictionary*, Oxford, 1899.

India. The most frequently mentioned tree in the *Ṛgveda* is the tree described above, the *aśvattha* tree? In *Ṛgveda*, it is called the *aśvattha* (the tree that the horses stand under). In addition to being the holy fig tree, it is quite interesting to note that it was also used in another religious capacity: its wood was used to make vessels which would hold the spiritual intoxicating drink (*soma*) (*Ṛgveda* 1.135.8 and 10.97.5).[50]

The *aśvattha* tree (*pippala* or *pīpala*) grows in India, Burma (Myanmar), Sri Lanka, Pakistan and Afghanistan; it has been painted on early Haṛappan pottery since about (5,000 years ago) 3000 BCE.[51]

1.26 Ṛgveda Composed near River Sarasvatī by "Natives"

Even in *The Cambridge History of India*, the British scholar mentioned above, A.B. Keith, in commenting on the notion of the Aryan Invasion Theory, said that the bulk of *Ṛgveda* was composed near river Sarasvatī; that the *Ṛgveda* not only has the omission of movement into India, but tells its story *from the point of view of inlanders not invaders*[52] which is a very important distinction. One would suppose that if a more sophisticated people came from "outside" and took over the less sophisticated land and population by force, then the story would abound with details of the glorious "invasion" and the glories of the country of origin of the invaders, their Motherland or Fatherland. No such mention is made in the *Ṛgveda*.

There are other means to support the "No Aryan Invasion Theory." Sometimes the order of certain items in a category can provide a valuable clue to scholars looking to piece together past history. We know that rivers were very important to the

---

50. See B.B. Lal, *The Homeland of the Aryans, Evidence of Ṛgvedic Flora and Fauna and Archaeology*, Aryan Books International, 2005, pp. 1-4.
51. Ibid., pp. 5-6.
52. See K.D. Sethna, *The Problem of Aryan Origins*, S&S Publishers, 1980, p. 11.

people who composed the *Ṛgveda*. Some rivers annually overflowed, such as the river Sarasvatī, providing the people with rich soil to sow their crops. The rivers allowed for local and international trade with distant people.

It is extremely telling, according to some archaeologists, that the *Ṛgveda*, when mentioning the rivers that were of utmost importance to them, lists rivers of what we now call north-west India and Pakistan (and not Afghanistan, as some early historians thought), from east-to-west and not west-to-east as we should expect of people (or invaders) who are claimed to have travelled from west-to-east.[53] This is another major clue as to the "origin" of the Aryan people. If they were "invaders" coming in from the west to the east, they would have seen the rivers also from the west to the east and recorded them in that order as they passed them. Hence, the "invasion order" of the rivers would be opposite to the way in which they were chronicled in *Ṛgveda*, from east-to-west, especially since the east was an important direction to the people of the *Ṛgveda* and also the people of the Indus/Haṛappan Civilisation.

1.27 Skeletal Remains Disprove Aryan Invasion

Other clues can be gathered from skeletal remains. Anthropologists who have examined skeletons in the Indus/Haṛappan Civilisation cities of both Haṛappā and Lothal and modern-day Indian skeletons have concluded that the population has remained the same to the present day; it is as if there was no invasion by the Aryans at all to make any difference.[54]

If there had been an "Aryan Invasion," modern scientists examining skeletons should have found a distinct difference at the "invasion" time-point when the skeletal remains changed. The fact that no change can be detected speaks volumes regarding the lack of new blood or a new race entering India. This is yet

53. See K.D. Sethna, *The Problem of Aryan Origins*, S&S Publishers, 1980, p. 13.
54. Ibid., p. 19.

another fact that is difficult to explain for those who cling to the Aryan Invasion Theory in spite of scientific evidence available to the contrary.

1.28 Gene Pool Disproves Aryan Invasion

Not only have no biological discontinuities been found in India between 4500 BCE and 800 BCE; the north and south Indian gene pool is the same and differs markedly from the gene pool of western Eurasia.[55]

These are two very important facts that should be given more attention. The first is that the north and south Indian gene pool is the same. Previously, some Western scholars held the theory that the people from the southern part of India were both darker-skinned and of a different race than those people originating from the northern part of India. In general, people throughout India look very similar. There are some individuals throughout India that have lighter skin colour and some individuals throughout India that have darker skin colour. Now the scientific findings that the gene pool from the north and the south of India is the same, verifies what the observer can see with one's own eyes, that north and south Indians are from the same gene pool. The second scientific finding of interest to this discussion is that the gene pool of the people from India is different from the gene pool of the people of western Eurasia. This is yet another marker to help prove the invalidity of the Aryan Invasion Theory. If Aryan Invasion Theory was correct, one would expect to find a similar gene pool between the people of India and the "Aryan Invaders" who supposedly came from outside of India and took over. Even the great American archaeologist, George Dales, wrote in 1966 that the Aryans have not yet been identified archaeologically.[56]

---

55. See Shivaji Singh, "Vedic Culture and its Continuity Paradigm and Dimensions", in Sita Ram Dube (ed.), *Vedic Culture and Its Continuity*, Pratibha Prakashan, 2006, p. 27.

56. See K.D. Sethna, *The Problem of Aryan Origins*, S&S Publishers, 1980, p. 4.

1.29 Where are the Wooden Ṛgveda Chariot Wheels with "Spokes"?

Other scholars who have championed the Aryan Invasion Theory have stated that *Ṛgveda* mentions chariots with wheels that had spokes and that no such wheels with spokes have been found in the excavations of the Indus/Haṛappan Civilisation. The first thing to consider is that most wheels with spokes were made out of wood. And wood is one thing that did not seem to survive from the Indus/Haṛappan Civilisation. It could easily be that the climate of India destroyed all of the wheels, especially if they were all made of wood. There is evidence of the use of wood for chariot wheels; in fact, it is very likely that all of the chariot wheels were made out of wood. Some chariots that were made in India during the Indus/Haṛappan Civilisation were shipped to Egypt and Mesopotamia; some of these chariots have been successfully preserved and these chariots had wheels with spokes made of wood. In 1926, a famous archaeologist, Gordon Childe, cited a chariot, which he found in Florence, dating from the eighteenth Egyptian dynasty about 2,500 years ago (1550 BCE), whose axle is birch bark, which most likely came from what is now the Indian State of Kashmir.[57]

Many of the Haṛappan seals have pictures of wheels with spokes, including one from Lothal, which reminds one of a charioteer riding a two-wheeled chariot with spokes.[58] A "wheel with spokes" is depicted on the underside of the flat covers of Cemetery H, and around the shoulders of jars.[59] Haṛappan terracotta wheels with either painted or low relief spokes have been found in Banawālī, Kālibaṅgan and Rākhīgaṛhī.[60]

57. See M.K. Dhavalikar, *The Aryans: Myth and Archaeology*, Munshiram Manoharlal, 2007, p. 6.

58. See K.D. Sethna, *The Problem of Aryan Origins*, S&S Publishers, 1980, p. 47.

59. See H.D. Sankalia, *Pre-Historic Art in India*, Carolina Academic Press, 1978, pp. 18-19.

60. See B.B. Lal, *The Sarasvatī Flows On*, Aryan, 2002, p. 74.

1.30 Only Non-Wood Terracotta Model Wheels have "Spokes"

Many terracotta wheels have been found from Indus/Haṛappan Civilisation excavations. The author has verified for himself such terracotta wheels with spokes at the National Museum of India in New Delhi and at the museum next to the ancient ruins of the Indus/Haṛappā city of Lothal. But one can imagine that if a model out of clay (terracotta) is being fashioned, it is fairly difficult to actually make a wheel with spokes. It is much easier to make a model of a chariot or bullock cart with wheels that are all one piece. And that is exactly what the author saw in both the museums relating to the Indus/Haṛappan Civilisation: models of terracotta with wheels that were all in one piece, but with indications of spokes. This distinction needs to be emphasised. Photographs of Indus/Haṛappan Civilisation terracotta wheels reveal "spokes" either painted or low relief spokes. These have been found in Banawālī, Kālibaṅgan and Rākhīgaṛhī of the Indus/Haṛappan Civilisation, definitely showing that the artists making the wheels meant to show spokes.

These photographs reveal that "spokes" on those terracotta wheels do not at all look simply like a half-hearted attempt at a fantasy vehicle that did not exist at the time. These were apparently real attempts to represent what was very difficult to fashion in clay: real, thin, spokes on a bulky model made of terracotta. The fact that such "wheel with spokes" models have been found at more than one Indus/Haṛappan Civilisation site, indicates the possibility of universality throughout the civilisation; it is not as if just one model in one city was found and no other models existed throughout the realm.

1.31 Where is the "Iron" Spoken of in Ṛgveda for Time-Line Purposes

Another topic that has puzzled scholars for many years is the Sanskrit word, *ayas*, which has been translated by some scholars as "iron." Possibly when William Jones translated the *Manusmṛti* and other Europeans translated the *Ṛgveda,* they must have asked Sanskrit speakers and scholars in India what each word meant. When the word *ayas* came up in India in the 1700s and 1800s, the English word "iron" must have come back as the then accepted translation of the word.

The current majority theory is that smelted, man-made iron was widely available in India between the sixth and eighth century BCE.[61] What is not known is whether or not the metallurgists of the Indus/Haṛappan Civilisation were able to occasionally use their well-developed heating techniques to produce a type of iron later known as "pig iron" or occasionally use iron from fallen meteors. We do know now that some English translations of some words in *Ṛgveda* are incorrect.

1.32 "Ayas" may not mean "Iron"

Of course, various other possibilities exist: one that the original term *ayas* meant "metal" or a particular type of metal, such as copper or bronze, or a special blend of metal which was especially strong; another possibility, as mentioned above, is that iron was available in small quantities from meteors that had fallen from space, crashed into earth and these were found and used by people of Ṛgvedic era. In most passages of the *Ṛgveda,* the word *ayas* seems to mean "metal," however that is not so in the lạter-in-time translation, "iron," because it is said that the people of *Ṛgveda* times had forts that were made of this *ayas*. Hence, even if some iron was discovered in ancient India, it was certainly not a sufficient quantity so as to actually make complete forts out of iron.

Generally the Sanskrit term *ayas* was meant to indicate copper and the meanings "bronze" and "iron" are seen as later semantic

61. See K.D. Sethna, *The Problem of Aryan Origins*, S&S Publishers, 1980, p. 37.

developments.[62] Monier-Williams defines *ayas* to signify both "iron" and "metal"; sometimes *ayas* even meant "gold."[63]

It has also been shown that bronze was well known in the Indus/Haṛappan Civilisation. Since bronze is copper with different alloys added, usually tin, the craftsmen of the Indus/Haṛappan Civilisation exhibited great skill in their bronze-making art. In certain Indus/Haṛappan Civilisation sites, bronze objects having different percentages of tin in their composition have been found, and thus, it was observed that the bronze objects did not have a single uniform percentage. This seems to be another indication of the sophisticated knowledge of the processes of making different types of bronze and the effect different techniques would have.

Other scholars have found instances of the word *ayas* to really mean bronze or copper and not iron. Some scholars do not even find literary evidence of iron. They say that no conclusion can be drawn form the word *ayas* (which, as mentioned above, can also mean gold, etc.). For instance, a copper razor for shaving and cutting hair is called *aluhāyasa kṣura* or "razor of red *ayas*"; hence, it could be concluded that what was taken for iron was actually brass.[64]

1.33 Bronze "Handsaw" Hard as Iron

Another piece of evidence regarding bronze that was "as hard as iron" in the Indus/Haṛappan Civilisation was the "bronze handsaw." Bronze handsaws were used in the Indus/Haṛappan Civilisation technology of jewellery-making, especially bracelets called bangles. In India today, bracelets that are not flexible are often called bangles. And in the Indus/Haṛappan Civilisation times, bangles were often made out of seashells and shipped either inside the Indus/Haṛappan Civilisation realm or to foreign

62. See R.S. Sharma, *Looking for the Aryans*, Orient Longman, 1995, p. 62.
63. See Monier-Williams, *A Sanskrit-English Dictionary*, Oxford, 1899.
64. See K.D. Sethna, *Karpasa in Prehistoric India*, Biblia Impex, 1981, p. 54.

places. What is interesting about the Indus/Haṛappan Civilisation seashell bangle making technology is that the bronze handsaw that was used, was able to cut the shells for bangle-making as efficiently as modern-day steel saws, which in turn implies that Indus bronze workers were able to produce a bronze as hard as steel.[65] If bronze as hard as modern steel could be produced back then, then it is no wonder that there was so much linguistic confusion regarding interpretation of the Sanskrit word *ayas*.

Other scholars have reported that iron, which may have been meteoric, was reportedly found in some sites in West Asia belonging to the third millennium BCE; but now it is believed that the term *ayas* in the *R̥gveda* means copper and not iron.[66]

Interestingly enough, as described above, the craftsmen of the Indus/Haṛappan Civilisation hardened copper into bronze by alloying it with tin; after the decline of the Indus/Haṛappan Civilisation, no tin-based bronze objects were produced in India for over a millennium.[67]

1.34 Sophisticated Thought of R̥gveda may Correspond with Sophisticated High Temperature Technology of the Indus/Haṛappan Civilisation

R̥gveda, and the Sanskrit language itself shows a level of highly sophisticated thought. Some scholars believe that the High Temperature Technology of the Indus/Haṛappan Civilisation shows a similar level of sophisticated thought.

With regard to high temperature technology, especially in the craft of making "artistic beads" and particularly faience, the

65. See J.M. Kenoyer, *Ancient Cities of the Indus Valley Civilization*, Oxford University Press, 1998, p. 96.

66. See M.K. Dhavalikar, *The Aryans: Myth and Archaeology*, Munshiram Manoharlal, 2007, p. 73.

67. See Shivaji Singh, "Vedic Culture and Its Continuity: Paradigm and Dimensions", in Sita Ram Dube (ed.), *Vedic Culture and Its Continuity*, Pratibha Prakashan, 2006, p. 27.

Indus/Haṛappan Civilisation faience was much more advanced than in any other part of the known world at that time. To make faience beads, the Indus/Haṛappan Civilisation craftsmen heated their ground rock crystal and coloured stones, which they again cooled, ground up, combined with other things and fired a second time at high temperature.[68] The technological "know-how" must have been quite sophisticated in order to produce a controlled heat which was above 1200°C, which is almost 2200° Fahrenheit.

1.35 Conclusion

The West "discovered" the *Manusmṛti* in the late 1700s with the translation from the Sanskrit by a British judge in India, William Jones and its publication in England. The older philosophical or spiritual work, which was more carefully preserved by oral tradition, the *Ṛgveda*, was translated and published in England in the 1800s.

Although Jones believed that Sanskrit was the "mother" of many languages and that law in India was 3,800 years old, some Westerners theorised that "light" skinned "Aryans" migrated to India 3,500 years ago (1500 BCE) and brought with them Sanskrit and the *Ṛgveda*.

Such "evidence" of an "Aryan Invasion" in ancient India has been rapidly shrinking over the last 100 years due to the discovery of the Indus/Haṛappan Civilisation sites (including Mohenjo-Dāṛo, Haṛappā (1920) and Mehrgaṛh (1974)) horse bones, clay models of chariot wheels with spokes, bronze handsaws as hard as steel, space satellite pictures (1970) of the dried-up river (probably the river Sarasvatī) and Indian gene pool evidence of no invasion. If there is no "Aryan invasion", then no "Aryan invaders" came in to India 3,500 years ago (1500 BCE) to influence the composition of the *Ṛgveda* or the *Manusmṛti*. Other means of establishing a "Time-Line" can now be examined.

68. See Jane McIntosh, *A Peaceful Realm*, Westview Press, 2002, p. 71.

2

History of Law Code of Manu (Manusmṛti/Manu-Dharmaśāstra)

2.1 Oldest Law Code in India

THE Law Code of Manu also called *Manusmṛti* or *Manu-Dharmaśāstra,* appears to be the oldest Law Code from India (as opposed to the *Ṛgveda,* which is said to contain "natural law"). In order to take a fresh look as to when the *Manusmṛti* was composed, it is useful to examine the clues given to us from the *Manusmṛti* itself, from the *Ṛgveda* and possibly from the Indus/Haṛappan Civilisation archaeological remains in India and Pakistan and from the "Time-Line" of the Indus/Haṛappan Civilisation.

2.2 Oral Tradition Preservation

The *Manusmṛti* itself, even though not dated, nor originally written down, contains references to various practices of the people it was meant to inspire and govern. The *Manusmṛti* was apparently memorised and recited by legal advisers to chiefs of towns and major and minor kings, although it appears that there were some "revisions" over time. The *Ṛgveda,* on the other hand, was apparently memorised precisely word-for-word, with exact pronunciation and meter recitation requirements and recited everyday for many thousands of years. The *Ṛgveda* contains clues relating to the history and dating of the *Manusmṛti* and pre-dates the Law Code of Manu. The majority of Indus/Haṛappan Civilisation archaeological remains in India and Pakistan have been carbon-14 dated to between 4,000 and 5,000 years ago (2000 to 3000 BCE). Some are much older, for instance, the close-by city of Mehrgaṛh having been dated from about 8,000 to 9,000 years ago (6000 to 7000 BCE) and a minority of sites, for a short time, outlasted the rapid decline of the Indus/Haṛappan Civilisation and are just a little younger (some of those sites date back to 3,500 years ago (about 1500 BCE).

From excavations of Indus/Haṛappan Civilisation sites, archaeologists have found many similarities of the Indus/Haṛappan Civilisation culture to "Vedic Culture," the culture and practices described in the *Ṛgveda*. Some scholars are beginning to advance the theory of the two together and are coining the term: "Vedic-Haṛappā Civilisation." This book advances the theory that similarities also exist between the *Manusmṛti* and the Indus/Haṛappan Civilisation.

2.3 Similarities among Ṛgveda, Manusmṛti and Indus/Haṛappan Civilisation

There appears to be a related level of intellectual sophistication between the *Ṛgveda*, the *Manusmṛti* and the archaeological findings from the Indus/Haṛappan Civilisation. Such intellectual sophistication does not seem to have been found before the Indus/Haṛappan Civilisation, nor afterwards for at least 1,000 or more years. Once the sophisticated level of urbanisation, international trade and standardisation of the Indus/Haṛappan Civilisation ended, the next period of unification and sophistication in Indian history was approximately 2,300 years ago (from 322–232 BCE), around the time of the Emperors Candragupta Maurya and Aśoka.

The majority of Indus/Haṛappan Civilisation archaeological remains have been carbon-14 dated to between 4,000 and 5,000 years ago, (2000 to 3000 BCE). The "pre-Indus/Haṛappan Civilisation" time period starts with Mehrgaṛh, time-dated 8,000 to 9,000 years ago (6000 to 7000 BCE) and the "post-Indus/Haṛappan Civilisation" or "declining-Indus/Haṛappan

Civilisation" commences from the date that the river Sarasvatī dried up, approximately 3,900 years ago (about 1900 BCE). There exist different scholarly opinions about the dates of the post-Indus/Haṛappan Civilisation, but the ones given above are accepted today by the majority of scholars.

2.4 Manusmṛti Composed after Ṛgveda

It seems certain that the *Manusmṛti* was composed after the *Ṛgveda*. The easiest way to prove this is through the fact that the *Manusmṛti* does mention the Vedas, including *Ṛgveda*, in glowing terms, but *Ṛgveda* does not mention the *Manusmṛti* even once. The *Manusmṛti* does not just mention the *Ṛgveda* only in passing, but as the cornerstone of its civilisation's philosophical and spiritual thought. (Originally, the composition was just called the Veda, then later divided or added to in order to make up three and later four divisions, the apparent oldest and most important being *Ṛgveda*.) The *Manusmṛti*, chapter one, verse 23, says:

> But from fire, wind, and the sun he (the Creator) drew forth the threefold eternal Veda, called *Ṛk* (*Ṛg*), *Yajus*, and *Sāman*, for the due performance of the sacrifice.[1]

2.5 River Sarasvatī dates Ṛgveda and Manusmṛti

The dried-up river, possibly the river Sarasvatī may also help to date *Ṛgveda* and the *Manusmṛti*. Most scholars now agree that modern space satellite images show the dried-up path of a once great and mighty river flowing through what is now north-west India and Pakistan. Many scholars believe that this was the river Sarasvatī and further believe that the evidence shows that this river, the river Sarasvatī, dried up about 3,900 years ago (1900 BCE). Both the *Ṛgveda* and the *Manusmṛti* mention the river Sarasvatī in glowing terms, especially the *Ṛgveda*, praising the river as a "great and mighty river" flowing all the way from "the mountains to the sea."

1. See G. Buehler, *Laws of Manu*, Oxford (Sacred Books of the East, v. XXV), 1896, p. 5.

The *Manusmṛti* mentions the river Sarasvatī as a "divine river," but does not "bestow praises" upon the river as the *Ṛgveda* does. The *Manusmṛti* seems to treat the river Sarasvatī more as a boundary or as a geographical marker. Even this fact, the river Sarasvatī as a geographical marker, probably meant that the river had not dried up at the time of the composition of the *Manusmṛti*, otherwise, most likely, the reference would have been to the dried-up river Sarasvatī and not the "divine river Sarasvatī," as appears from the text. Specifically, the *Manusmṛti* in chapter 2, verse 17, says, "That land, created by the gods, which lies between the two divine rivers Sarasvatī and Dṛṣadvatī, they (sages) call Brahmāvartta."[2]

Many scholars believe that at least part of river Sarasvatī dried up because of earthquakes prior to 3,900 years ago (1900 BCE), preventing the river from flowing from the "mountains to the sea" and making the river much less "mighty" to those who would compose hymns about this "divine river." That alone is reason enough to see why more and more scholars have concluded that the *Ṛgveda* has an extremely strong possibility of being composed prior to 3,900 years ago (1900 BCE) and almost no possibility of being composed after.

That same argument can be advanced for the *Manusmṛti*. As described above, the *Manusmṛti* mentions, "That land, created by the gods, which lies between the two divine rivers Sarasvatī and Dṛṣadvatī, they (sages) call Brahmāvartta" in chapter 2, verse 17.[3] Similarly, the analysis that placed the composition of *Ṛgveda* prior to 3,900 years ago (1900 BCE), (the date of the earthquakes that dried up the river Sarasvatī), the *Manusmṛti* should survive that exact same test of being composed prior to 3,900 years ago (1900 BCE).

---

2. See G. Buehler, *Laws of Manu*, Oxford (Sacred Books of the East, v. XXV), 1896, p. 20.

3. Ibid.

This part of the analysis concerning the date of composition of the *Manusmṛti* is as follows: The *Manusmṛti* would not describe a thriving and desirable tract of land such as "Brahmāvartta" if that tract of land was already abandoned (as was the case soon after the drying up of river Sarasvatī 3,900 years ago (1900 BCE) (according to modern archaeological findings). Since that river had not dried up yet, one could and should logically conclude that, therefore, that certain tract of land known as "Brahmāvartta" must have been vibrant, alive and comprised a thriving community during the time of composition of the *Manusmṛti*. The "philosophy" espoused in the *Manusmṛti* was Vedic philosophy, not the later Jain or Buddhist philosophy.

This theory appears to give evidence of the correlation between the *Manusmṛti* and the civilisation known as the Indus/ Haṛappan Civilisation. Both seem to have some relationship (if not exactly the same relationship) with a not-yet-dried-up river Sarasvatī (meaning both should have existed prior to 3,900 years ago (1900 BCE). If those earthquakes rendered part of the river Sarasvatī to become dried up, then it makes sense that the *Manusmṛti* was composed prior to the earthquakes, prior to the river Sarasvatī drying up and therefore prior to 3,900 years ago (1900 BCE).

2.6 The Physical Location Similarities/ Location of River Sarasvatī

The physical location (the exact "real estate" location) where *Ṛgveda* seems to have been composed is very similar to the one major location identified in the *Manusmṛti* and also very similar to one huge tract of land belonging to the Indus/ Haṛappan Civilisation. Since these locations appear to be very similar, additional location analysis may help in "time-dating" the *Ṛgveda* and the *Manusmṛti*.

The *Ṛgveda* location or the "Land of the Vedas" was between the river Sarasvatī and river Dṛṣadvatī.[4] The first issue is the exact location of the Sarasvatī River.

Some scholars have contended that river Sarasvatī is in Afghanistan. The biggest problem with this theory is that Afghanistan is landlocked and, therefore, does not have an ocean. The *Ṛgveda* clearly states that river Sarasvatī flows from the "mountains to the sea." Most scholars today believe that river Sarasvatī ran east of the current Indus or Sindhu River that in large part is located in what is now Pakistan.

More than one hundred years ago, a British officer named Oldham discovered the large dried-up "river-bed" of what he believed to be the seasonal river, river Ghaggar (later scholars believed that to be the Sarasvatī). Oldham's conclusion was that a seasonal river could not create a river-bed so vast; thus the Ghaggar River must be flowing (during its seasonal flow) on the river-bed of an older dried-up river.

In the early 1970s space satellite photographs were taken of many parts of the world, including India, in part showing underground channels of water where scholars believed that river Sarasvatī had partially dried up and partially gone underground.

2.7 Location of River Dṛṣadvatī

River Dṛṣadvatī is also another river, like river Sarasvatī, that is dried up and has not been located exactly. Some scholars believe that river Dṛṣadvatī was located north-east of river Sarasvatī and actually flowed into river Sarasvatī. This theory would then yield a region where the *Ṛgveda* could have been composed and also the same region, called "Brahmāvartta" by the *Manusmṛti*, where the *Manusmṛti* was composed. For purposes of our comparison,

4. David Frawley, "Geographical References: The Ocean and Soma", in Agrawal (ed.), *In Search of Vedic-Haṛappan Relationship*, Aryan Books International, 2005, p. 35.

   Ṛgveda III.23.4: "He set thee in the earth's most lovely station, in Indra's place, in days of fair bright weather. On man, on Āpayā, Agni! on the rivers Dṛṣadvatī, Sarasvatī, shine richly."

this tract of land is also the place where there are hundreds of Indus/Haṛappan Civilisation locations, many of which have yet to be completely excavated.

Alternatively, some other scholars believe that river Dṛṣadvatī was located just due east of river Sarasvatī and flowed almost parallel to river Sarasvatī. This second theory would then yield a similar region to the one described above: a location where the *Ṛgveda* could have been composed and also the same "Brahmāvartta" region, where the *Manusmṛti* was composed. Also, just like the above analysis, this similar location is also the place where there are many Indus/Haṛappan Civilisation sites.

In summary, although the precise boundaries are in dispute and the exact course of the river Sarasvatī and the river Dṛṣadvatī is still disputed, a number of. years ago, even prior to the discovery of numerous Indus/Haṛappan Civilisation sites, it was said that the ancient river Sarasvatī-Dṛṣadvatī zone (now dried up) yielded the discovery of 1,200 (the Indus/Haṛappan Civilisation) sites on these now dried-up rivers, out of a total of more than 1,600 sites in both India and Pakistan.[5] Since that time, more complete sites and more probable rivers Sarasvatī-Dṛṣadvatī zone sites have been discovered.

2.8 Additional Geography

There are additional geographical places mentioned in the second chapter of the *Manusmṛti*:

> 2.19. The plain of the Kurus, the (country of the) Matsyas, Pañcālas, and Sūrasenas, these (form), indeed, the country of the Brahmarṣis (Brāhmanical sages, which ranks) immediately after Brahmāvartta. (This section is not too far from the modern day capital of India, New Delhi, where additional Indus/Haṛappan Civilisation sites have been discovered.)

---

5. See I.K. Sharma, "The Sarasvatī-Sindhu Civilization and Vedic Co-relations", in Agrawal (ed.), *In Search of Vedic-Haṛappan Relationship*, Aryan Books International, 2005, p. 149.

More than 100 years ago, scholars wrote about a "middle district" mentioned in *Yajurveda*. *Yajurveda* is one of the Vedas composed after *Ṛgveda* and mentioned in the *Manusmṛti*. With the advent of *Yajurveda*, the geographical centre changed. There is a "middle district" near modern Delhi and spreading out in an eastern direction to Kurukṣetra or the Plain of the Kurus, and further east, south of Nepal (rivers Jumnā [Yamunā] and Ganges).[6]

Several other geographical places mentioned in the second chapter of the *Manusmṛti*:

> 2.21. That (country) which (lies) between the Himavat and the Vindhya (mountains) to the east of Prayāga and to the west of Vinasana (the place where river Sarasvatī disappears) is called Madhyadeśa (the central region).

The extra addition of "the place where river Sarasvatī disappears" is added by the translator, George Buehler, not in the original text. The addition gives us additional information. First, either the translator himself, or a commentator after the composition of the *Manusmṛti* knew of the beginning of the drying-up of river Sarasvatī. This also seems to indicate that even this addition, "the place where river Sarasvatī disappears," is prior to the large earthquakes and more extensive drying-up of river Sarasvatī 3,900 years ago (1900 BCE).

The Himalayas are the high range of mountains, located in part in northern India. The Himalayas are also personified as Himavat, mythologically considered to be the father of Gaṅgā (river Ganges). The Vindhya range is the mountain range separating northern from southern India, beginning in Gujarat that goes north-east to river Ganges. Prayāga is the ancient name for the modern Indian city of Allahabad, in the north-east.

Some scholars are now advancing the theory that there are ancient cities in the eastern part of India that are as old or almost

6. Edward Washburn Hopkins, *The Religions of India*, Ginn and Co., 1895, pp. 176-79.

as old as the Indus/Haṛappan Civilisation.[7] The author himself has visited museums in Kolkata (Calcutta) and verified himself archaeological artefacts from the Kolkata region that seem very similar to Indus/Haṛappan Civilisation artefacts found elsewhere in India.

The *Manusmṛti* also states in verse 2.22:

> But (the tract) between those two mountains (just mentioned), which (extends) as far as the eastern and the western oceans, the wise call Āryāvartta (the country of the Aryans).

This may give credence to the theory that the Indus/Haṛappan Civilisation was larger than previously thought.

The famous epic concerning Kṛṣṇa, the *Mahābhārata,* says that river Sarasvatī dried up in a desert (at a place called Vinasana or Adarsana). Since the *Mahābhārata* mentions the dried-up river Sarasvatī, and the *Manusmṛti* did not mention such a major occurrence, it is reasonable to conclude that the *Manusmṛti* was composed before the *Mahābhārata* took place, before the "Sarasvatī dried up in a desert."

2.9 Ṛgveda Preserved Orally Word-for-Word

As mentioned above, the *Ṛgveda* was memorised thoroughly, hence the entire text was transferred from one generation to the next orally word-for-word. Most other cultures preserved oral knowledge just by vaguely repeating a story.

In ancient India, it was discovered that writing on acid-dipped palm leaves or clay tablets lasted a long time, but could be destroyed by the ravages of time, the elements and the insects. Apparently, there was also a fear of losing the "power" of the *Ṛgveda* by losing the ability to chant it as closely as possible to the original. The only way to be certain of exact preservation of

7. See Sambhu Nath Mondal, *Decipherment of the Indus-Brahmi Inscriptions of Chandraketugarh (Gangahrada): The Mohenjodaro of East India*, S.P. Saha, 2006.

knowledge was to convince a certain percentage of the population with a talent for memorisation to dedicate their lives to memorising and preserving knowledge. Not just vaguely memorising a story, as was the custom in other contemporaneous cultures, but exactly memorising word-for-word.

2.10 Brāhmaṇas, "Mouths of the Creator" or "Human Library Books" or "Human Computers"

Brāhmaṇas were the people with a talent for memorisation and a willingness to dedicate their lives to memorising and preserving knowledge and the author refers to these people as "mouths of the creator" or "human library books" or "human computers." These "mouths of the creator" or "human library books" or "human computers" seem to have functioned like computers of our time; they had to memorise certain compositions, and then, upon being prompted, they probably could start anywhere and go forward in the text, as a small percentage of current Brahmins (brāhmaṇas) can still do today in India.

Using the terms, "mouth of the creator" or "human library book" or "human computer" is possibly a new way of expressing the concept of how the *Ṛgveda* was preserved intact and unchanged by the practice of daily recitation. And that information has been handed down, seemingly unchanged, generation after generation, apparently for thousands of years. Compelling evidence exists to point to the conclusion that such oral transmission occurred in India for a large body of knowledge, in addition to the *Ṛgveda*, although not so precisely transmitted, such as the *Manusmṛti*. Although it is relatively easy in India today to find those who recite *Ṛgveda* everyday, it is now much more difficult, if not impossible to find those who can recite the *Manusmṛti*. Obviously, memorisation is a difficult process. The study of the Vedas by the simple and arduous process of memorising was so accurate and minute that, with a view to establishing the text and preventing interpolation, every verse, word, and syllable has been counted."[8] Because of the impermanency of writing on clay pots, clay seals or even carving on stone that could be broken or on palm leaves, parchment or leather that could be lost or burned by an enemy, the idea of preserving important knowledge by writing was most probably rejected in ancient India.

2.11 Examples of Modern-day Indians able to Memorise Large Body of Knowledge

Two modern-day examples from India, that the author personally knows well, with amazing abilities to memorise large amounts of information and recall such information upon a moment's notice, are an Āyurvedic physician, Dr Vasant D. Lad and a professor of music, V.V. Shrikande.

Both these individuals have an extraordinary capacity to have committed to memory unbelievable amounts of knowledge in their individual fields and upon request can immediately summon up that knowledge from the depths of their minds and produce it for an audience of one or 1,000.

During the time of extensive use of the *Manusmr̥ti*, those "human library books" who devoted themselves to memorising the *Manusmr̥ti* could, the author theorises, with exact precision, recite any law, on any topic, especially since the *Manusmr̥ti* prescribed a study period for those who studied, to be either 36 years or 18 years. These Brāhmaṇa "human library books" could, the author theorises, probably recite all of the relevant sub-texts and commentaries to the laws, if it was required by the "king sitting as judge" or one of the other Brāhmaṇas when he was "sitting as judge" (just to confirm the text of the *Manusmr̥ti*). This topic will be further explained in a later chapter.

8. See Zenaide A. Ragozin, *History of Vedic India*, 1984, rpt. 2003, p. 119.

2.12 Vedas Spiritually Oriented

The Vedas were very spiritually oriented (lots of hymns in praise of various *devas* or "shining ones" or "gods" of creation, such as fire, wind, etc.). The Vedas and the compositions that followed contained information on geography, history, astronomy, astrology, mathematics, medicine and law. Although the *Manusmṛti* also contained many verses that could be classified as spiritual or religious laws, such laws will not be examined here other than those that give us insight into the formation of the *Manusmṛti*.

The *Manusmṛti* refers to brāhmaṇas, being spiritually-minded and "begging" for their food each day (although begging could be done from family and their relatives); that in addition to their spirituality, the brāhmaṇas were hierarchically placed at the top of society. The brāhmaṇas were not required to do manual labour.

When the brāhmaṇas committed crimes, the punishments for their crimes were less harsh than for other members of society. Although in some parts of the *Manusmṛti*, the brāhmaṇas were not supposed to lend money, in other parts, the brāhmaṇas were allowed to loan money and to charge the maximum amount of interest on a loan, more than any other class or caste of society at the time of Manu. Brāhmaṇas could charge interest rates of up to 60 per cent per year, compared to royalty/warriors called kṣatriyas who could charge up to 48 per cent per year, cattlemen/merchants called vaiśyas could charge up to 36 per cent a year, and even servants called śūdras could charge up to 24 per cent a year on a loan.[9]

Such "laws" regarding moneylending are not found in the *Ṛgveda*. As regards rate of interest, one can only speculate about the Indus/Haṛappan Civilisation society, since their script is not

9. Law Code of Manu: 8:142. "Just two in the hundred, three, four, and five (and not more), he may take as monthly interest according to the order of the castes (*varṇa*)."

yet fully deciphered, and other clues are not yet available to us. Giving food or other gifts to a brāhmaṇa was considered to be a practice that would earn the other members of the *Manusmṛti* society a type of "spiritual merit" and was thereby encouraged.

2.13 Brāhmaṇas Not "Priests"

Some modern translators of the *Manusmṛti* have translated the word, brāhmaṇa, to mean the English word, "priest." This translation does not seem to be entirely correct. When Europeans began translating the *Manusmṛti* and the *Ṛgveda*, many of the translators were probably member of European Christian churches and were used to seeing members of the clergy of the Roman Catholic, Anglican or Lutheran Church, dressed in a black robe, "interceding" between "God" and the non-priests or "lay" members of that church.

Even though the brāhmaṇa class or caste was treated as the highest level of the society of ancient India, this was, most likely, the price that the society found it had to "pay" in order to maintain its "mouths of the creator" or "human library books" or "human-computers." (Later on, many scholars argue today that members of the higher classes or castes have tried to keep the caste system intact for reasons of political or economic gain.)

When one person (especially a major or minor king or chief of a village) wanted to hear a legal brāhmaṇa recite any piece of knowledge, on a particular law, one had to call in the legal brāhmaṇa to start reciting. When one person (especially a major or minor king or chief of a village) wanted to hear a *Ṛgveda* brāhmaṇa recite a "prayer" to any force of "nature," such as the god of fire, "Agni," or the goddess "Sarasvatī," who was the personification of river Sarasvatī, or start singing one particular verse or song, complete with correctly-memorised words, correct pronunciation and correct rhythm, one had to call in the *Ṛgveda* brāhmaṇa to start reciting. It was almost as if the "mouths of the creator" or "human library books" or "human computers" were asked to "switch the power on."

Furthermore, it is more likely that the brāhmaṇas had to perform their "human library book"/"human computer" functions daily more than their "priestly" functions. Just as a modern computer memory gets "backed up" everyday, the brāhmaṇas probably had to recite all that they had memorised everyday, especially the *Ṛgveda* brāhmaṇas, so as to be able to remember the exact words, pronunciation and the rhythm.

The *Manusmṛti* seems to point to another important aspect — the legal brāhmaṇa "human computers" had to memorise and be able to recall on a moment's notice more information on topics other than prayers; the ability to recite the law must have been important to many of the citizens of the *Manusmṛti* society. The laws of the *Manusmṛti* contained important non-spiritual topics such as weights and measures. If one merchant-seller disagreed with another merchant-buyer about the proper way to judge the weight of a product to be sold, they would probably have gone to the king or chief of a village to help them decide. Then that king or village chief would have probably asked his law brāhmaṇas, his law "human library books" or "human computers," to recite the precise verse of the *Manusmṛti* on the origins and the exact way to determine correct weights and measures. That same king or village chief might also request the chanting of the verse of the *Manusmṛti* that proclaimed that the king or village chief was empowered to be the one to set weekly prices on certain commodities.

Probably a better comparison of *Manusmṛti* brāhmaṇas is not to "priests" in their sacerdotal capacities, but instead the European Middle Ages monastery, when all of the members of a monastery (whether lay members or clergy) spent their days copying books by hand (before the printing press), and reading out loud any passage that the non-monastery population (who could not read) requested. The books that were being copied mostly dealt with religious and Church matters, but occasionally non-Church matters as well. The *Manusmṛti* brāhmaṇas, in the author's opinion, probably were much more like medieval monastic scribes with excellent memories and without the aid of medieval pen and paper.

2.14 "Veda" Defined

The Concise Oxford Dictionary of Current English defines the word, *veda* as "the most ancient Hindu scriptures, comprising four collections called the *Ṛgveda, Sāmaveda, Yajurveda* and *Atharvaveda* (Sanskrit *veda,* literally (sacred) knowledge).[10]

2.15 Chanting of Ṛgveda as a Hymn

A more detailed discussion of the theory of the "human library book" or "mouth of the Creator" may help the reader's understanding. In ancient India, it must have been observed that any one human being could remember quite precisely (i.e. word for word) long passages of information, if such information was sung or chanted. In order for the hymn to be sung or chanted in the same way every time, different musical "beats" or "meters" were devised (or "heard" according to other theories), and the information was poetically and musically set to a particular musical pattern.

In order for anyone to want to give up their entire lives to becoming a brāhmaṇa or a "human library book," it was probably found to be necessary to elevate the social status of the brāhmaṇas, so that children could aspire to devote their lives to becoming a "human library book." Food and shelter were probably provided by the society, so that the brāhmaṇas could spend all of their time at their "work."

The main "work" that the brāhmaṇas, did apparently was

10. *The Concise Oxford Dictionary of Current English,* Oxford University Press, 1995, p. 1553.

to remember their "book" (their portion of the *Ṛgveda* or *Manusmṛti* or other important composition) by chanting it several times a day and by teaching it to the next generation. Originally, the older compositions that were memorised by brāhmaṇas mostly had philosophical or spiritual or religious content and prayers to some aspect of the "divine." Brāhmaṇas, probably also engaged in recitations to their families and others. The next generation of brāhmaṇas probably would be a child of the brāhmaṇa, usually a son, who was willing to devote his entire life to becoming a "human library book."

2.16 Ṛgveda: Multiple Layers of Messages

It now appears that the *Ṛgveda* content did not just serve a single purpose, nor even a dual purpose, but multiple purposes. For instance, each line of *Ṛgveda* seems to contain not only what appears to be spiritual prayers and stories on first blush, but upon a more detailed examination, reveal information about history, geography, astronomy, astrology and mathematics.

In ancient India, writing, it was likely considered, would make people lazy with their memories and actually shrink the human mind and the capacity for memorisation. It had been observed that any one human being could remember long passages of information quite precisely (i.e. word for word), as the brāhmaṇas remembered the Vedas. Actually, for modern students of ancient texts of India, such as *Ṛgveda* and the *Manusmṛti*, it is indeed very fortunate that writing had not "caught on" to any large extent in ancient India. Otherwise, most of *Ṛgveda* probably would have been written down on parchment or acid-dipped palm leaves and been lost, having been eaten by insects or destroyed through the ravages of time. Of course, there was the writing on domestic clay pots and probably "commercial writing" on domestic and internationally destined "seals." However, the people of ancient India seemed to realise, as few contemporaneous cultures did, that most writing would be destroyed, or that it might be extremely difficult to leave a type of "Rosetta Stone"[11] in a place where it would be easily found to aid in the decipherment of ancient texts.

Also, since the chanting of the Vedas requires precise meters, tones, and pronunciation, the people of ancient India provided the modern listener with a type of "time travel machine," almost like an ancient audio-recording device, available for listening today, to the hymns/chants of thousands of years ago.

2.17 Meaning of "Manu"

The word "Manu" (as in the *Manusmṛti*) has many different meanings depending on the context. "Manu" can mean: "thinking, wise or intelligent." "Manu" can also generally mean man or mankind, or "the Man *par excellence*" or the representative man and father of the human race. In the *Ṛgveda*, there is a "Manu" that is said to have been the first to have instituted sacrifices and spiritual/religious ceremonies. In general, although in most cases, the word "Manu" has to do with humanhood, the name "Manu" is also used to describe a divine being or a mythical progenitor of the earth.[12] At the time of composition of the *Ṛgveda*, human beings that were called *ṛṣi*, were supposedly very wise or "enlightened" beings or seers who were able to "see" or "hear" the songs of the Universe and sing or chant them out loud. Since the Sanskrit word *maha* roughly means great, then the two words together, *maharṣi*, means "Great Seer." Many of the original *ṛṣi*s of *Ṛgveda* were given the title *maharṣi*.

11. The Rosetta Stone is an artefact from Ancient Egypt, which allowed scholars to decipher Ancient Egyptian hieroglyphic writing. It is a stone carved with the same text in three languages, two Egyptian language scripts and one in classical Greek, discovered by a French army engineer under Napoleon, in 1799 at Rosetta, a port city in Egypt.

12. See Monier-Williams, *A Sanskrit-English Dictionary*, Oxford, 1899.

The *Manusmṛti* refers to a *maharṣi*, or a family or school of *ṛṣi* and *maharṣi*, who composed or compiled the *Manusmṛti*. In some stories, this *maharṣi* named "Manu" is regarded as the progenitor of the present race of living beings, and said, like the "Noah" of the biblical "Noah's Arc" fame, to have been preserved from a great flood and the father of a new race of humans. It bears noting that there is an etymological similarity of the word "Manu" to the German word for man, "Mann," and of course, the English word, "man."[13]

Another definition of the word Manu (*manu*) is: Thinking, wise, intelligent, "the thinking creature," man, mankind, the sons of man; the man *par excellence* or the representative man and father of the human race (regarded in the *Ṛgveda* as the first to have instituted sacrifices and religious ceremonies). The name Manu is especially applied to 14 successive mythical progenitors and sovereigns of the earth, the 7th Manu, called Vaivasvata, Sun-born regarded as the progenitor of the present race of living beings mentioned by Tacitus, in his work (Germania), as the mythical ancestor of the Germans (mann), (man); Angl. Sax. (man); Eng. (man)."[14]

2.18 Manusmṛti: Alternate Names

The *Manusmṛti* is also called by various other names. One of them is Mānava-Dharmaśāstra. The word *mānava* means "descended from or belonging to man or Manu, human; favouring men, the children of men, mankind; the races of men."[15] The word *dharma* means "that which is established or firm, steadfast decree, statute, ordinance, law, usage, practice, customary observance or prescribed conduct, duty; right, justice (often as a synonym of punishment; virtue, morality, religion, religious merit, good; holding to the law, doing one's

13. See Monier-Williams, *A Sanskrit-English Dictionary*, Oxford, 1899.
14. Ibid.
15. Ibid.

duty), law or justice personified as a bull. . . ."[16] The word *śāstra* means an order, command, precept, rule; teaching, instruction, direction, advice, good counsel; any instrument of teaching, any manual or compendium of rules, any book or treatise, any sacred book.

2.19 Buddhist Law of Dharma

In Thailand, Buddhist law codes are ascribed to the *Manusmṛti*. One of the writers on Buddhist Law, Andrew Huxley, talks about the reduction to writing of Buddhist Law/Dharma from oral memorised texts. The *Vinayapāli* (which was collated and reduced to writing in the first century BCE) consists of oral memorised texts and jottings of various kinds from the prior Buddhist centuries, the core of which must have been fixed during the reign of King Aśoka.[17]

Sompong Sucharitkul, in his article, "Thai Law and Buddhist Law," wrote about the Vinaya:

> True it is that the Vinaya lacks some of the elements in the modern legal system from the perspective of the Western world. There is no Court of Appeal, no prison wardens, no bailiffs to compel or enforce compliance with the verdict of monastic peers, while the most serious offenses are punishable with a form of *capitis diminutio* (defrocking or derobing of a monk). The Vinaya is nonetheless law, if only for application within the religious order, with inevitable repercussion for serious offences in the secular world.[18]

Sucharitkul has introduced well these "different" Eastern concepts to a Western audience.

---

16. See Monier-Williams, *A Sanskrit-English Dictionary*, Oxford, 1899.
17. See Andrew Huxley, *Buddhist Case Law on Theft: the Vinītavatthu on the Second Pārājika*, University of London Law Department School of Oriental and African Studies, 1999.
18. See Sompong Sucharitkul, "Thai Law and Buddhist Law", *American Journal of Comparative Law*, 1998.

2.20 Smṛti vs. Śruti

The Law Code of Manu is most often called *Manusmṛti* (that which is remembered by Manu). The word *smṛti* is also a difficult concept, and will be presented here by comparing and contrasting it with the word *śruti.*

In ancient India at the time of the composition of the *Manusmṛti,* there was a differentiation between information that was considered "divine in origin" and information generated by man. The compositions which were "divine in origin" were called Śruti and the human-generated compositions were called Smṛti.

Śruti is defined as:

> hearing, listening, related to the ear, organ or power of hearing, that which is heard or perceived with the ear, sounds, noise, etc. that which has been heard or communicated from the beginning, sacred knowledge orally transmitted by the brāhmaṇas from generation to generation, the Veda (i.e. sacred eternal sounds or words as eternally heard by those sages called ṛṣis, and so differing from Smṛti or what is only remembered and handed down in writing by human authors.[19]

Or in context:

> Śruti means that which is heard of or acquired by hearing. All the four Vedas together with all affiliated Upaniṣads are known as Śruti. They are regarded as primary scripture and the eternal truths stated in Śruti are considered divine in origin.[20]

In other words, Śruti was supposedly the divine sounds or songs that are being sung all the time and that any human being who could hear them (that person would then be called a *ṛṣi,* since such a divine song was only really available to a *ṛṣi*).

Smṛti, on the other hand, is defined as:

---

19. See Monier-Williams, *A Sanskrit-English Dictionary*, Oxford, 1899.
20. See E.T. Sankaran Kutty, *A Glimpse on Śruti*, Bharatiya Vidya Bhavan, 2006, p. 3.

> remembrance, reminiscence, the whole body of sacred tradition or what is remembered by human teachers (in contradistinction to Śruti or what is directly heard or revealed to the *ṛṣis*), the whole body of code of law as handed down by tradition (esp. the codes of Manu, Yājñavalkya and the 16 succeeding inspired lawgivers, viz. Atri, Viṣṇu, Hārīta, Uśanas or Śukra, Aṅgīras, Yama, Āpastamba, Samvarta, Kātyāyana, Bṛhaspati, Parāśara, Vyāsa, Śaṅkha, Likhita, Dakṣa and Gautama).[21]

Or in context:

> "Smṛti" means that which is remembered or written down from memory, "Smṛti" actually interpreted "Śruti" texts in a practical way that is intended for ordinary people or less intelligent people. . . .[22]

Smṛti is probably the precursor of the English word, "smart." In this context, one is smart if he or she can remember much information. Smṛti was not regarded on the same level as Śruti. Śruti, the song being constantly being sung by the divine, available to any human being, usually a *ṛṣi*, with a sufficiently powerful "radio-like" mind. Smṛti was much more common, "remembered" by human teachers (such as the *Manusmṛti*).

2.21 Ṛṣi Defined

A *ṛṣi*, as described above, was one who "received" Śruti. *Ṛṣi* is defined as:

> an inspired poet or sage, any person who alone or with others invoked the deities in rhythmical speech or song of a sacred character and was regarded by later generations as a patriarchal sage or saint, occupying the same position in Indian history as the heroes and patriarchs of other countries, and constituting a peculiar class of beings in the early mythical system. They are the authors or rather seers of the Vedic hymns. They are the inspired personages to whom these hymns were revealed.[23]

21. See Monier-Williams, *A Sanskrit-English Dictionary*, Oxford, 1899.
22. See E.T. Sankaran Kutty, *A Glimpse on Smṛti*, Bharatiya Vidya Bhavan, 2006, p. 22-23.
23. See Monier-Williams, *A Sanskrit-English Dictionary*, Oxford, 1899.

2.22 Spiritual Underpinnings of the Manusmṛti through Ṛgveda

In order to get some feel for the minds of the people who both composed and were influenced by the *Manusmṛti*, we need to examine briefly, the Vedas. *Ṛgveda* especially was the chief composition or "hymn" which was chanted or sung everyday and which was, as was pointed out above, the original "law composition," in the sense that this was a codification of everything that the average person of that time and place believed to be "natural law"; for instance, that there was a god, or force of nature called "Agni," who was responsible simultaneously for made-with-wood "fire," for the "fire of digestion" and the "spark" in human brains. And that all of those "fires" could be made better or stronger by "singing" or "chanting" hymns of praise to "Agni" (or getting others to chant for you). Correspondingly, a lack of chanting "Agni" praises would result in all of those "fires" not being "stoked" or cared for and result in a weakening or smothering of those fires whether it was a real made-with-wood "fire," the "fire of digestion" or the "spark" in a human brain.

It was, apparently, a rather simple formula: the "divine song" Śruti, had been "heard" by a spiritual person, a *ṛṣi*. Sing more "divine song" Śruti, receive more from the divine. Sing fewer "divine song" Śruti, receive less. Also, one could apparently sing the songs asking that as they got "more," their enemies got "less." Apparently, the gods or "Nature" were "fed" by the songs. Feed the gods to get fed yourself; starve the gods and receive starvation for yourself. It seems to have been based upon receiving tangible results and seemed to have only occasional references to worlds beyond this one.

2.23 Example of Śruti: Vedic "Text" of Ṛgveda

An example of Śruti from the Vedic composition, *Ṛgveda*, chapter II (second *maṇḍala*), hymn 1, directed to Agni: Fire And More:

> Thou, *Agni*, shining in thy glory through the days, art brought to life from out the waters, from the stone:
>
> From out the forest trees and herbs that grow on ground, thou, sovereign Lord of men art generated pure.
>
> Thine is the Herald's task and Cleanser's duly timed; Leader art thou, and Kindler for the pious man.
>
> Thou art Director, thou the ministering Priest: thou art the *Brahman*, Lord and Master in our home.
>
> Hero of Heroes, Agni! Thou art Indra, thou art Viṣṇu of the Mighty Stride, adorable:
>
> Thou, *Brahmaṇaspati*, the *Brahman* finding wealth: thou, O Sustainer, with thy wisdom tendest us.
>
> Agni, thou art King Varuṇa whose laws stand fast; as *Mitra*, Wonder-Worker, thou must be implored.
>
> Āryaman, heroes' Lord, art thou, enriching all, and liberal Aṁśa in the synod, O thou God.[24] (emphasis added)

This is a good example of text from *R̥gveda*, that spiritual and philosophical composition which pre-dated the *Manusmr̥ti* and was considered to be "sacred" by the authors of the Law Code of Manu, as we shall see below.

2.24 R̥gveda gives Immediate Divine Rewards or Punishments

In *R̥gveda* the gods bestow rewards or punishments to humans. In the *Manusmr̥ti* humans (such as kings or village chiefs, acting as judges) give out punishments, usually not rewards, and threaten punishments after death.

These R̥gvedic "divine rewards" came, for instance, in the form of sufficient rain for watering crops. People asked for large crop yields, freedom from sickness, defeat of their enemies, etc.

---

24. See Ralph T.H. Griffith, *Hymns of the R̥gveda*, 1889, Munshiram Manoharlal, 1999.

Sometimes "divine" punishments came in the form of little or no rain, many pests that ate the crops and defeat by enemies. And one of the means of "earning" specific rewards was "acceptable" sacrifices to the gods. The "rewards and punishments" mentioned in *Ṛgveda* also seemed much more immediate, that is, realised while one was still alive, not a reward or punishment after death.

On the other hand, in the *Manusmṛti*, much more of the time, the subject of rewards seems to have meant "after-death" rewards. Many of these rewards were not the immediate earthly rewards of the kind mentioned in the *Ṛgveda*, but rewards that were far off, such as going to one of the heavens. The punishments, in many cases, were also not immediate; many were described as punishments after death, for instance, being sent to one of the eighteen hells, or for people who were more afraid of reincarnation, the threat of being reincarnated as a very undesirable animal, such as a donkey.

2.25 Ṛgveda Words Packed with Multiple Meanings

Within each phrase of *Ṛgveda* there exist many references packed with meaning, "hidden" to the modern reader. We will examine next some of the myriad "hidden" meaning of these "packed" words.

2.26 Agni

"Agni" is defined as: "fire, sacrificial fire (of three kinds); the god of fire, the fire of the stomach, digestive faculty, gastric fluid; bile; gold; (Latin (ignis)."[25] When the listeners in ancient India heard the word *agni*, did they just think about the god of fire? Did they think about fire itself, sacrificial fire or non-sacrificial fire? Did they think about improving their own gastric fire (since their system of medicine, Āyurveda, says that most of the diseases were born from improper digestion, i.e. not enough "fire of

25. See Monier-Williams, *A Sanskrit-English Dictionary*, Oxford, 1899.

digestion")?[26] Did they think about gold? Or all of the above? Of course, there is no definitive way to find out. But if the word *agni* had all of those different meanings and if the average listener knew all of the meanings, then it is likely that all of the meanings were brought to the front of the listener's mind, to some extent or another.

Another question comes to mind, as to whether the listeners of the time of *Ṛgveda* composition (during ancient *Ṛgveda* Time) heard something different, or interpreted something differently than the listeners at the time of composition of the *Manusmṛti*. Did the listeners during the *Ṛgveda* Time simply think about increasing their own sacrificial or cooking fire or their own gastric fire? Did they ask their gods to destroy the cooking fire and gastric fire of their enemies? Did the listeners at the *Manusmṛti* Time interpret the *Ṛgveda* in a similar manner or were they more worried about heaven and hell or being reborn, for instance, as a donkey? That is to say, did the first group think more about the present and the second group think more about life after death? These and other similar questions have not been completely answered as of yet. But one can intelligently theorise, the more one studies the well-preserved oral texts. And if the emerging theories are correct, that there is a correlation between the *Ṛgveda* and the Indus/Haṛappan Civilisation, then additional information is available for scholars to analyse.

Some of the key words from the *Ṛgveda* text above will next be examined.

2.27 Brahman

The word *Brahman* means: the one self-existent Spirit, the Absolute. The word *Brahman* means growth, expansion, evolution, development, swelling of the spirit or soul, from (*bṛh*) pious effusion or utterance, outpouring of the heart in

26. See Vasant Dattatray Lad, MASc, *Textbook of Ayurveda*, The Ayurvedic Press, 2002, p. 81.

worshipping the gods; the sacred word, the Veda, a sacred text, a text or *mantra* used as a spell; the sacred syllable *Oṁ*; religious or spiritual knowledge; holy life; the Brahmā or one self-existent impersonal Spirit, the one universal Soul (or one divine essence and source from which all created things emanate or with which they are identified and to which they return), the Self-existent, the Absolute, the Eternal (not generally an object of worship but rather of meditation and knowledge; The word "Brahmin" (brāhmaṇa) means the class of men who are the repositories and communicators of sacred knowledge, the Brāhmanical caste as a body, one versed in sacred knowledge; the brāhmaṇa was the most learned of them and was required to know the three Vedas, to supervise the sacrifice and to set right mistakes.[27] A similar question arises here. When the people of the R̥gvedic era or *Manusmr̥ti* era heard the word *Brahman*, did they think of growth or expansion? Did they think of the brāhmaṇa men in their village, town or city? Or did all of these meanings cross their minds simultaneously?

2.28 Indra

"Indra" is defined as the god of the atmosphere and sky or lord of rain (who in Vedic mythology reigns over the deities of the intermediate region or atmosphere; he fights against and conquers with his thunderbolt (*vajra*) the demons of darkness, and is in general a symbol of generous heroism; (Indra) was not originally lord of the gods of the sky, but his deeds were most useful to mankind, and he was, therefore, addressed in prayers and hymns more than any other deity, and ultimately superseded the more lofty and spiritual Varuṇa; in the later mythology (Indra) is subordinated to the triad Brahmā, Viṣṇu, and Śiva, but remained the chief of all other deities in the popular mind.[28]

---

27. See Monier-Williams, *A Sanskrit-English Dictionary*, Oxford, 1899.
28. Ibid.

2.29 Viṣṇu

"Viṣṇu" is the "All-pervader" name of one of the principal Hindu deities (in the later mythology regarded as "the preserver"), and with Brahmā "the creator" and Śiva "the destroyer," constituting the well-known Trimūrti or triad; although Viṣṇu comes second in the triad he is identified with the Supreme Deity by his worshippers; in the Vedic period, however, he is not placed in the foremost rank, although he is frequently invoked along with the other gods, especially with Indra whom he assists in killing Vṛtra; as distinguished from the other Vedic deities, he is a personification of the light and of the sun, especially in his striding over the heavens, which he is said to do in three paces, explained as denoting the threefold manifestations of light in the form of fire, lightning, and the sun, in the brāhmaṇas he is identified with sacrifice, and in one described as a dwarf; in the *Mahābhārata* and *Rāmāyaṇa* he rises to the supremacy which in some places he now enjoys as the most popular deity of modern Hindu worship: the distinguishing feature in the character of the post-Vedic Viṣṇu is his condescending to become incarnate in a portion of his essence on ten principal occasions, to deliver mankind from certain great dangers.[29] Both Viṣṇu and Indra both drank the *soma-rasa* (intoxicating drink). (See below regarding *soma-rasa*.)

2.30 Varuṇa

"Varuṇa" is the "All-enveloping Sky"; he is often regarded as the Supreme Deity, being then styled "king of the gods" or "king of both gods and men" or "king of the universe." No other deity has such grand attributes and functions assigned to him; he is described as fashioning and upholding heaven and earth, as possessing extraordinary power and wisdom called (*māyā*), ascending his spies or messengers throughout both worlds, as numbering the very winkings of men's eyes, as hating falsehood,

29. See Monier-Williams, *A Sanskrit-English Dictionary*, Oxford, 1899.

as seizing transgressors with his noose (*pāśa*), as inflicting diseases, especially dropsy, as pardoning sin, as the guardian of immortality; yet he is often connected with the waters, especially the waters of the atmosphere or firmament, and in one place is called with Mitra (Sindhu-pati), "lord of the sea or of rivers"; hence in the later mythology he became a kind of Neptune, and is there best known in his character of god of the ocean.[30] Mitra is the "friend, companion, associate, sustaining earth and sky and beholding all creatures with unwinking (unblinking) eye."[31]

2.31 Conclusion

There is evidence that perhaps similar geographical locations were shared by the people of the *Ṛgveda*, later by the people of the *Manusmṛti* and perhaps contemporaneously by the people of the Indus/Haṛappan Civilisation, the land "which lies between the two divine rivers, Sarasvatī and Dṛṣadvatī, and which the sages refer to as Brahmāvartta."

Apparently, during the time of the extensive use of the *Manusmṛti*, legal brāhmaṇas, "mouths of the Creator" or "human library books" or "human computers" devoted themselves to memorising the *Manusmṛti* and could recite any law upon request. The *Manusmṛti* is a "man-made" "Smṛti" — "that which is remembered" (and could more easily be changed or added to), not a "more divine" "Śruti" "that which was heard" by a *ṛṣi*, such as the *Ṛgveda*, which contains much more "hidden" information.

30. See Monier-Williams, *A Sanskrit-English Dictionary*, Oxford, 1899.

31. Ibid.

3

Caste and Guilds in Ancient India

3.1 Originally no "Fixed Caste" in Ninth Chapter of Ṛgveda

CLASS divisions or a "caste" system existed at the time of the Law Code of Manu in ancient India and detailed in many verses. Prior to the *Manusmṛti*, it appeared that there was not a "fixed-caste" system in India. This supposition can be supported by examining the oldest compositions from India, the "Vedas," and particularly the oldest, the *Ṛgveda*.

The ninth chapter or *maṇḍala* (circular, round),[1] is the chapter that is almost exclusively devoted to the god Soma Pavamāna or Indu, of the magical, intoxicating drink (*soma*).

3.2 Individuals get to Choose Their Work or Class in Ṛgveda

In this ninth *maṇḍala* of *Ṛgveda*, hymn CXII, it appears that individuals get to choose their livelihood rather than being born into it. In verse 3, the "composer" of this verse (or the "seer" of the verse) calls himself "the singer" or "the poet." He says that his father is a physician (probably using the ancient Indian healing system of Āyurveda) and his mother is "grinding corn," which probably means either cooking or trading ground corn as a miller. The "singer" or "poet" of this verse has a different task in society than that of his mother or father, a reference to

1. See Monier-Williams, *A Sanskrit-English Dictionary*, Oxford, 1899.

not being trapped into one course of action or profession or caste or class:

> A bard (poet/singer/seer) am I, my dad's a leech (an Āyurvedic physician), mummy lays corn upon the stones (a miller);
>
> Striving for wealth, with varied plans, we follow our desires like kine. Flow, Indu, flow for Indra's sake.[2] (explanations added)

It does not appear from this verse that the class division within society had yet begun. People do not seem to be "locked in" to one caste just by their birth to a father and mother of a particular profession, class or caste. The first verse of this chapter refers to groups based on the different tasks in society, not one based on class or birth and makes no reference to being required to pursue only one course of action or career. The passage immediately preceding the one above seems to clarify such divergent paths:

> We all have various thoughts and plans, and diverse are the ways of men. The brāhmaṇa seeks the worshipper, the wright seeks the cracked wheel, and leech (an Āyurvedic physician) (seeks) the maimed (or diseased). Flow, Indu, flow for Indra's sake. . . .[3]
>
> (explanations added).

3.3 Manusmr̥ti — Fixed Caste by Birth

In the first chapter of *Manusmr̥ti*, reference is made to the creation of human beings by the Creator and the division of human beings.

Manusmr̥ti — chapter 1, verse 31, William Jones' translation (1794):

> That the human race might be multiplied, he caused the brāhmaṇa, the kṣatriya, the vaiśya, and the śūdra (so named from the scripture,

2. See Monier-Williams, *A Sanskrit-English Dictionary*, Oxford, 1899.
3. See Ralph Griffith, *Hymns of The R̥gveda*, 1889, Munshiram Manoharlal, 1999.

protection, wealth and labour) to proceed from his mouth, his arm, his thigh, and his foot.[4]

Other translations are similar.[5]

There are philosophers from India who have read passages in *Ṛgveda* to mean that "the gods" actually "feed" on prayers and sacrifices made by human beings. And if such prayers and sacrifices are not made, the gods "starve," while longing for more human beings to "feed" them. Medhātithi wrote one of the earliest surviving written commentaries on the *Manusmṛti*. Records indicate that Medhātithi was a lawyer and law commentator who lived about 1,400 years ago (in the seventh century CE). Relevant parts of his commentary will be examined here. Medhātithi shares the view of "nourishment" of other worlds.[6]

---

4. See William Jones, *The Works of Sir William Jones (The Institutes of Hindu Law or The Ordinances of Manu)*, G.G. and J. Robinson, 1794.

5. Manmatha Nath Dutt's translation, 1895:

   "For the furtherance of the (good of the) world, he created brāhmaṇa, kṣatriya, vaiśya, and śūdra from his mouth, arms, thighs, and legs."

   George Buehler's translation, 1896:

   "But for the sake of the prosperity of the worlds he caused the brāhmaṇa, the kṣatriya, the vaiśya, and the śūdra to proceed from his mouth, his arms, his thighs, and his feet."

   Ganganath Jha's translation, 1920:

   "With a view to the development of the (three) regions, he brought into existence the brāhmaṇa, the kṣatriya, the vaiśya and the śūdra, from out of his mouth, arms, thighs, and feet (respectively)."

   Wendy Doniger and Brian K. Smith's translation, 1991:

   "Then, so that the worlds and people would prosper and increase, from his mouth he created the priest, from his arms the ruler, from his thighs the commoner, and from his feet the servant."

   Patrick Olivelle's translation, 2005:

   "For the growth of these worlds, moreover, he produced from his mouth, arms, thighs, and feet, the brāhmaṇa, the kṣatriya, the vaiśya, and the śūdra."

6. See G. Jha, *Manusmṛti with the Manubhāṣya of Medhātithi*, Motilal Banarsidass, vol. 6 (1st edn. 1920; 2nd 1999), p. 75: →

He wrote that since "prayers" and the "sacrifices" referred to here are the kind that are primarily verbal, it makes sense that this kind of philosophy would emphasise the human mouth as one of the most important organs of the human body. The logical continuance is true, say these philosophers, that the "god of creation" has a type of "body," similar in many ways to the human body, and that different human beings are formed from different parts of that body. Of course, it follows, under this theory, that human beings, whose humanly task it is to verbally recite (prayers, laws, teachings, etc.) that they would be born from the mouth of the god of creation. And that other classes or castes of human beings would be created from various other "parts" of that same god of creation.

Medhātithi explains and repeats part of the *Manusmr̥ti* relating to the castes being formed: "He brought unto existence," — i.e. produced, the brāhmaṇa and other castes, — "From out of his mouth, arm, thighs and feet," respectively; i.e. the brāhmaṇa from out of his mouth, the kṣatriya out of his arms, the vaiśya out of his thighs and the śūdra out of his feet.[7]

3.4 Caste attributed to the Creator in Manusmr̥ti

In ancient India, the people who were governed by the *Manusmr̥ti* apparently subscribed to the theory that there was a creator, and that different classes or caste of people were created from different organs of that spiritual creator.

→ "*With a view to the development of the regions*, terrestrial and the rest; *development* stands for *Nourishment* and *expansion*; it is only when the four castes, brāhmaṇa and the rest, are there that there is development of the three regions; for the Gods live upon offerings made by these castes — these castes alone being entitled to the performance of sacrifices; so that the action done by these nourishes the two regions (celestial and subterranean); then again, the gods also are prompted by men's action to act; from the Sun-God comes rain; and thus the said creation (of the brāhmaṇa) tends to the nourishment of this (terrestrial) region also."

7. See G. Jha, *Manusmr̥ti with the Manubhāṣya of Medhātithi*, Motilal Banarsidass, vol. 6 (1st edn. 1920; 2nd 1999), p. 75.

Medhātithi found a justification of caste by saying that in reality, what is stated in the *Manusmṛti* is merely commendatory, intended to show the relative superiority and inferiority of the castes. "Of all beings Prajāpati (the creator) is the highest — among all the limbs of Prajāpati, the mouth is the highest — similarly the brāhmaṇa is the highest, most praiseworthy, of all the castes; and on the basis of this similarity the brāhmaṇa is described as produced out of Brahmā's mouth."

Medhātithi also said that the description of the brāhmaṇa coming out of Brahmā's mouth may be due to the fact that the work of the mouth, such as teaching and the like, belongs preeminently to the brāhmaṇa; to the kṣatriya belongs the work of the arms, fighting; to the vaiśya the work of the thighs, such as wandering about with the cows, when tending cattle, and also travelling for trade on land and water; and to the śūdra belongs the work of the feet, i.e. service.[8]

3.5 M.N. Dutt says no Original Oppression, Just "Division of Labour"

M.N. Dutt, one of the translators of the *Manusmṛti*, is of the opinion that originally there was no prejudice in dividing society into various castes or classes. He writes of a theory called "universal evolution" which states that people wanted to be born at the ". . . beck and call of Ideation (brāhmaṇa), Protectiveness (kṣatriya), and Sustentative function (vaiśya), they respectively gave them the names of kṣatriya (soldier), vaiśya (merchant or farmer) and śūdra (artisan or servant). *Śūdratvam* is held identical with *karmatvam*, work, action, or service. Originally a śūdra meant an evangelist of service to mankind, although by an unfortunate degeneration of its meaning, it subsequently came to be synonymous with something low or vile.[9]

8. See G. Jha, *Manusmṛti with the Manubhāṣya of Medhātithi*, Motilal Banarsidass, vol. 6 (1st edn. 1920; 2nd 1999), p. 75.

9. See M.N. Dutt, *Manusmṛti*, Chaukhamba Sanskrit Pratishthan, 1998, p. 11.

Perhaps Dutt's point of view may have made sense in the time prior to the *Manusmṛti*, during the time of the *Ṛgveda*. As was pointed out above, the Ṛgvedic society seems to be much more flexible, allowing one to move from group to group based on one's "self-decided" livelihood in life, not based on the livelihood of one's parents. The *Manusmṛti* seems to have evolved to, or at least reflected, a relatively inflexible, "fixed-caste" society.

Dutt continues his analysis by advancing the theory that the members of these different castes accepted this classification within their society and that it was much different than the divisions in modern society, which he considers arbitrary:

> These distinctions of castes have nothing of the hatred and the sense of inequality, which prompted many a civilised society of modern times to lay down an arbitrary barrier between man and man, to create an artificial gulf between the classes and the masses, only on the basis of money-qualification. The framers of the ancient Saṁhitās recognised the inevitable necessity of organising a division of labour among the several orders of the society.[10]

3.6 Dutt claimed that Servants / Śūdras were Free

Dutt's theory postulates co-operation as the basis of the caste system:

> The caste system had its origin in the principle of co-operation and reciprocal help, and not in contempt and spitefulness as it is now erroneously believed in certain quarters. A good śūdra (an artisan) was as much free and as much honourable as any kṣatriya, or any vaiśya or even any brāhmaṇa in ancient India.[11]

Dutt claims that śūdras enjoyed all the civic rights that every other member of society enjoyed and that this was very different from the slaves that existed in most other societies and

10. See M.N. Dutt, *Manusmṛti*, Chaukhamba Sanskrit Pratishthan, 1998, p. 11.
11. Ibid.

civilisations throughout the world at that time. Dutt's theory does not seem to stand up to his own translation of the *Manusmṛti*, for instance, even his translation regarding the three higher castes that were considered "twice born" and therefore "better than" those below that level of society: *Dvija* is defined as: "twice-born; a man of any one of the first three classes, any Aryan, (especially) a brāhmaṇa (re-born through investiture with the sacred thread (*upanayana*). . . ."[12]

Since the *Manusmṛti* stated that the most honoured members of the society of that time were produced from the Creator's mouth (near the brain), then perhaps it was easier to convince the general populace of that time of the "correctness" of this philosophical position: that some human beings were better than others. And the judgement had to do with a person's birth, and whether or not that person's parents were of a particular class or caste.

3.7 Movement between Classes Forbidden in Manusmṛti

Movement from one class or caste to another was technically forbidden by the *Manusmṛti*, as was intermarriage between the classes, although in practice, marriage between castes must have been not uncommon, because one part of *Manusmṛti* has classifications for all of the children of the different combinations.

The belief in reincarnation must have been strong at the time, and it was said that the only means by which a person could hope to change their class or caste was by doing a "good job" for an entire lifetime and hoping and praying that they would advance in class or caste during their next incarnation.

Separate Duties For Each Caste Depending on their Origin: *Manusmṛti* — chapter 8, verse 87: William Jones' translation (1794):

---

12. See Monier-Williams, *A Sanskrit-English Dictionary*, Oxford, 1899.

> For the sake of preserving this universe, the Being, supremely glorious, allotted separate duties to those who sprang respectively from his mouth, his arm, his thigh, and his foot.[13]

Other translations are similar.[14]

Some scholars see the caste system as an extremely clever way of convincing people to "stay in their place" in society. Or that those people "in power" were telling the powerless people that they are "locked in" to a certain role in society, and the only way out is by reincarnation.

3.8 Brāhmaṇas to Teach and Perform Sacrifices

Brāhmaṇa's Duties: The *Manusmṛti* — chapter 8, verse 88: William Jones' translation (1794):

---

13. William Jones, *The Works of Sir William Jones (The Institutes of Hindu Law or The Ordinances of Manu)*, vol. 3, 275, 1794, rpt. 1909.

14. M.N. Dutt's translation, 1895:

    "For the preservation of all this creation, He, of great effulgence, laid down separate duties for those originated from His mouth (brāhmaṇas), from His arms (kṣatriyas), from His thighs (vaiśyas) and from His legs (śūdras)."

    George Buehler's translation, 1896:

    "But in order to protect this universe He, the most resplendent one, assigned separate (duties and) occupations to those who sprang from his mouth, arms, thighs, and feet."

    Ganganath Jha's translation, 1920:

    "With a view to the protection of this entire creation, the Resplendent One ordained the distinct functions of those who sprang from the mouth, the arms, the thighs and the feet."

    Wendy Doniger and Brian K. Smith's translation, 1991:

    "But to protect this whole creation, the lustrous one made separate innate activities for those born of his mouth, arms, thighs, and feet."

    Patrick Olivelle's translation, 2005:

    "For the protection of this whole creation, that One of dazzling brilliance assigned separate activities for those born from the mouth, arms, thighs, and feet."

> To brāhmaṇas he has assigned the duties of reading the Veda, of teaching it, of sacrificing, of assisting others to sacrifice, or giving alms, if they be rich, and, if indigent, of receiving gifts.[15]

Other translations are similar.[16]

This is another example of the *Manusmṛti*'s "split personality." The above verse sounds as if brāhmaṇas' duties were primarily sacerdotal, whereas, later in the work, it sounds as if a goodly percentage of brāhmaṇas were law brāhmaṇas, assisting the village chief or king in administering the laws.

But, obviously, teaching and studying the Vedas was considered to be such an important activity for the entire community, that it became codified that others in the society were to support that activity. It became "accepted" that one person from another class of society would receive "spiritual merit" by giving money and other goods to brāhmaṇas. In

---

15. William Jones, *The Works of Sir William Jones (The Institutes of Hindu Law or The Ordinances of Manu)*, vol. 3, 275, 1794, rpt. 1909.

16. M.N. Dutt's translation, 1895.

    "Study (of the Vedas), teaching, performance of sacrifices, officiating as priests at other men's sacrifices, gift-making and acceptance of gifts are the duties of brāhmaṇas."

    George Buehler's translation, 1896:

    "88. To brāhmaṇas he assigned teaching and studying (the Veda), sacrificing for their own benefit and for others, giving and accepting (of alms)."

    Ganganath Jha's translation, 1920:

    "For the brāhmaṇas he ordained teaching, studying, sacrificing and officiating at sacrifices, as also the giving and accepting of gifts."

    Wendy Doniger and Brian K. Smith's translation, 1991:

    "For priests, he ordained teaching and learning, sacrificing for themselves and sacrificing for others, giving and receiving."

    Patrick Olivelle's translation, 2005:

    "To brāhmaṇas, he assigned reciting and teaching the Veda, offering and officiating at sacrifices, and receiving and giving gifts."

addition to their memorising functions, this then, was the "sacerdotal" portion of the caste.

Throughout most of the ancient world, the idea of primogeniture (the eldest son inheriting everything) was popular. Medhātithi has something to say about the order of birth of the different castes, which has something to do with primogeniture: "The best part of the body," the head; from out of that sprang, was born, the brāhmaṇa — he is also the eldest of all, the brāhmaṇa was produced before the other castes — "because he upholds the *Brahman*, i.e. Veda"; the upholding of the Veda has been specifically prescribed for him. Hence, for all these reasons, the brāhmaṇa is the lord, i.e. as if he were the lord of this whole world, i.e. he should be approached (treated) like the lord and people should obey his orders in matters relating to *dharma*. *Dharmataḥ prabhuhu* means *dharme prabhuhu* Lord in matter regarding *dharma*."[17]

3.9 Kṣatriyas to Protect the People

Kṣatriyas Duties: The *Manusmṛti* — chapter 8, verse 89: William Jones' translation (1794):

> To defend the people, to give alms, to sacrifice, to read the Veda, to shun the allurements of sensual gratification, are, in a few words, the duties of a kṣatriya.[18]

Other translations are similar.[19]

---

17. G. Jha, *Manusmṛti with the Manubhāṣya of Medhātithi*, Motilal Banarsidass, vol. 6 (1st edn. 1920; 2nd 1999), p. 1.

18. William Jones, *The Works of Sir William Jones* (*The Institutes of Hindu Law or The Ordinances of Manu*), vol. 3, 275, 1794, rpt. 1909.

19. M.N. Dutt's translation, 1895:

    "Protection of the people, gift-making, performance of sacrifices, study of the Vedas, and abstention from luxury are, in general, the duties of kṣatriyas."

    George Buehler's translation, 1896:

    "89. The kṣatriya commanded to protect the people, to bestow gifts, to offer sacrifices, to study (the Veda), and to abstain from attaching himself to sensual pleasures." →

If kṣatriyas were the warriors, kings, village chiefs, soldiers and police, it was likely believed that such activities required courage and strength. Courage and strength might be weakened by anger and attachment to sensual pleasures and thus the *Manusmṛti* composed a verse against any such behaviour that would weaken courage and strength in members of that class.

3.10 Vaiśyas to Raise Cattle and become Traders

Vaiśya's Duties: The *Manusmṛti* — chapter 8, verse 90: William Jones' translation (1794):

> To keep herds of cattle, to bestow largesses, to sacrifice, to read the scripture, to carry on trade, to lend at interest, and to cultivate land are prescribed or permitted to a vaiśya.[20]

Other translations are similar.[21]

→ Ganganath Jha's translation, 1920:

"For the kṣatriya he ordained protecting of the people, giving of gifts, sacrificing and studying, as also abstaining from being addicted to the objects of sense."

Wendy Doniger and Brian K. Smith's translation, 1991:

"Protecting his subjects, giving, having sacrifices performed, studying, and remaining unaddicted to the sensory objects are, in summary, for a ruler."

Patrick Olivelle's translation, 2005:

"To the kṣatriya, he allotted protecting the subjects, giving gifts, offering sacrifices, reciting the Veda, and avoiding attachment to sensory objects."

20. See William Jones, *The Works of Sir William Jones (The Institutes of Hindu Law or The Ordinances of Menu)*, G.G. & J. Robinson, 1794.

21. M.N. Dutt's translation, 1895:

"Rearing of cattle (sheep, etc.), gift-making, performance of sacrifices, study (of the Vedas), merchandise, moneylending and agriculture are the duties of vaiśyas."

George Buehler's translation, 1896:

"The vaiśya to tend cattle, to bestow gifts, to offer sacrifices, to study (the Veda), to trade, to lend money, and to cultivate land."

Ganganath Jha's translation, 1920:

→

The vaiśyas were the original businessmen of Indian society at the time of the *Manusmṛti*. They controlled the biggest businesses of the society at the time of the *Manusmṛti*: the farming of crops and the running of dairy farms. Most probably, there must have been merchants in this class that were just traders.

3.11 Śūdras to Serve Everyone Else

The *Manusmṛti* — chapter 8, verse 91: William Jones' translation (1794):

> One principal duty the supreme Ruler assigns to a śūdra; namely, to serve the before-mentioned classes, without depreciating their worth.[22]

Other translations are similar.[23]

"For the vaiśya, tending of cattle, giving of gifts, sacrificing and studying; as also trade, moneylending and cultivating of land."

Wendy Doniger and Brian K. Smith's translation, 1991:

"Protecting his livestock, giving, having sacrifices performed, studying, trading, lending money, and farming the land are for a commoner."

Patrick Olivelle's translation, 2005:

"And to the vaiśya, looking after animals, giving gifts, offering sacrifices, reciting the Veda, trade, moneylending, and agriculture."

22. See William Jones, *The Works of Sir William Jones (The Institutes of Hindu Law or The Ordinances of Manu)*, G.G. & J. Robinson (1794).

23. M.N. Dutt's translation, 1895:

"Only one work did the Lord ordain for śūdras, viz. to ungrudgingly serve the three above-said social orders."

George Buehler's translation, 1896:

"One occupation only the Lord prescribed to the śūdra, to serve meekly even these (other) three castes."

Ganganath Jha's translation, 1920:

"For the śūdra, the Lord ordained only one function; the ungrudging service of the said castes."

Wendy Doniger and Brian K. Smith's translation, 1991:

"The Lord assigned only one activity to a servant: serving these (other) classes without resentment."

→

3.12 Smart Servants were denied Advancement for Life

This was, by far, in the opinion of the author, one of the most insidious ideas of the *Manusmṛti*: that if you are born to a father and mother who were servants, you would automatically be expected to be a servant for your entire life. It apparently did not matter if you had more intelligence than a soldier or a dairy farmer. It did not matter if you were born with the skills of an excellent businessman. You were "stuck" as it were, to serve meekly the other three castes, and then patiently wait, and hope and pray that you would be born to a higher class in your next lifetime. As the *Manusmṛti* reminded the members of its society: The Lord, Prajāpati, ordained one function, for the śūdra (in the form): Thou shalt perform the service of the said castes, i.e. of the brāhmaṇa, kṣatriya and vaiśya, ungrudgingly, i.e. without complaining; no resentment should be felt even in the mind.[24]

By the time the *Manusmṛti* was composed (or altered), perhaps foreign influences became stronger in India, since there are similarities in text to the Code of Hammurabi and other Codes. In any case, probably the strength of the brāhmaṇa class or caste was growing and it was probably the desire of certain members of that caste to "carve out" a protected niche in their society of the time.

3.13 Ṛgveda had Changeable Class; Manusmṛti had Fixed Caste

Even though some portions of the *Manusmṛti* seem to have copied directly from the *Ṛgveda*, the interpretations apparently were different. The passage in the *Manusmṛti* that was used to justify fixed caste was copied from *Ṛgveda* division of tasks or non-

---

→ Patrick Olivelle's translation, 2005:

"A single activity did the Lord allot to the śūdra, however: the ungrudging service of those very social classes."

24.. See G. Jha, *Manusmṛti with the Manubhāṣya of Medhātithi*, Motilal Banarsidass, vol. 6 (1st edn. 1920; 2nd 1999), v. 3, p. 134.

fixed class. The Creation Hymn of *R̥gveda* (X.90.12), in part: ". . . brāhmaṇas sprang forth from his (Primordial Man) mouth, kṣatriyas were originated from his arms, vaiśyas came out from his thighs while śūdras were born from his feet."[25] As pointed out above, other verses in *R̥gveda* seem to indicate that people were classified by the work they chose, apparently not fixed and especially not fixed by birth.

3.14 "Man-Made Law" for Manusmr̥ti

Everyday life in ancient India must have undergone a transformation from a fluid society to more fixed society by the time of the composition of the "Man-Made Law" *Manusmr̥ti*. The laws of the *Manusmr̥ti* dictate the change and codify the change. Every citizen is locked into a societal position based on birth and the social position of one's parents. The only availability for social mobility is reincarnation into a higher (or as punishment for wrong action — lower) social position.

3.15 Guilds: Important in the Indus/Haṛappan Civilisation

J.P. Joshi believes that in the Indus/Haṛappan Civilisation mature internal trade could have been done by guilds in an organised fashion.[26] Indus/Haṛappan Civilisation crafts were very specialised; people probably devoted their lives to their specialities, like the carnelian necklaces that took a craftsman a whole year to make.[27] All of these engraved seals point to the existence of a guild of engravers.[28]

---

25. Pranati Ghosal, *Lifestyle of the Vedic People*, D.K. Printworld, 2006, p. 180.
26. See D.P. Sharma, and Madhuri (eds.), *Panorama of Harappan Civilization*, Kaveri Books (2003), p. 60.
27. See Jane McIntosh, *A Peaceful Realm*, Westview Press, 2002, p. 81.
28. H.D. Sankalia, *Pre-Historic Art in India*, Carolina Academic Press, 1978, p. 64.

3.16 Guilds: Important in Manusmṛti and Ṛgveda

In the *Manusmṛti*, guilds were in existence and certain laws were composed specifically for guild members. For instance, *Manusmṛti* (8.41):

> (A king) who knows the sacred law, must inquire into the laws of castes (*jāti*), of districts, of guilds, and of families, and (thus) settle the peculiar law of each.[29]

Manusmṛti: Guilds (8.219):

> If a man belonging to a corporation (guild) inhabiting a village or a district, after swearing to an agreement, breaks it through avarice, (the king) shall banish him from his realm.[30]

Medhātithi commented about Guilds this way: that the King is the most superior member of society, followed by persons authorised by the king, then Tribes, the Guilds, then Families:

> If however one party should have no confidence in these, and should say these persons are more nearly related to you, then the case shall be referred to the guilds, this term "guild" standing for a body of traders and others who may be following the same profession.[31]

Guilds are weightier than relatives, because they are more careful before the king, require members to pay fines for wrongdoing, etc. This must have been an interesting "business-type" of association, popular and powerful during the time of the *Manusmṛti*.

3.17 Breach of "Guild" Contract in Manusmṛti

Breach of "Guild" Contract by Greedy Member: The *Manusmṛti* — chapter 8, verses 219-21: William Jones' translation (1794):

---

29. See G. Buehler, *Laws of Manu*, Oxford (Sacred Books of the East, v. XXV) (1896).
30. Ibid.
31. See G. Jha, *Manusmṛti with the Manubhāṣya of Medhātithi*, Motilal Banarsidass, vol. 6 (1st edn. 1920; 2nd 1999), p. 6.

> The man, among the traders and other inhabitants of a town or district, who breaks a promise through avarice, though he had taken an oath to perform it, let the king banish from his realm. Or, according to the circumstances, let the judge, having arrested the promise breaker, condemn him to pay six *niṣkas*, or four *suvarṇas*, or one *śatamāṇa* of silver, or all three if he deserves such a fine. Among all citizens and in all classes, let a just king observe this rule for imposing fines on men, who shall break their engagements.[32]

Other translations are similar.[33]

---

32. See William Jones, *The Works of Sir William Jones (The Institutes of Hindu Law or The Ordinances of Manu)*, G.G. & J. Robinson (1794).

33. M.N. Dutt's translation, 1895:

    "Him, who having promised on oath to abide by the rules of the guild or assembly of his village or country, breaks that promise (i.e. transgresses the rules) out of greed, (the king) should banish from the country. Having thus punished the breaker of promise, (the king shall impose upon him) a fine of four *suvarṇas*, or six *niṣkas*, or one hundred silver coins. A virtuous king shall adopt this law of penalty (i.e. inflict these penalties on) in respect of persons who have violated their compacts with their caste-guilds or village-assemblies."

    George Buehler's translation, 1896:

    "If a man belonging to a corporation inhabiting a village or a district, after swearing to an agreement, breaks it through avarice, (the king) shall banish him from his realm.

    And having imprisoned such a breaker of an agreement, he shall compel him to pay six *niṣkas*, (each of) four *suvarṇas*, and one *śatamāṇa* of silver. A righteous king shall apply this law of fines in villages and castes (*jāti*) to those who break an agreement.

    Ganganath Jha's translation, 1920:

    "If a man, after having entered into a compact under oath *with* a village, a country or a confederation, should break it, through greed, him the king shall banish from his kingdom. (emphasis added) Having caught such a breaker of compact, he shall make him pay six *niṣkas* of four *suvarṇas* each and also one *śatamāṇa*. This is the law of punishment which the king shall follow in the case of the breakers of compacts relating to villages and caste-federations."

    Wendy Doniger and Brian K. Smith's translation, 1991:

    "If a man enters into a sworn agreement with a group from a village →

William Jones translates that *Manusmṛti* passage: "among the traders and other inhabitants of a town or district who breaks a promise"; Dutt translates: "oath to abide by the rules of the guild or assembly of his village or country"; Buehler translates: "belonging to a corporation inhabiting a village or a district, after swearing to an agreement"; Jha translates: "having entered into a compact under oath with a village, a country or a confederation"; Doniger and Smith translate, "sworn agreement with a group from a village or district"; and Olivelle translates, "belonging to a village, region or corporate entity enters into a contract."

These are all very different concepts. Is it just "any contract"? Is it a "compact under oath with a village, a country or a confederation"? Or is it an "oath to abide by the rules of the guild or assembly of his village or country"?

Patrick Olivelle, in his commentary on verse 219, says,

> The contract dealt with here is not a private one but pertains to a corporate body. When a contract is made with the stipulation that all those who belong to that corporate entity will do something, then each individual is bound by it. Here the corporate entities are a village, a region (group of villages) and a corporation (traders, artisans, etc.). Some interpret the compound *grāmadeśasaṁgha* as a corporation located in a village or region (so see Buehler). The term

---

→ or district and then breaks it out of greed, (the king) should banish him from the kingdom. He should arrest a man who violated an agreement and make him pay a fine of four 'gold coins,' six 'gold ornaments' and a silver 'hundred-weight.' A just king should apply this rule of punishment to those who violate agreements with village or caste communities."

Patrick Olivelle's Translation, 2005:

"When a man belonging to a village, region or corporate entity enters into a contract truthfully and then breaks it out of greed, the king should banish that man from his realm. He should arrest that man who has violated the compact and fine him six *niṣka*s, each weighing 4 *suvarṇa*s and a silver *śatamāṇa*. In this manner, righteous king should apply the rules of punishment to individuals who violate compacts within a village, caste or association."

satyena (*satya*) is also interpreted by some to mean an oath. . . ."[34]
(emphasis added).

Olivelle's commentary seems much more correct than his translation, as will be explained below.

3.18 "Village" is a Group of Households

Medhātithi defines "village" as a group of households, and the term here stands for the inhabitants of the village, as it is only among men that there can be a compact; similarly, "country" is a group of villages.[35] First, it appears that women cannot enter into such agreements. Second, there is nothing like modern law that allows corporations or villages to enter into a contract.

The next part refers to an inhabited place or a village. But the word "village," translated from the English to the Sanskrit, can give us some additional insight into the general concept and framework of the word "village." Village can also mean: "*kalāpa* 'that which holds single parts together,' a bundle, band; a bundle of arrows, a quiver with arrows . . . totality, whole body or collection of a number of separate things."[36] If "that which holds single parts together" is broken, by one "weak link," then potentially, the whole chain can fall apart.

Kheta is a village, residence of peasants and farmers, small town. Village can additionally mean: "*pura* a fortress, castle, city, town (a place containing large buildings surrounded by a ditch and extending not less than 1 *kosa* in length; if it extends for half that distance it is called a *kheta*, if less than that, a *karvata* or small market town; any smaller cluster of houses is called a *grāma* or village."[37]

---

34. See Patrick Olivelle, *Manu's Code of Law, a Critical Edition and Translation of the Mānava-Dharmaśāstra*, South Asia Research, 2005, p. 317.
35. See G. Jha, *Manusmṛti With the Manubhāṣya of Medhātithi*, Motilal Banarsidass, vol. 6 (1st edn. 1920; 2nd 1999), p. 266.
36. See Monier-Williams, *A Sanskrit-English Dictionary*, Oxford, 1899.
37. Ibid.

3.19 "Confederation" can contain Different Castes and Foreigners

"Confederation" is a combination formed by persons professing the same faith or path, even though inhabiting different countries and belonging to different castes. For instance, there is a confederation of mendicants, the confederation of traders, the confederation of persons learned in the Vedas and so forth.[38]

> What kinds of people make "combinations" among themselves, one of the most common one being cattle-owning vaiśyas, who unite to prevent the encroachment of neighbours' cattle on their grazing land. There are several kinds of business in which inhabitants of villages, etc. make a combination among themselves. For instance, "our village is being encroached upon by the inhabitants of another village, very frequently they graze their cattle on our pasture-lands, they cut our embankments and carry away water, if you be all agreed, then we shall prevent their doing all this, and when we prevent this, it is possible that we may come to blows, or may have to appear before the court; if we remain combined in all this, then we shall go forward to prevent the encroachment; otherwise we shall let it be." On this compact being proposed, men may agree to it saying yes, why should the ancient privileges of our village be trespassed by them? Now, after having thus entered in compact and encouraged it, if someone were to shirk away and make common cause with the other party, and become lukewarm towards his own neighbours, such a person should be banished by the king from his kingdom.[39]

3.20 "Greed" : Selfish Interests

Next, greed is defined: "greed" here stands for succumbing to one's own selfish interests as served by the inhabitants of the rival village. "For cases of such breach, through ignorance, there is another remedy."[40]

38. See G. Jha, *Manusmṛti with the Manubhāṣya of Medhātithi*, Motilal Banarsidass, vol. 6 (1st edn. 1920; 2nd 1999), pp. 266-67.

39. Ibid.

40. Ibid.

If Medhātithi's commentary (in Jha's translation of the *Manusmṛti*) is correct and Ganganath Jha's translation of Medhātithi is correct, then all three of the translations of this section of the *Manusmṛti* are somewhat misleading, with Jha's being the most correct. The commentary by Olivelle seems to correct his misleading translation. Olivelle's translation uses the words "corporate entity," which the modern legal reader would probably misinterpret. Medhātithi's use of the word "confederation" is clearer than Olivelle's "corporation," although both seem to correct the misunderstanding in their respective commentaries.

One part of Medhātithi's commentary is somewhat surprising, that "confederation" is a combination formed by persons professing the same faith or path, even though inhabiting different countries and belonging to different castes. For instance, there is a confederation of mendicants, the confederation of traders, the confederation of persons learned in the Vedas and so forth.

It makes sense that there is a confederation of mendicants, traders, etc., but the fact that they might "belong to different castes," seems to indicate that with regard to guilds, the *Manusmṛti* was not followed closely with regard to caste separation rules. Perhaps that is why there were so many inter-caste marriages, since *Manusmṛti* has one part that just gives the technical names for all of the children of these "mixed" marriages.

A confederation, according to Medhātithi, can be composed of individuals inhabiting different countries and belonging to different castes. This is different from the Olivelle commentary. The Medhātithi's commentary seems to indicate the seriousness of promising "just to join" or to be a member of a type of "mutual aid society." If Medhātithi's commentary is correct, then, for instance, if 100 per cent of the cattle-owning vaiśya men of a village unite to prevent the encroachment of neighbours' cattle on their grazing land and those men of that village agreed to form a confederation to defend the village grazing field against encroachment, and when the time came to "come to blows" with the neighbours who did the encroaching, and, for example, 50 per cent of the confederation members quit during the battle, having been bribed the night before, those 50 per cent who actually went into battle might well be injured or killed. The injury would have been the direct result of the greed of the members who accepted the bribe (through greed), quit the confederation and refused to join in the fight.

The rule for the people of the time might have been: don't enter into any confederations (guilds) lightly, without much thought of the requirements and consequences, and the possibility of permanent banishment from the kingdom, don't go back on your "membership required" promises because of greed.

3.21 Precursor of Crime of Treason

Jha's translation may actually indicate a precursor of the future modern Nation-State crime of treason:

> If a man, after having entered into a compact under oath with a village, a country or a confederation, should break it, through greed, him the king shall banish from his kingdom.[41]

This may have been the first, or one of the first codified legal concepts of the crime of treason. It seems similar to laws in future civilisations relating to military rules of war, joining an army and then becoming a "traitor" and/or "giving comfort to the enemy" for money or a bribe. If the inhabitants of Village A form a confederation (just like a tiny army) to enter into a kind of "battle" with Village B, even if the "battle" is a battle of words or the threat of force (which might lead to minor physical skirmishes), then those citizens of Village A who had agreed to

41. See G. Jha, *Manusmṛti with the Manubhāṣya of Medhātithi*, Motilal Banarsidass, vol. 6 (1st edn. 1920; 2nd 1999), p. 267.

become a "soldier" of Village A, but were then persuaded by greed (e.g. a bribe paid by Village B) to not "fight" on behalf of Village A, must be punished (by banishment or another monetary fine).

3.22 Guilds vs. Tribes vs. Families

Medhātithi points out the difference between Guilds and Tribes. "Tribes" consist of persons who always move about in groups, e.g. masons, temple priests, and so forth. They would investigate the cases of disputes arising among themselves and for the enforcing of decisions they shall appoint committees. The difference between these two ("Guilds" and "Tribes") is that the former (Guilds) consists of persons following the same profession and they can act singly also, whereas Tribes always act collectively. And it is because the Tribes act collectively that the disputants are afraid of them. According to others however, the term "families" stands for neutrals; and such persons, even though not members of the same guild, are conversant with all the ins and outs of the case, and as such capable of coming to a decision.[42]

3.23 Conclusion

The non-fixed class system seemed to be apparent from verses of the *Ṛgveda*. A person would be defined by their work, not by their birth. By the time of the composition of the *Manusmṛti*, the caste system was "fixed" by law, probably by the "higher" classes (and probably by men in the "higher" classes, since women were given fewer rights than men in the *Manusmṛti*).

The *Manusmṛti* has many laws pertaining to guilds. Some scholars have analysed the "production of goods" by the Indus/Haṛappan Civilisation and have concluded that guilds must have been used to facilitate such production. The *Manusmṛti* may thus be related to the Indus/Haṛappan Civilisation.

---

42. See G. Jha, *Manusmṛti with the Manubhāṣya of Medhātithi*, Motilal Banarsidass, vol. 6 (1st edn. 1920; 2nd 1999), p. 7.

4

Advanced Thought in Ancient India

4.1 Ṛgveda as an Ultimate Source of Science

ṚGVEDA is held by some scholars in India to be the ultimate source of science. Albert Einstein said that cosmic religious experience is the strongest and noblest driving force behind scientific research. Dr Shri Ram Verman, in his book, *Vedas: The Source of Ultimate Science,* starts out by defining the world "Veda" from *Ṛgveda* as "knowledge," coming from the Sanskrit verb root *vid,* which means "to know" and saying that the 10,552 verses of *Ṛgveda* contain not only many scientific provisions, but also mythology, cosmology and religion intermixed. India believed in the superiority of intuition to intellectual reasoning. Vedic *ṛṣis* believed that what they saw and heard from a superior spirit are the Vedas.[1]

In *Ṛgveda,* the word *deva* is used. Western scholars usually translate the words *deva* or *devatā* to mean "deity or god." Monier-Williams seems to agree in part, but also expands the definition, defining *deva* as heavenly, divine . . . the shining ones (also said of terrestrial things of high excellence).[2] Verman cites the ancient Indian reference book, *Nirukta,* to show that the word *deva* is derived from *da, dur, dip* and *divu* or "knowledge, light, peace and delight." The word *agni* is used quite often in *Ṛgveda. Agni* sometimes means God, sometimes the sun or light and heat or

1. See Shri Ram Verma, *Vedas: The Source of Ultimate Science,* Nag Publishers, 2005, p. 3.
2. Ṣee Monier-Williams, *A Sanskrit-English Dictionary,* Oxford, 1899.

bodily heat. Another word used quite a bit is *soma*. *Soma* means Lord of delight and nectar. All this, according to Verman, is Vedic symbolism, riddles to be interpreted with great difficulty.[3]

4.2 Astronomy Advancement in Ṛgveda and Manusmṛti

There has been a recent shift in the dating of Indian astronomy. The archaeological discovery that the river Sarasvatī dried up more than 3,900 years ago (before 1900 BCE) make ancient texts, such as *Ṛgveda*, older than that and the discovery of astronomy in the Vedic texts older than previously thought.[4]

Ṛgveda says that the moon's path was divided into 27 equal parts, each part was called a *nakṣatra*; modern science says that such a conclusion was close to reality, the moon takes about 27 and one-half days to complete its cycle.[5] This conclusion required fairly precise and accurate observation.

Another astronomical leap for Vedic people was the realisation that the moon received its light by way of the sun. The moon was called *sūrya raśmi*, the "one that shines by sunlight"; Vedic ritual was based on the times for the full and new moon, solstices and equinoxes.[6]

4.3 Calendar Invented in Ancient India

A fairly precise calendar seems to have been invented in ancient India. It is not exactly known when this calendar was invented, but some scholars believe that perhaps it was invented at the

3. See Shri Ram Verma, *Vedas: The Source of Ultimate Science*, Nag Publishers, 2005, pp. 15-16.
4. See Subhash Kak, "Birth and Early Development of Indian Astronomy", in H. Selin (ed.), *Astronomy across Cultures, The History of Non-Western Astronomy*, Kluwer Academic Publisher, 2000, p. 303.
5. See Bhagwan Singh, *The Vedic Harappans*, Aditya Prakashan, 1996, p. 409.
6. See Subhash Kak, "Birth and Early Development of Indian Astronomy", in H. Selin (ed.), *Astronomy across Cultures, The History of Non-Western Astronomy*, Kluwer Academic Publisher, 2000, p. 308.

same time as the civilisation in Mehrgaṛh. Apparently, the calendar used the observation of the Pole Star. The location of the Pole Star keeps changing over time due to the "precession" of the earth's polar axis, with a period of roughly 26,000 years. Polaris is the Pole Star now, but about 5,000 years ago (around 3000 BCE) it was Draconis.

According to some scholars, the *Ṛgveda* had the earliest calendar, which is believed by some to probably be the *saptarṣi* calendar (*ṚV*, 1.164.48)[7] That verse in *Ṛgveda* speaks about the twelve months, and the days of the year, which were said to be 360 (with additional make-up periods of time): "Twelve are the fellies, and the wheel is single; three are the naves. What man hath understood it? Therein are set together spokes 360, which in nowise can be loosened."

The Greek historians, Pliny and Arrian, say that the earliest calendar in India had a cycle of 2,700 years, called the *saptarṣi* calendar. The *saptarṣi* calendar is still in use in some parts of India today. Pliny suggested that it was that very same *saptarṣi* calendar which was the one that the people of India began to use almost 9,000 years ago (in 6676 BCE).[8] If this is true and if that calendar was used in Mehrgaṛh, then Mehrgaṛh is certainly one of the oldest "cradles of civilisation."

4.4 Sidereal Time used by Modern Astronomers

Today, the way in which most people living in the world determine "what is the time of day" is just to look at a clock. Many people do not realise that there is more than one way to determine "what time it is." One of the ways to "tell time" is to look at the stars. This is called "sidereal time," which is based on "star time" rather than the "sun time." Modern-day

7. See S.R. Verma, *Vedas: The Source of Ultimate Science*, Nag Publishers, 2005, p. 1.

8. See Subhash Kak, "The Mahābhārata and the Sindhu-Sarasvatī Tradition", in Agrawal (ed.), *In Search of Vedic-Haṛappan Relationship*, Aryan Books International, 2005, p. 82.

astronomers spend their time looking at stars. They find it convenient to use sidereal time. Most planetary and stellar observatories in the world today are equipped with a "sidereal clock" that gives modern-day astronomers the correct sidereal time. The astronomers from the Vedic time apparently "discovered" sidereal time.[9]

It seems amazing that the star-gazers from the time of the *Ṛgveda* discovered sidereal time in addition to the regular solar time that most of us use today in order to determine the time of day. Many Westerners think that it was Greek astronomers in about 2,350 years ago (250 BCE) who discovered the precession of the earth's polar axis and sidereal time. Rather it was the Vedic people, as described by Greek historians, who discovered sidereal time.[10]

The people who lived at the time the *Manusmṛti* was composed were also deeply interested in astronomical observations. In the *Manusmṛti*, chapter 1, verse 67, astronomical observations were recorded,

> A year is a day and a night of the gods; their division is (as follows): the half year during which the sun progresses to the north will be the day, that during which it goes southwards the night.[11]

4.5 Mathematic Genius in Ṛgveda, Manusmṛti and Indus/Haṛappan Civilisation

M.D. Pandit is of the opinion that one of the most accurate means to measure the development of a civilisation is to study its mathematical knowledge contained in its literature. He believes

9. S.R. Verma, *Vedas: The Source of Ultimate Science,* Nag Publishers, 2005, pp. 255-56.
10. See Subhash Kak, "Birth and Early Development of Indian Astronomy", in H. Selin (ed.), *Astronomy across Cultures, The History of Non-Western Astronomy,* Kluwer Academic Publisher, 2000, pp. 311-12.
11. See Buehler, *Laws of Manu*, Oxford (Sacred Books of the East, v. XXV), 1896, p. 10.

that no civilisation can develop without mathematics. One of the ways to measure development of a civilisation's mathematical knowledge is to look at its knowledge of numbers.

The highest number mentioned in *Ṛgveda* is one hundred thousand.[12] This seems incredible as compared to comparable cultures around the world that were far behind in high numbers.[13] In another composition from ancient India, the *Rāmāyaṇa*, there were names for numbers of powers of ten up to ten to the sixty-second; this is to be compared to the ancient Greeks, who had no names for numbers beyond ten to the fourth.[14]

The *Manusmṛti* also mentions a very large number, "one million": 3. 131. "Though a million of men, unacquainted with the *ṛkas*, were to dine at a (funeral sacrifice), yet a single man, learned in the Veda, who is satisfied (with his entertainment), is worth them all as far as the (production of) spiritual merit (is concerned)."[15]

Fire altars were built in Vedic times to comply with the duty of fire worship. The construction of the fire altars required solving geometric and algebraic problems.[16] There are also examples of mathematical multiplication in *Ṛgveda* (1.122.13): "We will rejoice to drink the *tenfold present when the twice five* come bearing sacred viands." Ancient India seems to have had addition, subtraction, multiplication, division, squaring, finding the square root, finding the cube and finding out the cube root. One of the

12. See M.D. Pandit, *Mathematics as Known to the Vedic Saṁhitās*, Sri Satguru Publisher, 1993, p. 10.

13. See Bhagwan Singh, *The Vedic Harappans*, Aditya Prakashan, 1996, p. 408.

14. See George Gheverghese Joseph, *The Crest of the Peacock, The Non-European Roots of Mathematics*, Princeton University Press, 2000, p. 242.

15. See G. Buehler, *Laws of Manu*, Oxford (Sacred Books of the East, v. XXV), 1896, p. 68.

16. See Subhash Kak, "Birth and Early Development of Indian Astronomy", in H. Selin (ed.), *Astronomy across Cultures, The History of Non-Western Astronomy*, Kluwer Academic Publisher, 2000, p. 313.

greatest inventions by Vedic mathematicians was the development of the concept of zero.[17]

Mathematical thought in Vedic times seemed to be very complex. If the mathematical ability was that advanced, one can only wonder about the advanced thinking in other areas.

4.6 Śrī-Yantras are 51½ Degrees, Similar to Great Pyramid in Egypt

One hymn from one of the Vedas is dedicated to a written meditation diagram called a *śri-yantra* (a great object; a tāntric meditation device), consisting of nine interwoven isosceles triangles. Four of these triangles point upwards, representing Śakti, primordial female dynamic energy and five of the triangles point downwards, representing Śiva, primordial male essence of wisdom. The triangles are arranged to produce subsidiary triangles, at the centre of which is a dot (*bindu*). In all correctly constructed *śri-yantra*s the base angle of the largest triangles is about 52½ degrees. The slope of the base of the Great Pyramid at Gizeh in Egypt, built around 2600 BCE, is approximately the same, both the *śri-yantra*s and the Great Pyramid using the "golden ratio" or "divine proportion," with links to Fibonacci numbers.[18]

4.7 Śulbasūtras (Mathematics)

The precision of some of the calculations needed to arrive at the above mathematics, seems to have been first written down in the Śulbasūtras, about 2,800 years ago (between 800 and 600 BCE), although passed down orally for an unknown period of time prior to that. But there are clues from the archaeological remains that Śulbasūtra mathematics was used in the Indus/Haṛappan Civilisation. The Śulbasūtras contained both religious and secular mathematics. They contain a general statement of the

---

17. See M.D. Pandit, *Mathematics as Known to the Vedic Saṁhitās*, Sri Satguru Publisher, 1993, p. 133.

18. See G.G. Joseph, *The Crest of the Peacock, The Non-European Roots of Mathematics*, Princeton University Press, 2000, pp. 236-37.

Pythagorean Theorem, a method for calculating the square root of two, correct to five decimal places. The Śulbasūtras give a remarkable approximation of constructing a square twice the area of a given square, "A", with no clue as to how this was arrived at. The formula is: increase the measure by its third and this third by its own fourth less the thirty-fourth part of that fourth.[19]

4.8 Weights and Measures of Indus/Haṛappā and Manusmṛti

The *Manusmṛti*, chapter 8, verse 131 goes into great detail about weights and measures.[20] That seed of the *guñjā* creeper (also known as a *guñjā*-berry or *raktikā* or *rattī*) was used as a unit of measurement, which, apparently, was also used by the Indus/Haṛappan Civilisation. The cubical stone weights of the Indus/Haṛappan Civilisation were based on a complex system of measurements. The base weight appears to have been that same tiny black and red seed known as the *guñjā*, which is still used by jewellers in Pakistan and India. In the *Manusmṛti*, that unit of measurement was called a *kṛṣṇalā*, which the translators say is the same as one *guñjā*-berry or one *raktikā* (or *rattī*).

The author verified the apparent precision of the weights and measures from the Indus/Haṛappan Civilisation during visits to the National Museum in New Delhi, India and the museum located at the Indus/Haṛappan Civilisation site of Lothal.

The Indus/Haṛappan Civilisation culture was a highly organised society with a number of different plumb-bobs of uniform size and weight. The weights were "decimal," that is, if we take 27.584 as standard, the other weights are .05, .1, .2, .5, 5, 10, 20, 50, 100, 200 and 500.[21] Once again, this is another means

19. See G.G. Joseph, *The Crest of the Peacock, The Non-European Roots of Mathematics*, Princeton University Press, 2000, pp. 234-35.
20. See Buehler, *Laws of Manu*, Oxford (Sacred Books of the East, v. XXV), 1896, p. 193.
21. See G.G. Joseph, *The Crest of the Peacock, The Non-European Roots of Mathematics*, Princeton University Press, 2000, p. 222.

to prove up the sophistication of the Indus/Haṛappan Civilisation and see how it was possible to achieve the uniformity in cities and towns throughout this vast ancient civilisation.

Some scholars believe that eight *guñjā* seeds equal the smallest known Indus weight, which by our modern standards equals .871 grammes; the largest weight found at Mohenjo-Dāṛo weighs 10,865 grammes, about 25 pounds, which is almost 100,000 times the weight of the *guñjā* seed.[22] Other scholars believe something very close, but not precisely similar: that the most common Indus weight was equivalent to about 13.7 grammes. The people of the Indus/Haṛappan Civilisation used smaller weights that were as little as one-sixteenth of this and as much as 800 times the most common unit. The basis was probably the *rattī* (seed of a *guñjā* creeper) about 0.109 gramme, one/one hundred twenty-eighth (1/128) of the most common unit.[23]

The people of the Indus/Haṛappan Civilisation had two systems of weights, one for internal trade and the other for international trade. The Indus unit weight of 27.584 grammes seems to have been the basis of the later Greek uncial system of weight of 27.2 grammes. A series of small gold discs found at the Indus/Haṛappan Civilisation city of Lothal weigh 50 mg to 3250 mg in the ratio of 1 : 2 : 4 : 5 : 10 : 20 : 30, etc. Research on the *guñjā* seed, also called a *rattī*, the seed of the *guñjā* creeper, reveals that it is now almost certain that the accepted weight of a *guñjā* was 100 mg.[24]

The *Manusmṛti*, chapter 8, verse 131 goes into great detail about weights and measures, especially the weight that pertains to copper, silver and gold:

---

22. See J.M. Kenoyer, *Ancient Cities of the Indus Valley Civilization*, Oxford University Press, 1998, p. 98.
23. See Jane McIntosh, *A Peaceful Realm*, Westview Press, 2002, p. 124.
24. See S.R. Rao, *New Frontiers of Archaeology*, Popular Prakashan, 1994, p. 13.

Those technical names of (certain quantities of) copper, silver, and gold, which are generally used on earth for the purpose of business transactions among men, I will fully declare.

(Verse 132): The very small mote which is seen when the sun shines through a lattice, they declare (to be) the least of (all) quantities and (to be called) a *trasareṇu* (a floating particle of dust).

(Verse 133): Know (that) eight *trasareṇus* (are equal) in bulk (to) a *likṣā* (the egg of a louse), three of those to one grain of black mustard (*rāgasarṣapa*), and three of the latter to a white mustard seed.

(Verse 134): Six grains of white mustard are one middle-sized barley-corn, and three barley-corns one *kṛṣṇalā* (*raktikā*, or *guñja*-berry); five *kṛṣṇalās* are one *māśa* (bean), and sixteen of those one *suvarṇa*.

(Verse 135): Four *suvarṇa*s are one *pala*, and ten *pala*s one *dhāraṇā*; two *kṛṣṇalās* (of silver), weighed together, must be considered one *māṣaka* of silver.

(Verse 136): Sixteen of those make a silver *dhāraṇā*, or *purāṇa*; but know (that) a *karṣa* of copper is a *kārṣāpaṇa*, or *paṇa*.

(Verse 137): Know (that) ten *dhāraṇā*s of silver make one *śatamāṇa*; four *suvarṇa*s must be considered (equal) in weight to a *niṣka*.

(Verse 138): Two hundred and fifty *paṇa*s are declared (to be) the first (or lowest) amercement, five (hundred) are considered as the mean (or middlemost), but one thousand as the highest.[25]

In addition to the numerous cities and towns of the Indus/ Haṛappan Civilisation that emerged about 4,600 years ago (2600 BCE), there was also uniformity in the system of weights. The uniformity also emphasised considerable trade.[26] In the Indus/ Haṛappan Civilisation, one finds that weights of various kinds

25. See G. Buehler, *Laws of Manu*, Oxford (Sacred Books of the East, v. XXV), 1896, pp. 193-94.

26. See Subhash Kak, "The Mahābhārata and the Sindhu-Sarasvatī Tradition", in Agrawal (ed.), *In Search of Vedic-Haṛappan Relationship*, Aryan Books International (2005), p. 82.

of stone followed a standardised weight system used throughout the realm.[27]

There seems to be a relationship between the Indus/Haṛappan Civilisation weight system and the *Manusmṛti* weight system. That is to say, the archaeological remains of the Indus/Haṛappan Civilisation produced weights and a system of weights that bear a striking similarity to the weights and system of weights described in the *Manusmṛti*.

4.9 Speed of Light in Ancient India

In the Purāṇas, another composition from ancient India, time was defined as 15 *nimeṣa*s equal to one *kāṣṭhā*. When this statement is converted into modern units (one *nimeṣa* equals sixteen over seventy-five seconds) it comes very close to the correct figure of 186,000 miles per second. If this is true, this is much earlier than what most people think, that the speed of light was first determined in the year 1675.[28]

A very similar number was given in the *Manusmṛti*. The *Manusmṛti* has its own definition of a *nimeṣa*, just slightly different, but very similar. If the above calculation is correct, then this means that the speed of light was either discovered and passed down by the composers of the *Manusmṛti*, or that the Purāṇas preceded the *Manusmṛti* and those Purāṇic physicists passed it down to the composers of the *Manusmṛti*.

The actual text of this part is: *Manusmṛti*, chapter I.64:

> Eighteen *nimeṣa*s (twinklings of the eye) are one *kāṣṭhā*, thirty *kāṣṭhā*s one *kalā*, thirty *kalā*s one *muhūrtta*, and as many (*muhūrtta*s) one day and night.[29]

27. See Jane McIntosh, *A Peaceful Realm*, Westview Press, 2002 (colour plate 19).
28. See Subhash Kak, "Birth and Early Development of Indian Astronomy", in H. Selin (ed.), *Astronomy across Cultures, The History of Non-Western Astronomy*, Kluwer Academic Publisher, 2000, p. 331.
29. See G. Buehler, *Laws of Manu*, Oxford (Sacred Books of the East, v. XXV), 1896, p. 10.

4.10 Complexity of Sanskrit Language and the Ṛgveda

The Ṛgvedic hymns were apparently the composition of ten families and individuals, all called *ṛṣi*. Some hymns, 1,028 of them, comprising 10,552 verses were collected into books or *maṇḍalas* called *Ṛgveda* or *Ṛk Saṁhitā*.[30] Many scholars speak of the tremendous intellectual power that was needed to create the Sanskrit language. There must have been a mathematical consciousness on the part of the Vedic speakers of Sanskrit that is an intellectual development and speaks for a sufficiently advanced state of civilisation. Such a mathematical consciousness, some scholars say, has not been found in any other contemporary language.[31] Other scholars concur. The *Ṛgveda*, they say, represents a "Developed Stage" of human civilisation, witness the abstract thought, the hallmark of a high level of intellectualism. The language of the hymns is also quite developed.[32]

In 1786, as mentioned above, in his famous address to the Asiatic Society of Bengal, William Jones said: The Sanskrit language, whatever be its antiquity, is a wonderful structure, more perfect than the Greek, more copious than the Latin and more exquisitely refined than either: yet bearing to both of them a stronger affinity, both in roots of verbs, and in the forms of grammar, than could possibly have been produced by accident.[33]

Sanskrit is considered by many people to be a difficult language to learn because of its sometimes overwhelming

---

30. S.P. Gupta, "The Sarasvatī and the Homeland of Early Ṛgvedic Ṛṣis", in Agrawal (ed.), *In Search of Vedic-Haṛappan Relationship*, Aryan Books International, 2005, p. 55.

31. See M.D. Pandit, *Mathematics as Known to the Vedic Saṁhitās*, Sri Satguru Publisher, 1993, p. xi.

32. S.P. Gupta, "The Sarasvatī and the Homeland of Early Ṛgvedic Ṛṣis", in Agrawal (ed.), *In Search of Vedic-Haṛappan Relationship*, Aryan Books International, 2005, p. 70.

33. Devendra Handa, "Vedic vis-à-vis Harappan Culture", in Agrawal (ed.), *In Search of Vedic-Haṛappan Relationship*, Aryan Books International, 2005, p. 75.

complexity. Sanskrit words, besides conveying meaning, also convey the correct gender, number and mutual relations very accurately.

The way in which the Vedas are chanted is also of high intellectual complexity. The Vedic "beat" or "metre" is called *chandas*, and is governed by the principle of measurement by number of syllables. For example, the Gāyatrī metre has 24 syllables.[34] The knowledge of how many syllables were contained in the Gāyatrī metre was one of the ways in which the number of syllables contained in *Ṛgveda* was able to be counted. If one knew precisely which metre was assigned to which hymn, and the number of verses in a hymn, one could easily count the total number of syllables.

4.11 High Level of Development

The Ṛgvedic *ṛṣis*, those poet-composers who would "sing" or "chant" the *Ṛgveda*, used words for themselves, their "listeners" and the "subjects of their hymns" that show a high level of mental, moral and cultural development. For instance the *Ṛgveda ṛṣi* used words that mean "knowing the inner working of another's mind," "being law abiding," "prudent," "earnest," "highly cultured" and "enlightened."[35]

Music was also important in Vedic times. *Ṛgveda* has the concept of seven musical notes (*Ṛgveda* 10.32.4).[36] This may very well be the oldest reference to the seven notes of the musical scale.

---

34. See M.D. Pandit, *Mathematics as Known to the Vedic Saṁhitās*, Sri Satguru Publisher, 1993, p. xiv.
35. See Bhagwan Singh, *The Vedic Harappans*, Aditya Prakashan, 1996, p. 38-39.
36. See P. Ghosal, *Lifestyle of the Vedic People*, D.K. Printworld, 2006, p. 139 (This beauteous place of meeting have I looked upon, where, like milch-cows, the kine order the marriage train; Where the Herd's Mother counts as first and best of all, and round her are *the seven-toned people of the choir*).

4.12 Government

The Ṛgvedic village, *grāma*, probably had a population of about 100 people known as a *jana* or *viṣ* and had a king, *rājā* ruling over it.[37] Monier-Williams defines (*rājā*) as not only a king, but also a sovereign, a chief or best of its kind.[38] The Vedic people had *sabhā*s and *samiti*s whose functions seem to have been both legislative and to give advice to rulers. The rulers had a hierarchical status, for example, *rājan*, kings. The smallest rulers were called *rājaka*, next *rājan*, then *samrāṭ*.[39]

In the 1800s in India, a settlement with a population of 300 inhabitants was described as an important settlement, therefore, 4,000 years ago, a place with a population of 200 may well have been considered a major settlement.[40] So today, when we speak of a settlement, or a village, or a town or city, we must be careful with population estimates.

Ṛgveda lists many occupations related to the administration of government, including officer, minister, architect, treasurer, tax collector, courier, commander, village headman, warrior, archer, ambassador/envoy, spy, police officer and guard.[41] There are so many governmental and administrative functionaries mentioned in the *Ṛgveda*. It is impossible to think that the people living at the time of the composition of *Ṛgveda* were simple nomads. Other terms which refer to kingdoms and rulers of different stature are *rāṣṭra, rājā, jyeṭharāja, samrāṭ, janarāja*. Terms existed for councils and assemblies such as *saṁsad, sabhā, samiti* and terms for various categories of administrative posts such as

37. See M.K. Dhavalikar, *The Aryans: Myth and Archaeology*, Munshiram Manoharlal, 2007, p. 53.
38. See Monier-Williams, *A Sanskrit-English Dictionary*, Oxford, 1899.
39. See B.B. Lal, "Search for Vedic-Harappan Relationship", in Agrawal (ed.), *In Search of Vedic-Haṛappan Relationship*, Aryan Books International, 2005, p. 5.
40. See M.K. Dhavalikar, *The Aryans Myth and Archaeology*, Munshiram Manoharlal, 2007, p. 53.
41. See P. Ghosal, *Lifestyle of the Vedic People*, D.K. Printworld, 2006, p. 99.

adhyakṣa, dūta, nidhapti, rathaspati and *senarni*. Vedic society was not merely in a rural stage. The *R̥gveda* refers to great assemblies (9.92.6), major and minor kings (8.21.18), riches pouring forth from four seas (9.33.6) and boats with one hundred oars (1.116.5); this was not a simple society.[42]

Dholavīra, situated in the isolated island of Khadir in the Great Rann of Kutch in modern day Gujarat, India, has remains from both the Indus/Haṛappan Civilisation period and later. In the post-Indus/Haṛappan Civilisation period, the urban components rapidly diminish and disappear, along with the weights and many other sophisticated items of art and utility.[43] If the *Manusmr̥ti* did indeed have great influence during the rise of the Indus/Haṛappan Civilisation, then it stands to reason that the *Manusmr̥ti* might also have less influence with the decline of the Indus/Haṛappan Civilisation.

The Indus/Haṛappan Civilisation cities of Haṛappā, Moheṅjo-Dāṛo, Lothal, Kālibaṅgan and Dholavīra had both an upper town acropolis or citadel and a lower town. The upper town was reserved for the residence of the Ruler and his entourage and the lower town for the rest of the population.[44] In addition to the numerous cities and towns of the Indus/Haṛappan Civilisation that emerged about 4,600 years ago (2600 BCE), there was also uniformity that also emphasised social classes.[45] The archaeological evidence of the Indus/Haṛappan Civilisation division of upper and lower classes seems somewhat similar to the *Manusmr̥ti* division of classes.

42. See B.B. Lal, *It is Time to Rethink*, in N. Lahiri (ed.), *The Decline and Fall of the Indus Civilization*, Permanent Black, 2000, pp. 78-79.
43. R.S. Bisht, "Dholavira", in N. Lahiri (ed.), *The Decline and Fall of the Indus Civilization*, Permanent Black, 2000, pp. 305-14.
44. See S.R. Rao, *New Frontiers of Archaeology*, Popular Prakashan, 1994, p. 4.
45. See Subhash Kak, "The Mahābhārata and the Sindhu-Sarasvatī Tradition", in Agrawal (ed.), *In Search of Vedic-Haṛappan Relationship*, Aryan Books International, 2005, p. 82.

Behind the issuing of uniform weights and their use in the Indus/Haṛappan Civilisation realm, must have been a well-organised bureaucratic system capable of enforcing standardisation over this enormous area. There must have been centres of administration. A village was considered a collection of houses and nothing else. Towns were the home of the local chief, centre of an area's administration and a centre of craft production and trade.[46]

The total number of Indus/Haṛappan Civilisation sites that have currently been found is approximately 2,658. The Indus/Haṛappan Civilisation was greater in area than the contemporary civilisations of Egypt and Mesopotamia, in Iraq and Syria, in the valley of the Euphrates and Tigris rivers.[47]

4.13 Kings and Chiefs to Serve and Protect

The *Manusmṛti* refers to the kings and rulers not as demi-gods, as they were in Egypt and Mesopotamia, but almost as "servant-kings," whose chief task was to "protect the people." It was not within their "job description" to build themselves lavish palaces and live a life of luxury.

The *Manusmṛti* has an entire chapter devoted to laws and advice regarding kings and village chiefs. It is summed up in one verse in the first chapter, saying that the Creator commanded all members of the kṣatriya caste (the ruling and warrior caste) to protect the people. The *Manusmṛti*, chapter 1.89, "The kṣatriya commanded to protect the people, to bestow gifts, to offer sacrifices, to study (the Veda), and to abstain from attaching himself to sensual pleasures."[48] This is a very important verse, not only in "protecting the people," but also to abstain from

---

46. See Jane McIntosh, *A Peaceful Realm*, Westview Press, 2002, p. 83.
47. See D.P. Sharma and Madhuri, *Harappan Civilisation*, Kaveri Books, 2003, p. 17.
48. See G. Buehler, *Laws of Manu*, Oxford (Sacred Books of the East, v. XXV), 1896, p. 14.

attaching himself to sensual pleasures, something that archaeological evidence shows was different in the lives of other kings and rulers of other ancient civilisations.

In *Manusmṛti*, kings and village chiefs were also given the job of head administrator. They had to learn how to procure the right persons for administration and skills of management. The *Manusmṛti*'s references to "collection of revenue, (e.g.) in mines, manufactures, and storehouses" seem similar to the archaeological clues left by the ruins of the Indus/Haṛappan Civilisation. The *Manusmṛti*, chapter 7.62, "Among them let him (the King, the Chief) employ the brave, the skilful, the high-born, and the honest in (offices for the collection of) revenue, (e.g.) in mines, manufactures, and storehouses, (but) the timid in the interior of his palace."[49]

The people of the Indus/Haṛappan Civilisation must also have had a great ability to memorise. The architecture was complex, the mathematics complex, the engineering complex, and apparently was not written down. All that archaeologists have found written down are a number of repeated symbols, as-yet-undeciphered on Indus/Haṛappan Civilisation "seals."

The *Manusmṛti*, chapter 7.63, "Let him also appoint an ambassador who is versed in all sciences, who understands hints, expressions of the face and gestures, who is honest, skilful, and of (noble) family" and chapter 7.64, "(Such) an ambassador is commended to a king (who is) loyal, honest, skilful, possessing a good memory, who knows the (proper) place and time (for action, who is) handsome, fearless, and eloquent."[50]

There are very complicated local and international governmental practices described in the *Manusmṛti*, the ones that were apparently also needed at the time of the Indus/Haṛappan

49. See G. Buehler, *Laws of Manu*, Oxford (Sacred Books of the East, v. XXV), 1896, p. 157.

50. Ibid., p. 158.

Civilisation (due to its extensive international trade), and probably not needed again for at least 1,500 years after the decline of the civilisation. These practices may yet point to another relationship between the Indus/Haṛappan Civilisation and the *Manusmṛti* society. The *Manusmṛti*, chapter 7.66, "For the ambassador alone makes (kings') allies and separates allies; the ambassador transacts that business by which (kings) are disunited or not" and the *Manusmṛti*, chapter 7.67, "With respect to the affairs let the (ambassador) explore the expression of the countenance, the gestures and actions of the (foreign king) through the gestures and actions of his confidential (advisers), and (discover) his designs among his servants."[51] In this related area, high level diplomacy, such skills were necessary in the Indus/Haṛappan Civilisation time and not needed again for 1,500 years (until the re-emergence of complex societies in India.

The total number of Indus/Haṛappan Civilisation sites that have currently been found is approximately 2,658.[52] This means that there were quite a large number of villages, which also may correspond with the *Manusmṛti*. The *Manusmṛti*, chapter 7.115, "Let him appoint a lord over (each) village, as well as lords of ten villages, lords of 20, lords of 100, and lords of 1,000."[53]

In addition to the numerous cities and towns of the Indus/Haṛappan Civilisation that emerged about 4,600 years ago (2600 BCE), there was also uniformity that emphasised considerable trade.[54] Trade was the perfect opportunity to collect taxes, as

---

51. See G. Buehler, *Laws of Manu*, Oxford (Sacred Books of the East, v. XXV), 1896, p. 158.
52. See D.P. Sharma, and Madhuri, *Harappan Civilisation*, Kaveri Books, 2003, p. 17.
53. See G. Buehler, *Laws of Manu*, Oxford (Sacred Books of the East, v. XXV), 1896, p. 162.
54. See Subhash Kak, "The Mahābhārata and the Sindhu-Sarasvatī Tradition", in Agrawal (ed.), *In Search of Vedic-Haṛappan Relationship*, Aryan Books International, 2005, p. 82.

the *Manusmṛti* instructed rulers and chiefs to do. The *Manusmṛti*, chapter 7.127, "Having well considered (the rates of) purchase and (of) sale, (the length of) the road, (the expense for) food and condiments, the charges of securing the goods, let the king make the traders pay duty" and *Manusmṛti*, chapter 7.128, "After (due) consideration the king shall always fix in his realm the duties and taxes in such a manner that both he himself and the man who does the work receive (their due) reward." The *Manusmṛti*, chapter 7.129, "As the leech, the calf, and the bee take their food little by little, even so must the king draw from his realm moderate annual taxes"; the *Manusmṛti*, chapter 7.130, "A fiftieth part of (the increments on) cattle and gold may be taken by the king, and the eighth, sixth, or twelfth part of the crops"; *Manusmṛti*, chapter 7.131, "He may also take the sixth part of trees, meat, honey, clarified butter, perfumes, (medical) herbs, substances used for flavouring food, flowers, roots, and fruit"; and the *Manusmṛti*, chapter 7.132, "Of leaves, pot-herbs, grass, (objects) made of cane, skins, of earthen vessels, and all (articles) made of stone."[55]

The administration of the cities and towns of the Indus/Haṛappan Civilisation probably could not have been accomplished without revenue from collection of some sort of "taxes." Within the *Manusmṛti*, the amounts of taxes were described down to each level of society and means of production. These descriptions also give a glimpse into the lives of the people living under the *Manusmṛti*, who seem to have lived lives that seem to be similar to the people of the Indus/Haṛappan Civilisation.

4.14 Soma

Soma was considered both a "god" and a sacred intoxicating drink of the people of the time of *Ṛgveda* and perhaps not a "god" but

55. See G. Buehler, *Laws of Manu*, Oxford (Sacred Books of the East, v. XXV), 1896, p. 165.

still a sacred intoxicating drink by the composers of the *Manusmṛti*. Some scholars call this the "Soma cult," which they believe may have reached Babylonia and Egypt. Those same scholars say that this "Soma cult" pervades all of the Vedas and is a cult of all Vedic people, like the fire ritual. All the Vedic gods drank the *soma*, which gave them power. The *soma* plant was not just one plant, but a plant mixture or the sacred use of plants. That is why *soma* is mentioned relative to all plants. Ephedra does not resemble the characteristics of the *soma* plant as described in *Ṛgveda*. The *Ṛgveda* describes *soma* as a watery plant, growing near water and flowing with a milky juice gained by crushing the plant. Ephedra is a dry plant that has almost no juice.[56] *Soma* was an important ritual and was prepared three times a day, morning, noon and evening.[57] *Soma* was the most important intoxicating drink. It was a divine drink, consumed on sacrificial occasions as part of a ritual, it was difficult to obtain the actual *soma* plant and therefore several substitutes were used, other alcoholic beverages were consumed.[58]

The *Manusmṛti* regarding *soma*, chapter 11.14,

> If (a man) possessing 100 cows, kindles not the sacred fire, or one possessing 1,000 cows, drinks not the *soma*-juice, a (sacrificer) may unhesitatingly take (what he requires) from the houses of those two, even (though they be brāhmaṇas or kṣatriyas).[59]

According to the *Manusmṛti*, it was wrong to drink "un-blessed" regular alcohol and at the same time, very important to drink the "blessed," "transformed" alcohol, *soma*.

---

56. See David Frawley, "Geographical References: The Ocean and Soma", in Agrawal (ed.), *In Search of Vedic-Harappan Relationship*, Aryan Books International, 2005, p. 44.

57. See M.K. Dhavalikar, *The Aryans: Myth and Archaeology*, Munshiram Manoharlal, 2007, p. 67.

58. See P. Ghosal, *Lifestyle of the Vedic People*, D.K. Printworld, 2006, pp. 26-27.

59. See G. Buehler, *Laws of Manu*, Oxford (Sacred Books of the East, v. XXV), 1896, p. 295.

Some scholars are beginning to believe that *soma* may also have been important to the people of the Indus/Haṛappan Civilisation. The people of the Indus/Haṛappan Civilisation made extraordinary square and rectangular fired-soapstone (steatite) seals with pictures of animals and "Indus script." Many of the animals engraved on Indus/Haṛappan Civilisation seals were male bulls with a mysterious "offering stand" in front of them. Some scholars identify the offering stand as a filter for the preparation of the sacred intoxicating beverage called *soma*.[60]

The elephant or *hastin* is mentioned in *Ṛgveda* and appears on Mature Haṛappan seals and there is much evidence of objects made from ivory in the Indus/Haṛappan Civilisation. There are faunal remains from (about 9,000 years ago) the seventh to sixth millennium BCE.[61] There exists a miniature "offering stand" carved in ivory from Indus/Haṛappan Civilisation. This may be the same "offering stand" carved on so many seals of the Indus/Haṛappan Civilisation. If this can be further documented, that these "offering stands" were really filters for the preparation of *soma*, that would be another clue linking the Indus/Haṛappan Civilisation to *Ṛgveda* and the *Manusmṛti*.

The most frequently mentioned tree in the *Ṛgveda* is known as the *aśvattha* tree (*pīpala* tree). That tree was also important for another use, a *soma* use, since its wood was used to make vessels which would hold the *soma* (*Ṛgveda* 1.135.8 and 10.97.5).[62] Since the craftsmen of the Indus/Haṛappan Civilisation used the leaf of the *aśvattha* tree in many decorations and even as part of the early "writing," there seems to be another connection between *soma*, *Ṛgveda*, the Indus/Haṛappan Civilisation, and the *Manusmṛti*.

60. See J.M. Kenoyer, *Ancient Cities of the Indus Valley Civilization*, Oxford University Press, 1998, p. 86.

61. See B.B. Lal, *The Homeland of the Aryans: Evidence of Ṛgvedic Flora and Fauna and Archaeology*, Aryan Books International, 2005, pp. 43-46.

62. Ibid., pp. 1-4.

4.15 Traditions from Indus/Haṛappan Civilisation

Many "practices" that were evident in the Indus/Haṛappan Civilisation have been handed down from generation to generation and have survived as "traditions" in the Indian subcontinent.

One tradition that is praçtised in India today is Yoga. Yoga is defined both as yoking, joining, attaching and meditation, especially . . . as a system taught by Patañjali and called the Yoga philosophy; . . . its chief aim being to teach the means by which the human spirit may attain complete union with . . . the Supreme Spirit.[63] The practice of Yoga, especially the physical-posture Yoga, correctly called, *haṭha-yoga* seems to have been performed by the people of the Indus/Haṛappan Civilisation, as seen by the terracotta figures in *haṭha-yoga* positions.

The *Sanskrit-English Dictionary* of Monier-Williams is excellent in providing roots of each Sanskrit letter. In this case, the word, *yoga* means "the act of yoking, joining, attaching, generally understood to mean various practices that help one reach greater spirituality."

Apparently the Sanskrit word comes from:

ya — . . . joining, restraining

o — - an interjection

ga — . . . going, moving

Putting this all together, the roots seem to indicate: "one who joins or restrains one's self to go," and many Indian philosophers believe "yoga" means "to go towards yoking one's self with God, or to the divine." Yoga, as we know it today in the West, has two well-known paths, the one most people know as yoga, the physical stretching and postures, which is called *haṭha-yoga* (force *yoga*) and the meditation path, which is generally called *rāja-yoga* (royal *yoga*).

63. See Monier-Williams, *A Sanskrit-English Dictionary*, Oxford, 1899.

There is strong evidence that the people of the Indus/Haṛappan Civilisation practised *haṭha-yoga* and possibly *rāja-yoga*. There are many terracotta figurines from the Indus/Haṛappan Civilisation sites, terracotta figures in *haṭha-yoga* postures (*āsanas*). *Haṭha-yoga* seems to go back to early Indus/Haṛappan Civilisation times as we can surmise from terracotta figures.[64]

One *haṭha-yoga* posture that a Indus/Haṛappan Civilisation terracotta figure is performing, today in India, is called *añjalī-mudrā*. One Indus/Haṛappan Civilisation engraved seal is carved with someone shown seated with folded legs as in the *haṭha-yoga* posture. The figure is performing what is today called *padmāsana* or *vajrāsana*.[65] The author has personally verified terracotta Indus/Haṛappan Civilisation figures and the figure on seals apparently performing *haṭha-yoga* postures in the National Museum in New Delhi.

Other traditions born in the Indus/Haṛappan Civilisation survive today in modern India. For instance, one practice in India today is married Hindu women putting *sindūra* (vermilion) to the *māṅga* (line of partition of the hair on their head). This practice seems to go back to early Indus/Haṛappan Civilisation times as one can tell from Indus/Haṛappan Civilisation female terracotta figures.[66] Another practice that survives today in India is women putting a type of collyrium (eye salve) (often made from castor oil ash cooked on copper) on their eyes (in the same place where some modern women put eyeliners), which apparently goes back to early Indus/Haṛappan Civilisation times as we can also tell from Indus/Haṛappan Civilisation female terracotta figures.

---

64. See B.B. Lal, *The Sarasvatī Flows On*, Aryan, 2002, p. 127.
65. See H.D. Sankalia, *Pre-Historic Art in India*, Carolina Academic Press, 1978, p. 29.
66. See B.B. Lal, *The Sarasvatī Flows On*, Aryan, 2002, p. 82.

The *Manusmṛti* had laws pertaining to gambling.[67] The same was true for *Ṛgveda*. From the Indus/Haṛappan Civilisation city of Lothal, dice have been found, as well as gamesmen that look very much like the pieces of a chess game. The author has verified these dice and gamesmen at the museums in New Delhi and at Lothal. These Indus/Haṛappan Civilisation gamesmen have led scholars to theorise that the throwing of dice, as well as chess, goes back to early Indus/Haṛappan Civilisation times.[68] Cubical dice have also been found in both Mesopotamia and the Indus/Haṛappan Civilisation (dice are usually found as pairs; a single one of them is called a "die"); the arrangement of the dots on a die from a royal third millennium BCE cemetery (5,000 years ago) in Ur have the exact same arrangement of dots as dice from the Indus/Haṛappan Civilisation; there is also a modern three-in-one, tweezers-cum-toothpick gadget that is in use in India today. Objects that are extremely similar have been found in Indus/Haṛappan Civilisation sites.[69]

The *tandūra* (oven) is very popular in northern India cooking today. The *tandūra* (oven) dates back to 4,800 years ago (2800 BCE) to early Indus/Haṛappan Civilisation times as we can tell from examples in many Indus/Haṛappan Civilisation cities and towns.[70] This is another example of Indus/Haṛappan Civilisation technological progress that has survived in India for thousands of years.

Easterly-facing "fire altars" are another "tradition" found in India today. The evidence suggests that fire worship had a religious role in Indus/Haṛappan Civilisation life. At Indus/Haṛappan Civilisation sites such as Kālibaṅgan, Lothal, Banawālī

---

67. See G. Buehler, *Laws of Manu*, Oxford (Sacred Books of the East, v. XXV), 1896, p. 261.

68. See B.B. Lal, *The Sarasvatī Flows On*, Aryan, 2002, p. 91.

69. See S. Ratnagar, *Trading Encounters from the Euphrates to the Indus in the Bronze Age*, Oxford University Press, 2006, p. 200.

70. See B.B. Lal, *The Sarasvatī Flows On*, Aryan, 2002, p. 95.

and Rākhīgaṛhī, bathing facilities are associated with what are taken to be fire altars.[71] Even more recent Kālibaṅgan excavations revealed "fire-altars" to be seven in number, considered a "sacred number" among some modern Hindus. The fact that those using Indus/Haṛappan Civilisation fire altars had to face east is something that is very common in Indian Hindu "fire rituals" of today. Kālibaṅgan excavations also revealed a terracotta specimen which is clearly a *liṅga* with *yoni*, symbols of creativity and fertility, something that is very common in Śaivite Indian Hindu temples today.[72] Fire worship and bathing were described by *Ṛgveda* and also prescribed in the *Manusmṛti*.

Mother Goddess-type of worship is another "tradition" found in India today. Aditi, the Mother Goddess, is mentioned frequently in the *Ṛgveda* and was the Mother of every god; worship of her could clearly be the Mother Goddess-type of worship that was apparently present in the Indus/Haṛappan Civilisation.[73]

Having one's right arm uncovered is another "tradition" found among Hindu practitioners in India today. Many of the male statues belonging to the Indus/Haṛappan Civilisation have their right arm uncovered, as one can tell from the terracotta figures and some stone statues. The *Manusmṛti* tells one to keep one's right arm uncovered, chapter 1.193, "Let him always keep his right arm uncovered, behave decently and keep his body well covered. . . ."[74]

Worship of the bull is another "tradition" found in India today. The bull in the *Ṛgveda* is spoken of as Puruṣa, the Supreme Being or Soul, as is Indra and Agni. Worship of the bull in the

71. See Jane McIntosh, *A Peaceful Realm*, Westview Press, 2002, p. 110.

72. See B.B. Lal, *The Sarasvatī Flows On*, Aryan, 2002, p. 119.

73. See K.D. Sethna, *The Problem of Aryan Origins*, S&S Publishers, 1980, p. 38.

74. See G. Buehler, *Laws of Manu*, Oxford (Sacred Books of the East, v. XXV), 1896.

Vedas is common.[75] A very large percentage of the Indus/ Haṛappan Civilisation seals have a carving of a bull on them.

4.16 Eternal Law from Ṛgveda is Ṛta

In *Ṛgveda*, the concept of "Eternal Law" is introduced and it is called *ṛta*. *Deva*s (who are defined sometimes as gods, sometimes as angels, sometimes as "shining beings") are the personified agents of *ṛta*. Cosmic order is that harmony (law) whose ordinances shine through *ṛta* (*Ṛgveda* X.65.5).[76] "Bring gifts to Mitra and to Varuṇa who, Lords of all, in spirit never fail the worshipper, whose statue shines on high through everlasting Law, whose places of sure refuge are the heavens and earth."

> *mitrāya śikṣa varuṇāya dāśuṣe yā samrājā manasā na prayuchataḥ* ।
> *yayordhāma dharmaṇā rocate bṛhad yayorubhe rodasīnādhasī vṛtau* ॥

Monier-Williams-defines *ṛta* as proper, right, fit, apt, suitable, able, brave, honest, law, rule, divine law, divine truth.[77] One hymn in *Ṛgveda* praises certain *deva*s as "True to Law, born in Law the strengtheners of Law, terrible, haters of the false" (*Ṛgveda* VII.66.13).[78] *Ṛta*, according to some scholars, is the universal law which all gods and humans must obey.[79]

4.17 The Manusmṛti Regarding Origins of Law

The *Manusmṛti*, chapter 2.6, "The whole Veda is the (first) source of the sacred law, next the tradition and the virtuous conduct of

75. See K.D. Sethna, *The Problem of Aryan Origins*, S&S Publishers, 1980, pp. 40-41.
76. See S.R. Verma, *Vedas: The Source of Ultimate Science*, Nag Publishers, 2005, p. 26.
77. See Monier-Williams, *A Sanskrit-English Dictionary*, Oxford, 1899.
78. See Bhagwan Singh, *The Vedic Harappans*, Aditya Prakashan, 1996, p. 313.
79. See S.R. Verma, *Vedas: The Source of Ultimate Science*, Nag Publishers, 2005, p. 57.

those who know the (Veda further), also the customs of holy men, and (finally) self-satisfaction." The *Manusmṛti*, 2.7, "Whatever law has been ordained for any (person) by Manu, that has been fully declared in the Veda, for that (sage was) omniscient."[80] The *Manusmṛti* seems to be trying to justify its differences with the Vedas by saying that all of the *Manusmṛti* has been declared in the Vedas (which appears to be untrue, since many "new" restrictive laws and punishments are in the *Manusmṛti* that are nowhere mentioned in *Ṛgveda* or any of the other Vedas). The *Manusmṛti*, 2.8, "But a learned man after fully scrutinising all this with the eye of knowledge, should in accordance with the authority of the revealed texts, be intent on (the performance of) his duties."[81] In the author's opinion, this sounds as if it is man-made law designed for social order, not one "heard" or composed by an "enlightened" Ṛgvedic *ṛṣi*.

The *Manusmṛti*, 2.9, "For that man who obeys the law prescribed in the revealed texts and in the sacred tradition, gains fame in this (world) and after death unsurpassable bliss."[82] In the *Manusmṛti*, there is an emphasis on "rewards" in the life hereafter, and not on the life of the present. The *Manusmṛti*, 2.10, "But by Śruti (revelation) is meant the Veda, and by Smṛti (tradition) the institutes of the sacred law: those two must not be called into question in any matter, since from those two the sacred law shone forth."[83]

As was remarked above, Smṛti, man-made, which was "remembered" was not as "high and mighty" as Śruti. Śruti was the song that was constantly being sung by the divine, available to any human being, usually a *ṛṣi*, with a sufficiently subtle "radio-like" mind. Smṛti was much more common,

80. See G. Buehler, *Laws of Manu*, Oxford (Sacred Books of the East, v. XXV), 1896.
81. Ibid.
82. Ibid.
83. Ibid.

"remembered" by human teachers. Here, it appears that the composers of the *Manusmṛti* were trying to elevate their "man-made" Smṛti to become a composition that was "not-to-be-questioned," similar to the "divine song" Śruti, the *Ṛgveda*.

The *Manusmṛti*, 2.11, "Every twice-born man, who, relying on the institutes of dialectics, treats with contempt those two sources (of the law), must be cast out by the virtuous, as an atheist and a scorner of the Veda."[84] Obviously, the composers of the *Manusmṛti* found that some of the population did not wish to obey the *Manusmṛti*, and that therefore, they should be punished. The *Manusmṛti*, 2.12, "The Veda, the sacred tradition, the customs of virtuous men, and one's own pleasure, they declare to be visibly the fourfold means of defining the sacred law."[85]

The *Manusmṛti*, 2.13, "The knowledge of the sacred law is prescribed for those who are not given to the acquisition of wealth and to the gratification of their desires; to those who seek the knowledge of the sacred law the supreme authority is the revelation (Śruti)."[86] The *Manusmṛti*, 3.133, "As many mouthfuls as an ignorant man swallows at a sacrifice to the gods or to the manes, so many red-hot spikes, spears, and iron (metal) balls must (the giver of the repast) swallow after death."[87] Unlike the *Ṛgveda* emphasising immediate rewards, the *Manusmṛti* centred around rewards and punishments after death.

4.18 Brāhmaṇas defined by the Manusmṛti

The *Manusmṛti*, 3.134, "Some brāhmaṇas are devoted to (the pursuit of) knowledge, and others to (the performance of) austerities; some to austerities and to the recitation of the Veda,

---

84. See G. Buehler, *Laws of Manu*, Oxford (Sacred Books of the East, v. XXV), 1896.

85. Ibid.

86. Ibid.

87. Ibid.

and others to (the performance of) sacred rites."[88] These are "human library books" or "human computers" as defined by the first phrase that "some are devoted to knowledge." This is not a "priest" performing a sacerdotal function. This is a scholar, a teacher, an inventor, much different than a "priest."

The *Manusmṛti*, 3.1, "The vow (of studying) the three Vedas under a teacher must be kept for 36 years, or for half that time, or for a quarter, or until the (student) has perfectly learnt them."[89] If one studies for 36 years, that is a long time, even if one begins in childhood. Again, this is more of a path of knowledge, rather than the path of just learning to perform sacerdotal functions as a "priest" for the people. Other passages in the *Manusmṛti* refer to the legal brāhmaṇas, helping a tired king, as opposed to the "priestly" ones.

The *Manusmṛti*, 7.141, "When he is tired with the inspection of the business of men, let him place on that seat (of justice) his chief minister, (who must be) acquainted with the law, wise, self-controlled, and descended from a (noble) family."[90] The king, or head of a village, when getting tired of acting as judge, must turn over the duties of judge to a brāhmaṇa who is acquainted with the law. This means someone who is not a "priest" but a lawyer or assistant judge who has helped the king or village head previously.

4.19 Conclusion

Ancient India seems to have been a "hotbed" of advanced intellectual thought. Evidence from Greek historians, from the *Ṛgveda*, from the archaeological remains of the Indus/Haṛappan Civilisation and the *Manusmṛti* all point to mathematical, astronomical and linguistical development that far outpaced much of similar development in the rest of the world.

---

88. See G. Buehler, *Laws of Manu*, Oxford (Sacred Books of the East, v. XXV), 1896.
89. Ibid., p. 51.
90. Ibid., p. 166.

5

Technology in Ṛgveda, Indus/Haṛappan Civilisation and Manusmṛti Society

5.1 Harnessing Animal Power and Division of Labour

AN example of the "brain-power" of the people of the Indus/Haṛappan Civilisation was their technology. One simple technology, probably one of the first, was making use of animal power. Harnessing the use of animal power in most early cultures made progress towards civilised life possible. The *Ṛgveda* mentions harnessing the use of animal power by training elephants and using animal reins and bridles.

Division of labour and specialisation was another simple, yet effective "technology" of the people of the Indus/Haṛappan Civilisation. Once there was division of labour together with sufficient food production, it was possible for some members of the Indus/Haṛappan Civilisation to specialise in a particular field or trade. Division of labour allowed for large amounts of local and international trade to flourish.

The *Ṛgveda* mentions similar division of labour, with the development of many different areas of work. Trades and professions mentioned in *Ṛgveda* include the following: surgeon, sailor, dancer, carpenter, guard, priest, trader, warrior, physician, navigator, architect, mason, potter and entertainer.[1]

---

1. See Bhagwan Singh, *The Vedic Harappans*, Aditya Prakashan, 1996, p. 162.

The *Manusmṛti* must have made use of the practice of division of labour because it also mentions laws that pertained to people of different trades and professions.

5.2 Indus/Haṛappan Civilisation Technology of Standardisation

Throughout the vast Indus/Haṛappan Civilisation empire merchants and craftsmen realised that standardisation helped mass production; for example, Indus/Haṛappan Civilisation copper and bronze arrowheads are of uniform size, shape and content; the bricks were mainly of two sizes depending on the particular type of construction.[2]

Standardisation throughout an entire realm that was geographically larger than the corresponding civilisations combined in Egypt and Iraq (Mesopotamia, Sumer, Ur) must have taken much planning, discussion and agreement. It is not something that could have happened overnight.

In the corresponding civilisations in Egypt and Iraq (Mesopotamia, Sumer, Ur), there existed kings that either believed themselves to be God or appointed by God. They had many statues carved of themselves, large, lavish palaces and often ruled with "an iron hand." The vast Indus/Haṛappan Civilisation seems not to have had any such kings. No large, lavish palaces have been found. No giant carved statues of kings have been unearthed. The Indus/Haṛappan Civilisation standardisation probably occurred under the leadership of a great many "minor" kings or tribal "chiefs" throughout the entire realm. These "minor" kings or tribal "chiefs" apparently did not care about giant statues of themselves being carved and did not care about palaces being built in their names. Perhaps they believed that it was their civic or spiritual duty to act as "servant kings," that is, kings who believed that "service to the people" was their foremost duty.

---

2. See S.R. Rao, *New Frontiers of Archaeology*, Popular Prakashan, 1994, p. 3.

If this is true, then part of the service to the people apparently must have been standardised throughout the entire Indus/ Haṛappan Civilisation realm. In the *Manusmṛti*, many laws were composed just for the class of kings, from major kings to tribal chiefs. The underlying philosophy was that the number one task of a king or chief was to protect the people.

5.3 World's Oldest "High-Fired" Ceramics and Jewellery

The artisans of the Indus/Haṛappan Civilisation crafted the world's oldest "high-fired" stoneware ceramics and were among the most highly skilled artists in antiquity; some stoneware bangles were made in such a complex manner than no one has been able to duplicate them today.[3] (Bangles are a type of bracelet, but most bracelets are flexible; bangles are one piece and do not bend.)

The "lost wax technique" in making metal statues and other objects usually starts with the artist making a model from clay or wax. Then a metal "mould" is made from the clay or wax model. Next the clay or wax is "lost" or destroyed when it is removed from the mould (usually two halves that can later be joined together), but when heated metal is poured into the mould, then cooled, an almost perfect metal replica of the original figure that was carved in clay or wax is the result. Metal figurines throughout the Indus/Haṛappan Civilisation sites, especially those at Mohenjo-Dāṛo, show that the Indus people were masters of complex casting using the "cire perdue" (lost wax) technique.

The Indus/Haṛappan Civilisation artisans also used various alloys of copper and other metals. Such alloys were carefully made; for example, 13 per cent tin added to copper was "conventional bronze"; sometimes it had added arsenic or lead.[4]

3. See J.M. Kenoyer, *Ancient Cities of the Indus Valley Civilization*, Oxford University Press, 1998, p. 75.
4. See Jane McIntosh *A Peaceful Realm*, Westview Press, 2002, p. 68.

It is almost unbelievable to modern researchers that the Indus bronze saw was able to cut ocean seashells for bangle-making as efficiently as modern-day steel saws, which means that Indus bronze workers were able to produce a bronze as hard as steel.[5]

Jewellery-making and particularly the craft of making "beads" was a specialty of the Indus/Haṛappan Civilisation. One type of manufactured bead today is called "faience." A "less sophisticated" type of "faience" was contemporaneously being created in Mesopotamia and Egypt. But in the Indus/Haṛappan Civilisation, the Indus technique for making "faience" was different than in Mesopotamia and Egypt. In the Indus/Haṛappan Civilisation, artisans carefully heated their ground rock crystal and coloured stones up to more than 1000°C, which they again cooled, ground up, combined with other things and fired a second time at high temperature.[6] D.K. Chakrabarti has written about J.F.S. Stone's analysis of the composition of faience beads found from the Minoan Civilisation in Crete — directly from the Indus/Haṛappan Civilisation culture; that faience consists almost entirely of finely ground quartz thermally cemented together, which was then glazed, most often with blue glass.[7]

5.4 Carnelian Beads

One of the semi-precious stone-beads that was made by the craftsmen of the Indus/Haṛappan Civilisation was made from the stone that is called, in English, "carnelian." These craftsmen were experts in crafting an extra-long bead that was high-fired to bring out the colour. The making of an Indus/Haṛappan Civilisation "long carnelian bead" must have been a difficult process. Apparently, the carnelian stone was mined in Khambhat

5. See J.M. Kenoyer, *Ancient Cities of the Indus Valley Civilization*, Oxford University Press, 1998, p. 96.
6. See Jane McIntosh, *A Peaceful Realm*, Westview Press, 2002, p. 71.
7. See D.K. Chakrabarti, *The External Trade of the Indus Civilization*, Munshiram Manoharlal, 1990, p. 43.

(formerly Cambay, which is now in the Indian state of Gujarat), dried, cut with a saw, heated and chipped to rough-cut. The carnelian bead must have been reheated to bring out colour. Next, probably using a fine-grained metamorphic drill, continuous drilling for three to eight days was needed to perforate the beads and finally the long carnelian beads were ground on stone with sand to polish them.[8]

Carnelian beads of this type were only made by the Indus/Haṛappan Civilisation artisans, and apparently nowhere else in the world at that time. For such a long and arduous process, the result was that these long carnelian beads were in great demand among the rich and powerful of Egypt, Mesopotamia and Sumeria. This fact turns out to be a great archaeological clue. Many jar fragments with Indus/Haṛappan Civilisation script on them have been found at many different Gulf state sites; kings and queens from Ur (modern Iraq) were buried with many treasures, including carnelian beads that were produced by the artisans of the Indus/Haṛappan Civilisation.[9] The etching of carnelian beads began in the Indus/Haṛappan Civilisation and the process has continued until the present day in India and Pakistan; nowhere else in the world does there exist such a record of production.[10]

5.5 White Micro-Beads

Some other "bead-making" by the Indus/Haṛappan Civilisation artisans resulted in beads so small that without archaeological finds of these beads, their size would be impossible to believe. The Indus/Haṛappan Civilisation "white micro-beads" are only 1 millimetre across and 1 to 3 millimetres long; some scholars

8. See D.P. Sharma and Madhuri, *Panorama of Harappan Civilization*, Kaveri Books, 2003, p. 176.

9. See J.M. Kenoyer, *Ancient Cities of the Indus Valley Civilization*, Oxford University Press, 1998, p. 97.

10. See D.K. Chakrabarti, *The External Trade of the Indus Civilization*, Munishiram Manoharlal, 1990, p. 111.

believe that no ancient hand-drill could be made small enough to drill such tiny beads and therefore, they theorise that the material was ground into powder, mixed to a paste, extruded with a fine copper wire for a hole, cut with a horsehair, then fired at around nine hundred degrees centigrade.[11]

The author has personally verified some Indus/Haṛappan Civilisation "white micro-beads" at the museum in Lothal, south of the modern-day city of Ahmedabad, in the Indian state of Gujarat. The Indus/Haṛappan Civilisation white micro-beads in the Lothal Museum were displayed in a small plastic bag. The bag of beads was behind a glass encasement and, attached to the outside glass of the encasement, was a magnifying glass. The magnifying glass was necessary, because most human eyes could not see clearly what was being displayed. When one looks through the magnifying glass, one can make out a collection of extremely tiny beads that were either carefully drilled or made according to the process theorised above. Some scholars believe that the beads were either used as jewellery or as a stringed ornament for the hair.

Indus/Haṛappan Civilisation craftsmen were also technically advanced when it came to woodworking tools. For instance, a handsaw has been discovered in an Indus/Haṛappan Civilisation site with undulating teeth, which allowed the dust to escape freely, something that seems ordinary in handsaw design today, but was far ahead of its time, more than 4,000 years ago.

5.6 Twisted Metal Drill / Compass / Bronze

In the Indus/Haṛappan Civilisation site of Lothal, a twisted metal drill has been discovered, which, some scholars say, represents a great moment in the history of civilisation.[12] No

11. See Jane McIntosh, *A Peaceful Realm*, Westview Press, 2002, p. 73.
12. See K.D. Sethna, *The Problem of Aryan Origins*, S&S Publishers, 1980, p. 51.

other contemporaneous civilisation invented a twisted metal drill. The United States Patent Office (incorrectly) gave a patent for the "brand-new invention" of the twisted metal drill almost 4,500 years later, in the 1860s. Drills of copper and chalcedony were needed for making holes in beads; those found in Lothal and the copper saw were probably the earliest of the kind in the world.[13] Lothal metalsmiths produced bronze as follows: bangles with 11.2 per cent tin, pins with 13.8 per cent tin and chisels with 9.62 per cent tin.[14]

Indus/Haṛappan Civilisation town-planning was accomplished with the geometric instruments that had been developed: the compass, the plumb bob and right-angle measuring instruments that have been found at many sites.[15] Many scholars now believe that a type of compass or sextant has been found in Indus/Haṛappan Civilisation sites. Two shell rings, one with eight slits and the other with twelve slits have been found at the Indus/Haṛappan Civilisation cities of Lothal and Dholavīra. Those "rings" measure not only the line, points and degrees on a plain surface, but also the eight or twelve whole section of the horizon; if held in suspension, it could even be used as a sextant.[16]

Some of the Indus/Haṛappan Civilisation "seals" depict the "mother goddess" and ritualistic scenes, giving the impression that the seals, although probably used as stamps of authority in trade, represented religious symbols used during the rituals.[17]

13. See M.K. Dhavalikar, *The Aryans Myth and Archaeology*, Munshiram Manoharlal, 2007, p. 63.
14. See S.R. Rao, *New Frontiers of Archaeology*, Popular Prakashan, 1994, p. 18.
15. See D.P. Sharma and Madhuri, *Panorama of Harappan Civilization*, Kaveri Books, 2003, p. 30.
16. See S.R. Rao, *New Frontiers of Archaeology*, Popular Prakashan, 1994, p. 15.
17. See D.P. Sharma and Madhuri, *Panorama of Harappan Civilization*, Kaveri Books, 2003, p. 47.

It is not entirely clear what the purpose was for all of the seals. The Haṛappans were highly literate and left behind more than 3,000 seals; 61 sealings at Lothal were probably used for sealing cargo.[18]

5.7 City-Planning in Ṛgveda, Indus/Haṛappā and Manusmṛti

Ṛgveda mentions similar material, style and workmanship as used by the Indus/Haṛappan Civilisation, including laying a foundation, framing of doors, laying of bricks, building gates, doors, entrances and load bearing girders, measuring width and breadth with a measuring rope.[19]

The *Manusmṛti* refers to drainage, engineering and architecture professionals in chapter 3, verse 163: "He who diverts water-courses, and he who delights in obstructing them, an architect, a messenger, and he who plants trees (for money). . . ."[20] Not only is this verse speaking in part about those who designed outside irrigation, but possibly also those who had the job of designing baths and indoor plumbing. This *Manusmṛti* description of professionals appears to be similar to professionals of the Indus/Haṛappan Civilisation, who obviously had architects and engineers to design the complicated urban bathrooms and drainage. The standard house of Indus/Haṛappan Civilisation times that survives even today in India was an open space in the centre with rooms on all sides.[21] Private houses were arranged around a central courtyard, a practice that is still maintained in traditional homes throughout northern India and

18. See S.R. Rao, *New Frontiers of Archaeology*, Popular Prakashan, 1994, p. 3.
19. See Bhagwan Singh, *The Vedic Harappans*, Aditya Prakashan, 1996, p. 285.
20. See G. Buehler, *Laws of Manu*, Oxford (Sacred Books of the East, v. XXV), 1896, p. 72.
21. See M.K. Dhavalikar, *The Aryans: Myth and Archaeology*, Munshiram Manoharlal, 2007, p. 55.

Pakistan.[22] There were later compositions of texts regarding architecture that required the open space in the centre with the rooms on all sides. In *Ṛgveda* III.55.14, a *ṛtasya sadma* is mentioned, or a "house of justice."[23] This seems very similar to the *Manusmṛti*, where the king or village chief, when sitting as judge, or his legal advisers, when sitting as judges, are advised to go to the "house of justice."

Sir John Marshall of England, who led the excavation of Mohenjo-Dāṛo in the 1920s, wrote about the relatively high degree of luxury of the Indus/Haṛappan Civilisation, denoted by the existence of roomy and well-built houses, their elaborate system of drainage, as well as the character of many of the smaller antiquities found within, seem to betoken a social condition of the people far in advance of what was then prevailing in Mesopotamia and Egypt.[24]

The Indus/Haṛappan Civilisation cities were oriented along cardinal directions (north-south and east-west) and that orientation is probably linked to religious beliefs, reflecting precise astronomical observations and movement of sun, moon and stars.[25] The streets of the Indus/Haṛappan Civilisation never diverge by more than two degrees.[26] Indus/Haṛappan Civilisation towns had well-planned wide straight streets and major roads running north-south and east-west and cutting each other at right angles with covered drains along the sides of streets; most were divided into two parts and fortified.[27] More

22. See J.M. Kenoyer, *Ancient Cities of the Indus Valley Civilization*, Oxford University Press, 1998, p. 58.

23. See Bhagwan Singh, *The Vedic Harappans*, Aditya Prakashan, 1996, p. 293.

24. See Jane McIntosh, *A Peaceful Realm*, Westview Press, 2002, p. 21.

25. See J.M. Kenoyer, *Ancient Cities of the Indus Valley Civilization*, Oxford University Press, 1998, p. 52.

26. See Jane McIntosh, *A Peaceful Realm*, Westview Press, 2002, p. 99.

27. See D.P. Sharma and Madhuri, *Panorama of Harappan Civilization*, Kaveri Books, 2003, p. 27.

than thirty-five Mature Haṛappan sites from the Indus/ Haṛappan Civilisation are located along the Gujarat coast, characterised by fabulous town planning and drainage systems, well-thought-out and proper layout of roads and fortification.[28]

The Indus/Haṛappan Civilisation was also well known for its incredibly strong bricks, most of which have survived until today. There are 15 different sizes of Haṛappan bricks, some with the ratio of 3 : 2 : 1, most with the ratio of 4 : 2 : 1, a ratio which, even today, is considered the optimal ratio for efficient strength and bonding.[29] In addition to the Indus bricks having the ratio of 1 : 2 : 4 (or 4 : 2 :1), these same ratios are reflected in the rooms of houses and in the construction of large public buildings.[30]

5.8 Lothal Bricks/Engineering Verified

The author has personally verified some of the bricks and engineering through his visit to the 5,000 years old Indus/ Haṛappan Civilisation site at Lothal. The bricks and brick walls at Lothal are amazingly straight considering that they are almost 5,000 years old. The quality of these Lothal sun-dried bricks and kiln-fired bricks and the brick walls were better than the modern-day simple brick structures dotting the farms surrounding Lothal. (When the author is describing simple modern-day Indian structures, the author is referring to small man-made structures made of brick for people or animals; the more expensive buildings in the area are similar to those in any Western country.)

The author next verified the seemingly perfect roundness of the water wells. The ancient inhabitants of Lothal must have been very intelligent people and obviously technologically

28. See Aniruddh Singh Gaur, *Harappan Maritime Legacies of Gujarat*, Asian Publishing Services, 2000, pp. 162-63.

29. See G.G. Joseph, *The Crest of the Peacock, The Non-European Roots of Mathematics*, Princeton University Press, 2000, p. 223.

30. See J.M. Kenoyer, *Ancient Cities of the Indus Valley Civilization*, Oxford University Press, 1998, p. 57.

advanced. They must have been first-class mathematicians, architects, engineers and builders. The Archaeological Survey of India (ASI) has covered the wells at Lothal (probably to prevent tourists from falling in), with a very strong, pre-fabricated modern, round metal screen. The interesting thing to the casual observer is that the modern, perfectly-round screen "fits like a glove." This seems to imply that the brick circles that the civil engineers of Lothal could achieve (and preserve for more than almost 5,000 years) in their water wells are extremely similar to the modern-day machine-made roundness. All of the above discussion is in addition to the engineering feat of the gigantic Lothal man-made, brick-lined dock. Apparently, the storehouses were built on brick platforms to perform efficiently even during floods.

5.9 Moheṅjo-Dāṛo and Haṛappā Excelled Egypt

Most archaeologists who have studied the Indus/Haṛappan Civilisation are very impressed. One summary is thus: Moheṅjo-Dāṛo and Haṛappā (of 5,000 years ago) were as old as the civilisations of Egypt and Iraq (Mesopotamia and Sumeria) and in many ways excelled them; the Indian cities were well planned with streets running north-south and east-west, whereas no such planning existed in Egypt and Iraq of that time, as well as kiln-fired bricks and superbly intricately carved steatite seals. Grain production went up with the building of circular silos plastered with lime and clay; objects were made with semi-precious stone in copper, silver and gold.[31] The Indus/Haṛappan Civilisation had fabulous town-planning and drains; important buildings were made of kiln-baked bricks; Dholavīra was divided into three divisions: Citadel, Middle Town and Lower Town and fortified with a thick brick wall.[32]

The division of the Indus/Haṛappan Civilisation site of

31. See B.B. Lal, *The Sarasvati Flows On*, Aryan, 2002, p. 30.

32. See Aniruddh Gaur, *Harappan Maritime Legacies of Gujarat*, 2000, p. 33.

Dholavīra into its three sections of Citadel, Middle Town and Lower Town seems similar to the division of caste or class from the text of the *Manusmṛti*. If, in general, as the *Manusmṛti* says, the brāhmaṇas were supposed to remain somewhat aloof from the rest of the population; the kṣatriyas and vaiśyas were supposed to remain separated from the servants, śūdras, then the three sections of Citadel, Middle Town and Lower Town of Dholavīra may very well be related to the *Manusmṛti*.

5.10 International Trade in Ṛgveda, Indus/Haṛappan Civilisation and the Manusmṛti

According to the *Ṛgveda*, in the beginning, there was no earth, just ocean; all things emerged from the primordial sea; God is the merciful supreme navigator.[33] There are many references in the *Ṛgveda* to travelling the oceans. Evidence of direct trade between the Indus/Haṛappan Civilisation and Mesopotamia can be found by the presence of seals, etched carnelian, terracotta statues and dice in Mesopotamia. Also, Mesopotamian goods have been found in the remains of the Indus/Haṛappan Civilisation: spiral and animal headed pins, segmented beads and pottery of the perforated knobbed and reserved slip ware type.[34] The *Ṛgveda* mentions fabulous profit from mining and shipping; words appear, such as, "having an abundant flow," "the speediest boat," "ships with three masts,". "ships with three sails," "the four seas filled full of riches thousandfold."[35]

Some scholars say that the dockyard of Lothal is a holding tank for water. The evidence points to it being a wharf. The Lothal dockyard measures 214 × 36 metres. A wharf would have served the purpose of handling cargo and lies along the western

33. See Bhagwan Singh, *The Vedic Harappans*, Aditya Prakashan, 1996, p. 228.

34. See Aniruddh Singh Gaur, *Harappan Maritime Legacies of Gujarat*, Asian Publishing Services, 2000, pp. 98-99.

35. See Bhagwan Singh, *The Vedic Harappans*, Aditya Prakashan, 1996, p. 237.

embankment wall. Since kiln-dried bricks were precious to the inhabitants of Lothal, they would not have used millions of fired-bricks to build this structure if it was only an irrigation water holding tank.[36] The dockyard at Lothal has been verified by the author and is a wonderful thing to behold, apparently a man-made dock, more than 4,000 years old, designed with very high technical skill and engineering skill, made with millions of kiln-dried bricks.

In the Indus/Haṛappan Civilisation, international trade was important. Many scholars believe that one means of identifying goods was the making of "seals" which were apparently attached physically to the internationally-traded goods. These extraordinary square and rectangular fired-soapstone (steatite) seals were made by Indus/Haṛappan Civilisation artisans with pictures of animals and Indus script; many animals were male bulls with a mysterious offering stand in front of them. The seals may have been used sometimes like credit cards today. Perhaps one would show his seal and get it "stamped" in clay. In ancient Mesopotamia, when a seal was lost, a herald announced the loss so that the seal would be invalidated. Some scholars identify the Indus/Haṛappan Civilisation "offering stand" (in front of the carved bull) as a filter for the preparation of a sacred intoxicating beverage called *soma*, which is used in Vedic rituals.[37] (The cone carved in ivory from the Indus/Haṛappan Civilisation city of Haṛappā lends credibility to this interpretation.)

Flat-bottomed boats used on the Indus River today resemble the terracotta boats made by artisans of the Indus/Haṛappan Civilisation. Many types of timber from the Indus/Haṛappan Civilisation are mentioned in Sumerian texts, including "sullum meluhhi," "black wood of Meluhha," probably ebony from south

---

36. See Aniruddh Singh Gaur, *Harappan Maritime Legacies of Gujarat*, Asian Publishing Services, 2000, p. 45.

37. See J.M. Kenoyer, *Ancient Cities of the Indus Valley Civilization*, Oxford University Press, 1998, p. 86.

India.[38] If this was ebony from south India, it shows even more clearly the trade within ancient India and internationally.

5.11 Indus/Haṛappan Civilisation Remains found in the Persian Gulf and Iraq

Bahrain is located in the Persian Gulf between Qatar and Saudi Arabia. One of the major excavated places in Bahrain was the ancient capital of Dilman (Dilum, Telmun), which, among other articles, yielded half a dozen stone weights, which in shape and weight agree completely with the weights found in the Indus/Haṛappan Civilisation.[39] Many Indus seals have been found in Bahrain, adding to the theory that the merchants of the Indus/Haṛappan Civilisation had colonies at in Bahrain. Shells were not available in Gulf countries and were, therefore, traded by merchants from the Indus/Haṛappan Civilisation city of Lothal to Bahrain and Mesopotamia; a special shell called *śaṅkha* (sacred conch) is very sacred today in Hindu temples and was also found to be important and traded throughout the Indus/Haṛappan Civilisation.[40]

We know from the *R̥gveda*, that the Vedic people engaged in sea trade. *R̥gveda* IX.33.6: "From every side, O Soma, for our profit, pour thou forth four seas; Filled full of riches thousandfold."[41] This has led some scholars to conclude that the Indus/Haṛappan Civilisation was the same as the Vedic civilisation. Those scholars say that the Vedic-Haṛappans engaged in sea trade.[42]

38. See Jane McIntosh, *A Peaceful Realm*, Westview Press, 2002, p. 169.
39. See D.K. Chakrabarti, *The External Trade of the Indus Civilization*, Munshiram Manoharlal, 1990, p. 13.
40. See Aniruddh Singh Gaur, *Harappan Maritime Legacies of Gujarat*, Asian Publishing Services, 2000, p. 110.
41. See Ralph T.H. Griffith, *Hymns of the R̥gveda*, 1889, Munshiram Manoharlal, 1999.
42. See B.B. Lal, "Search for Vedic-Harappan Relationship", in Agrawal (ed.), *In Search of Vedic-Haṛappan Relationship*, Aryan Books International, 2005, p. 5.

In Lothal (that Indus/Haṛappan Civilisation city located in modern-day Gujarat), a terracotta male head was found from Period A levels that looks like Sumerian figures, with a broad, stiff beard that was only known in Sumeria, not at all known at Lothal.[43]

A piece of evidence that Indus seals were used in foreign trade is a commodity sealing from Jokha (Umma) that bears an impress of woven material stamped with a square Haṛappan seal showing a unicorn and the written script of the Indus/Haṛappan Civilisation.[44]

Naeswar is another Indus/Haṛappan Civilisation site also in the modern-day Indian state of Gujarat and is located about 20 km north-east of Dvārakā. Naeswar was a major Indus/Haṛappan Civilisation period centre for shell works. In Naeswar, there have been discoveries of semi-precious stone, Indus/Haṛappan Civilisation beads and Indus/Haṛappan Civilisation seals from Ur, Brak, Nippur (all from Mesopotamia, or modern-day Iraq) and in Persian Gulf countries like UAE, Oman and Bahrain.[45]

5.12 Lothal and Dvārakā

Five "anchor stones" were found in the basin of the "dockyard" at Lothal; we thus assume that the ancient boats were made of wood such as teak, rope from vegetation fibre, cotton, flax or rush for sails, bamboo for masts; either wood or bronze for pegs and nails and stone for anchors, and perhaps bitumen (natural tar) or animal fat for caulking.[46] The Indus/Haṛappan

43. See D.K. Chakrabarti, *The External Trade of the Indus Civilization*, Munshiram Manoharlal, 1990, p. 63.

44. See S. Ratnagar, *Trading Encounters From the Euphrates to the Indus in the Bronze Age*, Oxford University Press, 2006, p. 259.

45. See Aniruddh Singh Gaur, *Harappan Maritime Legacies of Gujarat*, Asian Publishing Services, 2000, p. 7.

46. See S. Ratnagar, *Trading Encounters From the Euphrates to the Indus in the Bronze Age*, Oxford University Press, 2006, p. 226.

Civilisation site of Dvārakā has yielded more than 50 stone anchors, which have survived even if their wooden ships did not. Dvārakā must have been an important port in the past for local and international trading of the Indus/Haṛappan Civilisation.[47]

5.13 Sea Trade in Animals and Wood

The *R̥gveda* talks about sea trade (*R̥V*, 9.33.6) and boats with 100 oars (*R̥V*, 1.116.5).[48] The Sanskrit word for ocean, *samudra*, occurs about 100 times in the *R̥gveda*. It occurs many more times than any river or group of rivers by name. Other related terms meaning sea or ocean are *sāgara*, *arṇa*s, and *sindhu*. The main myth in the Vedas is of Indra slaying a dragon and releasing seven rivers to flow into the sea.[49] Terracotta model boats have been found at the Indus/Haṛappan Civilisation city of Lothal. These boats have a pointed or curved prow, a blunt stern and sharp keels, similar to Phoenician trading ships and Egyptian vessels of 4,000 to 5,000 years ago (between 2000 and 3000 BCE).[50]

R̥gveda I.51.1 mentions the god, Indra, as filling full like the sea. *R̥gveda*: I.52.4 says, "To Indra, even as rivers to the ocean, flow forth." *R̥gveda* X.45.1 says that "*Agni* sprang to life first from out of heaven, the second time from the Jātavedas and the third time from the waters."[51] *R̥gveda* in another section talks about the making of chariots and praises the Kiṁśuka and Śālmalī

---

47. See Aniruddh Singh Gaur, *Harappan Maritime Legacies of Gujarat*, Asian Publishing Services, 2000, p. 83.
48. See B.B. Lal, *The Sarasvatī Flows On*, Aryan, 2002, p. 71.
49. See David Frawley, "Geographical References: The Ocean and Soma", in Agrawal (ed.), *In Search of Vedic-Haṛappan Relationship*, Aryan Books International, 2005, p. 30.
50. See Aniruddh Singh Gaur, *Harappan Maritime Legacies of Gujarat*, Asian Publishing Services, 2000, pp. 141-43.
51. See Ralph T.H. Griffith, *Hymns of the R̥gveda*, 1889, Munshiram Manoharlal, 1999.

trees for the making of chariots (*Ṛgveda* 10.85.20); these trees are located only in India, Burma (Myanmar) and Sri Lanka.[52] Apparently, a chariot made of one of these woods was found in Egypt and is yet another example of the international trade that originated from the Indus/Haṛappan Civilisation. Wood was also a valuable trading commodity that was mentioned in Mesopotamian texts as being imported from Dilman, Magan and Meluhha.[53] Ivory was an important Indus/Haṛappan Civilisation export to Mesopotamia, used for making combs, pins, awls, hooks, gamesmen, buttons, scales, dice, and personal ornaments. *Lapis Lazuli* (the semi-precious blue stone) was desired by the ruling class of Mesopotamia for ideological reasons and used in temple consecrations and funerary offerings; it was a valuable trading commodity for the Indus/Haṛappan Civilisation.[54]

The *Ṛgveda* speaks of the *vibhītaka* trees for the making of dice, which were used in different types of games (*Ṛgveda* 7.86.6 and 10.34.1); these trees are located in India, Burma (Myanmar), Sri Lanka, Pakistan and Malaysia; Ṛgvedic "cucumbers" (wild version) are located in India, Pakistan and tropical Africa.[55] There is a well-known verse from *Ṛgveda* that is recited against sickness and says: just like the *urvāruka* (cucumber) being picked from its stem, so may the invoker of the hymn be released from death (*Ṛgveda* 7.59.12):

> *tryambakaṁ yajāmahe sugandhiṁ puṣṭivardhanam* ।
> *urvārukamiva bandhanānmṛtyormukṣīya māmṛtāt* ॥

Mesopotamia was a centre of making clothing from sheep-wool

52. See B.B. Lal, *The Homeland of the Aryans: Evidence of Ṛgvedic Flora and Fauna & Archaeology*, Aryan Book International, 2005, p. 11.
53. See Aniruddh Singh Gaur, *Harappan Maritime Legacies of Gujarat*, Asian Publishing Services, 2000, p. 128.
54. Ibid., p. 131.
55. See B.B. Lal, *The Homeland of the Aryans, Evidence of Ṛgvedic Flora and Fauna and Archaeology*, Aryan Books International, 2005, pp. 16-17.

and goat-wool; some Mesopotamian texts refer to a single commercial transaction involving 6,400 tons of wool.[56] Even by today's standards, that seems like an extremely large quantity of wool just for one commercial transaction.

The *gaura* or wild cow (*Bos gaurus*) mentioned frequently in the *R̥gveda*, has three sub-species in South and South-East Asia and has nothing to do with Europe or Western Asia, and the *mahiṣa* or water buffalo (*Bubalus bubalis*) also mentioned frequently in the *R̥gveda*, is from South and South-East Asia and has nothing to do with Europe or Western Asia.[57]

5.14 Further Evidence of International Trade

There is a significant amount of Sorath Haṛappan pottery located in what was called by the ancients, "Dilman," located in what we now know to be Bahrain, a country located in the Arabian Gulf.[58] The camel (*uṣṭra*) has been mentioned about a half-dozen times in the *R̥gveda*; there are many skeletal remains of camels at many Indus/Haṛappan Civilisation sites. The camels, though, never appeared on Haṛappan seals.[59] It is not known why camels did not appear on Indus/Haṛappan Civilisation seals. More study needs to be done in this area.

Different countries during the Indus/Haṛappan Civilisation time-period produced different "seals." One did not have to be literate to identify the seals of 5,000 years ago (the third millennium BCE). For instance, Haṛappans had the square Indus seals. Someone having the cylinder seal was identified as Mesopotamian.[60] The

56. See Aniruddh Singh Gaur, *Harappan Maritime Legacies of Gujarat*, Asian Publishing Services, 2000, p. 133.
57. See B.B. Lal, *The Homeland of the Aryans, Evidence of R̥gvedic Flora and Fauna and Archaeology*, Aryan Books International, 2005, pp. 38-39.
58. See Gregory Possehl, *The Indus Civilization*, Rowman Altamira, 2002, p. 60.
59. See B.B. Lal, *The Homeland of the Aryans, Evidence of R̥gvedic Flora and Fauna and Archaeology*, Aryan Books International, 2005, pp. 29-33.
60. See Gregory Possehl, *The Indus Civilization*, Rowman Altamira, 2002, p. 61.

people of the Indus/Haṛappan Civilisation traded in peacocks to Mesopotamia in the third millennium BCE and peacocks with coloured tails only come from South-East Asia.[61]

Indus/Haṛappan Civilisation products like seals, carnelian beads, figurines, shells and ivory dice have been reported from Tell Asmar, Kish, Lagash, Umma, Nippur, Tepa Gawra, Jokha, Tell Agrab and Ashur, which confirms Indus/Haṛappan Civilisation trade links with Mesopotamian Civilisation in what is now mostly modern-day Iraq.[62] Ample evidence exists of Indus Civilisation sea voyages, seafaring ships and sea trade; ships with three masts (*tirbandhura*) and/or ten oars (*daśaritra*) and even 100 oars (*śataritra*) were commissioned; the wealth thus achieved seems to have been tremendous.[63]

As mentioned above, the *Ṛgveda* had many references to ocean voyages. Scholars who previously believed that the *Ṛgveda* was composed in a land-locked country must have been mistaken. According to *Ṛgveda*, in the beginning, there was no earth, just ocean; all things emerged from the primordial sea; God is the merciful supreme navigator.[64]

In Mesopotamia in the third millennium BCE, no wood of the requisite strength for cart frames, wheels, sea boats or temple pillars or roofing was locally available apart from poplar; they could export cereals, oils and wool to the Indus/Haṛappan Civilisation in exchange for wood. In order to move textiles, wood and meals, boats of 5,000 years ago (the third millennium BCE) must have been constructed out of wooden planks; it is

61. See B.B. Lal, *The Homeland of the Aryans: Evidence of Ṛgvedic Flora and Fauna & Archaeology*, Aryan Books International, 2005, p. 51.

62. See D.P. Sharma and Madhuri, *Panorama of Harappan Civilization*, Kaveri Books, 2003, p. 61.

63. See B.B. Lal, "It is Time to Rethink", in N. Lahiri (ed.), *The Decline and Fall of the Indus Civilization*, Permanent Black, 2000, p. 89.

64. See Bhagwan Singh, *The Vedic Harappans*, Aditya Prakashan, 1996, p. 228.

believed that they retained their "spoon" shape and bipod mast; teak wood from India is an excellent shipbuilding wood because of its hardness and resistance to warping or swelling in water.[65]

The *Manusmṛti* had many references to trade, and some to long-distance trade. One such reference was: the *Manusmṛti*, 8.406, "For a long passage the boat-hire must be proportioned to the places and times; know that this (rule refers) to (passages along) the banks of rivers; at sea there is no settled (freight)."[66]

In Lothal, 64 clay sealings were found that seemed to be preserved because of a warehouse fire; the sealings prove that the Indus seals were used for a commercial purpose, to seal the cargo and authenticate the source and contents.[67]

There are few economic systems that are only concerned with obtaining and trading for food, shelter and clothing; status obligations and ruling-class ideologies are equally important; for instance, there was a royal Mesopotamian obligation to decorate temples with exotic materials which were only available at great distances. Ivory imported from the Indus/Haṛappan Civilisation became a favoured medium of art and carved objects in Mesopotamia and can be found today in many objects.[68]

5.15 Water Technology

Water technology is an important subject in the *Ṛgveda;* what we can guess by examining the ruins and excavating the cities, towns and villages is this: to the people of the Indus/Haṛappan Civilisation having sophisticated water technology was one of the most important aspects of their lives.

---

65. See S. Ratnagar, *Trading Encounters from the Euphrates to the Indus in the Bronze Age*, Oxford University Press, 2006, p. 215.
66. See G. Buehler, *Laws of Manu*, Oxford (Sacred Books of the East, v. XXV), 1896, p. 227.
67. See S.R. Rao, *New Frontiers of Archaeology*, Popular Prakashan, 1994, p. 9.
68. See S. Ratnagar, *Trading Encounters from the Euphrates to the Indus in the Bronze Age*, Oxford University Press, 2006, p. 159.

There is a rich terminology connected to water in the *Ṛgveda*, including a pond, a well, a spring or fountain, a canal, a leather bag for gathering water, an excavated well and irrigation. *Ṛgveda* also mentions the same material, style and workmanship as those used by the people of the Indus/Haṛappan Civilisation, including laying a foundation, frames of doors, bricklaying, gates, doors, entrances, load-bearing girder, measuring rope, width and breadth.[69]

The ancient Indus/Haṛappan Civilisation town of Kunal, in the State of Punjab, near Haryana, has undergone recent excavation. Bricks were found again to be standardised in two ratios of 1 : 2 : 3 and 1 : 2 : 4. A well-developed drainage system is in place, soakage jars fixed in street pits, to keep the streets neat and clean.[70] In general, one could say that the houses of the Indus/Haṛappan Civilisation were built of bricks and stone on high platforms, with stairs, bathrooms and a good drainage system both covered and open.[71]

In the Indus/Haṛappan Civilisation city of Lothal, not only annual flooding occurred, but also due to some severe floods the inhabitants had to rebuild their houses. Instead of just rebuilding in a replacement way, the inhabitants not only rebuilt their houses on higher platforms, but the opulence of inhabitants was increasing, judging from the number of spacious houses and industrial establishments, costly ornaments and imported goods.[72]

The dock at Lothal is the largest structure ever built by the

69. See Bhagwan Singh, *The Vedic Harappans*, Aditya Prakashan, 1996, p. 285.

70. See Khatri and Acharya, "Kunal Excavations", in Agrawal (ed.), *In Search of Vedic-Harappan Relationship*, Aryan Books International, 2005, p. 108.

71. See D.P. Sharma and Madhuri, *Panorama of Harappan Civilization*, Kaveri Books, 2003, p. 28.

72. See S.R. Rao, *Lothal: A Harappan Port Town*, in N. Lahiri (ed.), *The Decline and Fall of the Indus Civilization*, Permanent Black, 2000, p. 147.

Indus/Haṛappan Civilisation in any city. It was larger than 600 ft by 100 ft (210 × 35 m); there was a lock-gate system for low tide and it is estimated that as many as 30 ships of 60 tons or more could be berthed at the same time. Recent analysis of sediment from the floor of the basin at the Lothal Dock indicates the existence of a high tidal range in the Gulf of Cambay (Khambhat) during Indus/Haṛappan Civilisation times.[73]

5.16 Water in Ṛgveda, Indus/Haṛappā Civilisation and the Manusmṛti

Fire worship and bathing also seemed to go together in the *Manusmṛti* and in the Indus/Haṛappan Civilisation. At Kālibaṅgan, Lothal, Banawālī and Rākhīgaṛhī, bathing facilities are associated with what are taken to be fire altars.[74] Referring to students, the *Manusmṛti* says, chapter 2:176, "Everyday, having bathed, and being purified, he must offer libations of water to the gods, sages and manes, worship (the images of) the gods, and place fuel on (the sacred fire)."[75] Bathing and fire worship as described by *Ṛgveda* are prescribed in the *Manusmṛti* and apparently evidenced by archaeological remains in the Indus/ Haṛappan Civilisation.

The clearest examples of the important role that water played in the Indus/Haṛappan Civilisation occurs at Moheṅjo-Dāṛo and Dholavīra — many wells, elaborate drainage systems, bathing facilities in virtually all the houses and the Moheṅjo-Dāṛo Great Bath.[76]

"The World's First Swimming Pool," as some visitors call it, was built at Moheṅjo-Dāṛo, but it was probably used for

73. See S.R. Rao, *New Frontiers of Archaeology*, Popular Prakashan, 1994, p. 11.
74. See Jane McIntosh, *A Peaceful Realm*, Westview Press, 2002, p. 110.
75. See G. Buehler, *Laws of Manu*, Oxford (Sacred Books of the East, v. XXV), 1896, p. 42.
76. See Gregory Possehl, *The Indus Civilization*, Rowman Altamira, 2002, p. 57.

ritual bathing, not public swimming.[77] Even if the large pool at Moheñjo-Dāṛo was meant for ritual bathing, certainly all of the requirements given in the *Manusmṛti* could have been taken care of or satisfied. The *Manusmṛti* prescribes bathing three times a day in chapter 6.24: "When he bathes at the three *Savana*s (sunrise, midday, and sunset), let him offer libations of water to the manes and the gods, and practising harsher and harsher austerities, let him dry up his bodily frame."[78] If the *Manusmṛti* recommended bathing three times a day, that certainly would have seemed excessive to the average person living thousands of years ago. But to the people of the Indus/Haṛappan Civilisation, with all of their indoor plumbing and drainage, bathing three times a day would not be at all difficult or impossible, as it probably might have been at other periods in history in ancient India.

For almost every house in Moheñjo-Dāṛo, the bathroom was important; water was poured over the bather, over the brick floor, emptying into a brick outlet into an efficient drainage network of the city.[79] Similarly, the *Manusmṛti* prescribed depositing one's waste products far from home. Most of the inhabitants of other contemporaneous civilisations did not have the drainage of Indus/Haṛappan Civilisation, to accomplish this on a daily basis.

Water management was amazingly well developed in the Indus/Haṛappan Civilisation. The 18 reservoirs in Dholavīra suggest excellent water management by masters in hydraulic engineering in the Indus/Haṛappan Civilisation.[80] Those Indus/

77. See J.M. Kenoyer, *Ancient Cities of the Indus Valley Civilization*, Oxford University Press, 1998, p. 63.

78. See G. Buehler, *Laws of Manu*, Oxford (Sacred Books of the East, v. XXV), 1896, pp. 141-42.

79. See Jane McIntosh, *A Peaceful Realm*, Westview Press, 2002, p. 94.

80. See D.P. Sharma and Madhuri, *Panorama of Harappan Civilization*, Kaveri Books, 2003, p. 59.

Haṛappan Civilisation hydraulic engineers were at least 2,000 years ahead of their time because not for another 2,000 years did hydraulic engineers of that calibre emerge in Rome.[81] This is a fact, not to be underestimated, that the hydraulic engineers of the Indus/Haṛappan Civilisation achieved feats that were not seen again in the world for another 2,000 years.

Cleanliness is stringently enforced and water is recommended for cleaning purposes in another post-*Ṛgveda* composition, the Gṛhya-Sūtras. A regular daily bath was insisted upon. The sipping of water and washing of feet are insisted upon as preliminary to even the most trivial ritual act.[82] This is again just like the requirements of the *Manusmṛti*. Washing was one of the most important acts of many people in the *Manusmṛti* society. The baths at Moheṅjo-Dāṛo are large, thus suggesting that the daily bath was concurrent with the writing of the Gṛhya-Sūtras. It seems possible that the daily bath of the people of the Indus/Haṛappan Civilisation was in harmony with the laws of the *Manusmṛti*.

In the *Manusmṛti*, one was also supposed to bathe before eating, and in fact, eat with wet feet. In chapter 2:53, "Let a twice-born man always eat his food with a concentrated mind, after performing an ablution; and after he has eaten, let him duly cleanse himself with water and sprinkle the cavities (of his head)."[83] Not all people in ancient India lived near a body of water. Therefore, bathing before and after every meal would have been quite a task for many. But for the citizens of the cities and towns of the Indus/Haṛappan Civilisation there was no problem because of the technology of indoor plumbing, wells, toilets, baths and drains. The "wet feet" prescription was supposed to yield a long life; in the

81. See Jane McIntosh, *A Peaceful Realm*, Westview Press, 2002, p. 100.
82. See K.D. Sethna, *Karpasa in Prehistoric India*, Biblia Impex, 1981, p. 53.
83. See G. Buehler, *Laws of Manu*, Oxford (Sacred Books of the East, v. XXV), 1896, p. 25.

Manusmṛti, chapter 4. 76, "Let him eat while his feet are (yet) wet (from the ablution), but let him not go to bed with wet feet. He who eats while his feet are (still) wet, will attain long life."[84] This time, it is bathing before each meal, as well as some purification after each meal. All of this bathing required lots and lots of water, of course, available, if one lived in the Indus/Haṛappan Civilisation.

There were many wells throughout the Indus/Haṛappan Civilisation city of Moheṅjo-Dāṛo, essential for cleanliness and the drainage systems served to move the water away from the houses, below ground to prevent contamination. The builders of the Great Bath in Moheṅjo-Dāṛo used elevation and distance to set it apart from the rest of the city. The Great Bath was probably a ritual space that seems to have been reserved for the elites of the city, possibly the elites of the entire Indus world.[85] The fired bricks of the Great Bath were held together by *cūnā* mortar and asphalt to make them watertight for the bathers and so the water could be drained out by an opening in one corner.[86]

Drainage was also very important in the *Manusmṛti*. In the *Manusmṛti*, chapter 4:151, "Far from his dwelling let him remove urine (and ordure), far (let him remove) the water used for washing his feet, and far the remnants of food and the water from his bath."[87] The *Manusmṛti* insisted upon the removal of wastes and dirty water. This was easy for inhabitants of the Indus/Haṛappan Civilisation because of their marvellous drains,

84. See G. Buehler, *Laws of Manu*, Oxford (Sacred Books of the East, v. XXV), 1896, p. 96.

85. See Gregory Possehl, *The Indus Civilization*, Rowman Altamira, 2002, p. 58.

86. See D.P. Sharma and Madhuri, *Panorama of Harappan Civilization*, Kaveri Books, 2003, p. 40.

87. See G. Buehler, *Laws of Manu*, Oxford (Sacred Books of the East, v. XXV), 1896, p. 104.

house drains, street drains, city drains, but more difficult if one did not live as part of an Indus/Haṛappan Civilisation city or town.

A good example of an Indus/Haṛappan Civilisation toilet is in the town of Banawālī. In one of the houses the toilet has a washbasin high in the corner near the drain which carried off the waste water into a sullage jar placed outside on the street.[88] Probably the sullage jar had to be emptied by servants whose job it was to empty such jars. Excavators at the Indus/Haṛappan Civilisation city of Haṛappā have found what appear to be latrines in every house. The commodes were made of large jars sunk into the floor and many contained a small jar similar to the modern water jar (or plastic cup) used throughout India and Pakistan today for washing after using the toilet; clean sand was scattered on the floor of the latrine.[89]

The Law Code of Manu also suggests earth and water to be used to clean after using the toilet. In the *Manusmṛti*, chapter 5.134, "In order to cleanse (the organs) by which urine and faeces are ejected, *earth and water must be used*, as they may be required, likewise in removing the (remaining ones among) twelve impurities of the body.[90] Throughout the bathrooms and drains of the ruins of the Indus/Haṛappan Civilisation, one finds cakes of sand and earth; the inhabitants seem to have been very familiar with the practices apparently very similar to those contained in the *Manusmṛti*.

5.17 Mystery of Written Records from Indus/Haṛappan Civilisation

In spite of much archaeological evidence of advanced thinking

---

88. See B.B. Lal, *The Sarasvatī Flows On*, Aryan, 2002, p. 62.
89. See J.M. Kenoyer, *Ancient Cities of the Indus Valley Civilization*, Oxford University Press, 1998, p. 60.
90. See G. Buehler, *Laws of Manu*, Oxford (Sacred Books of the East, v. XXV), 1896, p. 134.

from the Indus/Haṛappan Civilisation, most of that advanced thinking must have been preserved by oral tradition. The Indus/Haṛappan Civilisation "script" that survives on thousands of small "seals" has not yet been translated to the satisfaction of a majority of scholars, and a minority of scholars call it "graffiti." The Indus/Haṛappan Civilisation "script" bears some resemblance to the less ancient Indian Sanskrit script of Brāhmī (dated from about 2,300 years ago — 300 BCE) and some resemblance to other ancient "foreign" scripts.

There are other theories regarding the small findings of the "written" word, including social control, i.e. keeping knowledge from the lower class and strengthening the mind through memorisation. Probably, until a "Rosetta Stone" is found, the Indus/Haṛappan Civilisation written "script" will remain a mystery. (The Rosetta Stone is an artefact from ancient Egypt, which allowed scholars to decipher ancient Egyptian hieroglyphic writing. It is a stone carved with the same text in three languages, two Egyptian language scripts and one in classical Greek, discovered by a French army engineer under Napoleon, in 1799 at Rosetta, a port city in Egypt.)

5.18 Conclusion

The Indus/Haṛappan Civilisation made progress towards "civilised life" by using the "technology" of harnessing the use of animal power and the "technology" of division of labour, in addition to urban planning, jewellery making, sanitation and long-distance maritime trade. Evidence of international trade abounds in foreign ports. Most of the above "technologies" were also mentioned in the *Ṛgveda* and the *Manusmṛti*. Throughout the vast Indus/Haṛappan Civilisation realm, standardisation helped mass production. Standardisation must have been brought about by the "servant kings," similar in concept to the *Manusmṛti* because there are no archaeological remains of large palaces or statues of kings, such as those found in foreign lands for contemporaneous cultures.

Other "overlaps" of technology and knowledge between Indus/Haṛappan Civilisation on the one hand and Ṛgvedic culture and *Manusmṛti* society on the other are water technology and efficient systems of government. *Soma*, the spiritual intoxicating beverage, was very important in *Ṛgveda* and *Manusmṛti* societies; it also seems to have been present and perhaps important in the Indus/Haṛappan Civilisation.

Many Indus/Haṛappan Civilisation practices have been preserved by modern-day citizens of the Indian subcontinent, including *haṭha-yoga*, make-up and jewellery. Many of these practices were also mentioned in the *Manusmṛti*, suggesting a possible link to the Indus/Haṛappan Civilisation.

6

Decline of the Indus/Haṛappan Civilisation

6.1 Earthquake 3,900 Years Ago (1900 BCE)

THERE is ample evidence of a large-scale volcanic-seismic-tectonic upheaval 3,900 years ago (in approximately 1900 BCE) involving a vast region, including a part of the Near East, the Arabian Sea and in India, the path of river Sarasvatī.[1] This was a major occurrence, something that happened around and beyond the Indian subcontinent. As the space satellite Landsat Imagery has shown, the palaeo-channels of river Sarasvatī relied on factors like the pattern of drainage scars, distinct tone, texture and surface manifestations such as younger alluvium and concentration of vegetation.[2] Some scholars summed it up succinctly, saying because of earthquakes, where once river Sarasvatī flowed, now remains only a desert.[3] There must have also been other rivers that dried up in the earthquakes, such as river Dṛṣadvatī, which resulted, in part, in the formation of the Thar Desert. River Sarasvatī was structurally controlled by enéchelon faults; hence even relatively minor tectonic

1. See O.P. Bharadwaj, "The Ṛgvedic Sarasvatī", in Agrawal (ed.), *In Search of Vedic-Haṛappan Relationship*, Aryan Books International, 2005, p. 17.
2. See O.P. Bharadwaj, "The Ṛgvedic Sarasvatī", in Agrawal (ed.), *In Search of Vedic-Haṛappan Relationship*, Aryan Books International, 2005, p. 24.
3. See Jane McIntosh, *A Peaceful Realm*, Westview Press, 2002, p. 185.

movements caused big changes in the configuration of the palaeo-channels.[4] There also exists evidence of other earthquakes prior to the large one 3,900 years ago, in 1900 BCE.

6.2 Earlier Earthquake in the Port City of Dholavīra

Evidence of an earthquake in the Indus/Haṛappan Civilisation city of Dholavīra, located in the western part of what is now the Indian State of Gujarat, has been dated to about 4,200 years ago (2200 BCE), which probably resulted in the diversion of the river drainage system; river Sarasvatī became shallower, probably resulting in some trade disaster.[5] Dholavīra was apparently a large and prosperous port city of the Indus/Haṛappan Civilisation, somewhat similar to the Indus/Haṛappan Civilisation city of Lothal. Both cities are located in what is modernly known in India as the State of Gujarat. Because of the number of earthquakes over the several hundred years prior to the big earthquake of 1900 BCE, some scholars speculate that by the time of the mature Haṛappan Civilisation, river Sarasvatī had dried up partially to cause it to terminate in an inland delta. This inland delta was located near the modern Pakistani city of Fort Derawar, where a large number of Haṛappan sites have been discovered.[6]

6.3 Overuse of Natural Resources by Indus/Haṛappan Civilisation

Another theory that is receiving the attention of scholars is the idea that the people of the Indus/Haṛappan Civilisation were not good at managing the natural resources around them. If true, that mismanagement had terrible consequences. The decline of the Indus/Haṛappan Civilisation in part was, as the

4. See B.B. Lal, *The Sarasvatī Flows On*, Aryan, 2002, p. 14.
5. See Aniruddh Singh Gaur, *Harappan Maritime Legacies of Gujarat*, Asian Publishing Services, 2000, pp. 153-54.
6. See Gregory Possehl, *The Indus Civilization*, Rowman Altamira, 2002, p. 9.

famous British archaeologist, Wheeler, said, "they were wearing out their landscape." If one does the calculations, one finds that a single-farmed-acre annually fed about 1.8 people; today in Pakistan, for example, 60 per cent of all milk production goes to human consumption and 12 per cent of all acreage is used for fodder production. Estimates are that there are 5,000,000 kiln-fired bricks at the Indus/Haṛappan Civilisation site of Moheṅjo-Dāṛo; in modern times, one tree provides enough fuel to fire 1,000 bricks; the people of the Indus/Haṛappan Civilisation must have denuded their forests; the evidence points to a precarious economic situation as a significant factor in the decline of this civilisation.[7]

This kind of "overuse" of natural resources was a relatively common phenomenon throughout history. The people of the Indus/Haṛappan Civilisation seemed sophisticated in many areas of their lives, such as technology. But perhaps the combination of the earthquakes and drying up of the rivers Sarasvatī and Dṛṣadvatī, along with the overuse of the natural resources, was just too much of a strain to sustain the complexities of the Indus/Haṛappan Civilisation.

6.4 3,900 Years Ago (1900 BCE) no More Indus/Haṛappan Civilisation Urban Centres

By about 3,900 years ago (1900 BCE), the Indus/Haṛappan Civilisation city centres were no longer functioning as urban centres. The Indus/Haṛappan Civilisation had come to an end as a complex socio-cultural system.[8] In one of the Indus/Haṛappan Civilisation cities, Dholavīra, a castle and a bailey were unearthed. Dholavīra, as stated above, is located in the modern-day Indian State of Gujarat, situated in the isolated island of

7. See Walter A. Jr. Fariservis, "The Origin, Character and Decline of an Early Civilization", in Nyanjot Lahiri (ed.), *The Decline and Fall of the Indus Civilization*, Permanent Black, 2000, pp. 251-62.

8. See Gregory Possehl, *The Indus Civilization*, Rowman Altamira, 2002, p. 2.

Khadir in the Great Rann of Kutch; in the post-Haṛappan period, the urban components rapidly diminished and disappeared, along with the weights and many other sophisticated items of art and utility.[9] One scholar summed up the thought that the majority of scholars are now concluding that the evidence shows that the urban phase of the Haṛappan Civilisation ended approximately around 4,000 years ago (2000 BCE) due to massive flooding, climatic changes, earthquakes and increased aridity and decline in trade.[10]

These are important historical markers. Many urban components, such as the use of weights and measures for local trade, as well as for international trade, were elements that seemed quite important and in frequent use during the Indus/Haṛappan Civilisation. If similar use of similar weights and measures were common in the *Manusmṛti* society, then perhaps there was an overlap between the Indus/Haṛappan Civilisation and the *Manusmṛti*. The possibility of this overlap becomes even stronger when examined in the light of such "trade components" such as similar descriptions of the *Manusmṛti* weights and measures to the many physical specimens of Indus/Haṛappan Civilisation weights and measures. Other "urban components" and sophisticated items of art and utility disappeared soon after the Indus/Haṛappan Civilisation earthquake 3,900 years ago (1900 BCE). The return of urbanisation in ancient India did not come thereafter for more than 1,500 years. There is much more of a chance of such an overlap between the Indus/Haṛappan Civilisation and the *Manusmṛti* society, rather than at any other later time.

6.5 No Sophisticated Bronze after Decline

Another area that bears examination is the technology of bronze

---

9. See R.S. Bisht, "Dholavira", in N. Lahiri (ed.), *The Decline and Fall of the Indus Civilization*, Permanent Black, 2000, pp. 305-314.

10. See D.P. Sharma and Madhuri, *Panorama of Harappan Civilization*, Kaveri Books, 2003, p. 64.

production. The craftsmen of the Indus/Haṛappan Civilisation hardened copper into bronze by alloying it with tin; after the decline of the Indus/Haṛappan Civilisation, no tin-based bronze objects were produced in India for over a millennium.[11] This provides another clue towards answering the question of the possible overlap between the Indus/Haṛappan Civilisation and the *Manusmṛti* society. Archaeological evidence reveals the bronze production of the Indus/Haṛappan Civilisation. The *Manusmṛti* tells us of its production of various metals, including bronze. This seems to be yet another piece of evidence possibly linking the Indus/Haṛappan Civilisation with the *Manusmṛti* society of ancient India.

6.6 1700 BCE: End of Indus/Haṛappan Civilisation Writing and Seal-Making

Some scholars advance the theory that the Indus/Haṛappan Civilisation "seals" were used by traders. Other scholars advance the theory that the "seals" with Indus "writing" were used only by a small group of political and ritual elites; the loss of power of that small group of political and ritual elites 3,700 years ago (1700 BCE) also coincided with the end of the seals and the Indus writing.[12]

This appears to be another interesting historical marker. With the falling apart of the urban centres and the corresponding decline of the Indus/Haṛappan Civilisation, there probably was no societal support for guilds to continue their work. No wonder there was also a sharp decline in production of the soapstone or steatite "seals" with their distinctive carvings and the accompanying writing of the Indus/Haṛappan Civilisation script.

---

11. See Shivaji Singh, "Vedic Culture and Its Continuity: Paradigm and Dimensions", in S.R. Dube (ed.), *Vedic Culture and Its Continuity*, Pratibha Prakashan, 2006, p. 27.

12. See J.M. Kenoyer, *Ancient Cities of the Indus Valley Civilization*, Oxford University Press, 1998, p. 79.

6.7 Cotton in Ancient India

Another way in which one can try to determine the dates of ancient cultures in India is through the study of certain archaeological finds, such as cotton. K.D. Sethna's book on the cotton of ancient India is an excellent example, *Karpasa in Prehistoric India*, analysing ancient texts, such as *Ṛgveda*, searching for the Sanskrit word for cotton, *karpāsa*.[13] One of the first facts that Sethna brings up is that cotton is not mentioned in the *Ṛgveda*, but remains of cotton were found in the ancient archaeological sites of the Indus/Haṛappan Civilisation in what is now north-west India and Pakistan.

D.P. Sharma and Madhuri Sharma edited a recent book about this time period. They called the Indus/Haṛappan Civilisation the Early Haṛappans and Indus-Sarasvatī Civilisation. The Sharmas looked at all of the evidence and concluded that at least from 4,000 to 5,000 years ago (2000 to 3000 BCE), a highly developed civilisation existed along the river Indus and (the now dried up) river Sarasvatī, in ancient India. Over the last 80 years more than 2668 sites from this civilisation have been discovered.[14] Although the *Manusmṛti* does not reveal its exact dates of composition, it does reveal its society as a highly developed civilisation, similar to the Indus/Haṛappan Civilisation. The *Manusmṛti* was also very sophisticated and seemed to apply to quite a number of urban and non-urban locations.

This is very different information from what was known in the 1920s, when the British archaeologist, Sir John Marshall, directed archaeological digs of just the two cities of the Indus/Haṛappan Civilisation, Moheṅjo-Dāṛo and sister-city, Haṛappā. In 1927, Sir John Marshall published his results in the Archaeological Survey of India. One of the things that he

13. See K.D. Sethna, *Karpasa in Prehistoric India*, Biblia Impex, 1981, p. x.

14. See D.P. Sharma and Madhuri (eds.), *Early Harappans and Indus-Sarasvatī Civilization*, Kaveri Books, 2006, p. 4.

announced was the discovery of cotton cloth. Sethna, as mentioned above, examined the ancient India text of *Ṛgveda*, and concluded that *Ṛgveda* did not mention cotton. Sethna concluded that if *Ṛgveda* did not mention cotton, *Ṛgveda* must have come before the Indus/Haṛappan Civilisation, i.e. 4,500 years ago (2500 BCE), which did have cotton and even traded internationally in cotton.[15] The *Manusmṛti* does mention cotton, therefore, this is another historical marker, giving another indication that the *Manusmṛti* was later in time than the composition of the *Ṛgveda* and possibly contemporaneous with the *Manusmṛti* society. The mention of cotton *karpāsa* in the *Manusmṛti* related to the sacrificial string of the brāhmaṇas, and specified that it be made of cotton. The references to cotton give us another clue as to the dating of the *Manusmṛti*; it cannot be dated in any case earlier than post-*Ṛgveda*.[16] Not only is the Sanskrit word for cotton *karpāsa* not mentioned in *Ṛgveda*, it is also not mentioned in the other three Vedas that follow *Ṛgveda*, nor the works that immediately followed the Vedas: the Brāhmaṇas, Āraṇyakas or Upaniṣads; according to *Ṛgveda*, clothes of that time period were woven of sheep's wool or goat's wool, sometimes adorned with gold.[17]

6.8 6,000 Year Ago (4000 BCE) Cotton: Ṛgveda Composed Before That Time

The Indian scholar, S.R. Rao, discovered that the evidence showed that pre-Haṛappans at Mehrgaṛh had domesticated cotton by 4000 BCE.[18] If we combined Sethna's research that *karpāsa* was not mentioned in the *Ṛgveda* and Rao's research that the pre-Indus/Haṛappan Civilisation had domesticated *karpāsa* 6,000 years ago (4000 BCE), that puts the date of composition of *Ṛgveda* much further back in time than the Max Müller "guess," i.e.

15. See K.D. Sethna, *Karpasa in Prehistoric India*, Biblia Impex, 1981, p. 18.
16. The sacrificial string of a brāhmaṇa shall be made of cotton.
17. See K.D. Sethna, *Karpasa in Prehistoric India*, Biblia Impex, 1981, p. 24.
18. See S.R. Rao, *New Frontiers of Archaeology*, Popular Prakashan, 1994, p. 3.

3,200 years ago (1200 BCE). If all of these facts and conclusions are correct, the composition of *Ṛgveda* must be dated earlier than 6,000 years ago (4000 BCE).

6.9 Climate Changes In India

Some scholars claim that the climate of India has not changed much over time. Perhaps they have not looked at all of the evidence when reaching such a conclusion. In what is now today called the Sind (located in what today is Pakistan) is partly a desert, which clearly at the time 2,300 years ago (the fourth century BCE), according to the records of Alexander the Great, was described as a fertile land.[19] If today's desert was a fertile land less than 2,500 years ago, we cannot be sure what the climate was another 2,000 years before that. We can only ask the questions as to possible climate and possible thinking regarding domestication of cotton and production of cotton goods.

6.10 Mesopotamia Traded With Dilman, Makan and Meluhha (Ancient India)

From Mesopotamia, on clay tablets, in cuneiform texts, often a faraway kingdom is inscribed, called Meluhha. Assyriologists tell us that the "h" is aspirated and hard, equivalent to the "kh". Thus Meluhha is to be pronounced Melukhkha, which could very well be the Mesopotamian pronunciation of Meluhha. This might be especially true if the traders from Haṛappā spoke the "corrupt" version of Sanskrit called Prākṛt, where the word would be pronounced (or mispronounced depending on one's adherence to Sanskrit purity) "Melakha."[20] Melakha or Meluhha is now widely accepted by scholars to mean the Indus/ Haṛappan Civilisation and this is one of the ways in which scholars infer that the international trade was carried on by the Indus/Haṛappan Civilisation from its ports such as Lothal.

19. See K.D. Sethna, *Karpasa in Prehistoric India*, Biblia Impex, 1981, p. 27.
20. Ibid., p. 69.

At the same time as the Indus/Haṛappan Civilisation appeared to engage in international trade, Sargon was a king of Mesopotamia. During Sargon's reign about 4,200 years ago (2250 BCE), ships from Dilman, Makan and Meluhha are said to have been moored in the harbour of his capital, Akkad.[21] Less than 150 years later, direct trade is reported only with Dilman and Makan. Meluhha seems to have become only an indirect supplier of goods. Finally, at the time of the Hammurabi Dynasty, about 3,700 years ago (1700 BCE) even Dilman loses trading contact not only with Meluhha but also with Makan.[22] The smaller earthquakes in ancient India prior to the large earthquake 3,900 years ago (1900 BCE) could have caused the drop in trade.

Meluhha was also referred to by a sailor returning to the city of Ur, the chief port-of-entry into Mesopotamia from the Persian Gulf. The three kingdoms were: Dilman (or Tilman or Telmun), Makan (or Makkan, or Magan) and Meluhha (or Miluhha). Whenever listed together, they also indicated their relative distances from Mesopotamia.[23]

The findings of Indus/Haṛappan Civilisation seals along with other pieces of evidence may lead one to conclude that at least during the period of the Mesopotamia ruler, Sargon, the Indus-Mesopotamia trade was direct and carried on by both land and sea. Mesopotamian literary references say that the products it received from Meluhha (the Indus/Haṛappan Civilisation) were goods made out of *lapis lazuli*, carnelian, gold, silver, copper, ebony, ivory and tortoise shell, peacocks and animals such as dogs and monkeys.[24]

This is perhaps another clue as to the Time Line of the *Manusmṛti*

---

21. See Aniruddh Singh Gaur, *Harappan Maritime Legacies of Gujarat*, Asian Publishing Services, 2000, p. 97.

22. See K.D. Sethna, *Karpasa in Prehistoric India*, Biblia Impex, 1981, p. 73.

23. Ibid., p. 72.

24. See D.K. Chakrabarti, *The External Trade of the Indus Civilization*, Munshiram Manoharlal, 1990, p. 144.

society. If the *Manusmṛti* society engaged in international trade, as appears to be the case, and Indus/Haṛappan Civilisation international trade was alive and well from about 4,000 to 5,000 years ago (2000 to 3000 BCE), and in steep decline after that, there exists the possible overlap of cultures. If it is clear that there were strong trading ties, i.e. transfer of goods (pre-Hammurabi Dynasty) between Mesopotamia and Meluhha (the ancient Indian Haṛappā Civilisation, especially its three large cities of Moheñjo-Dāṛo, Haṛappā and Lothal), there was, most likely, also trading of information and philosophy between Mesopotamia and Meluhha.

Since there are similarities between the Code of Hammurabi and the *Manusmṛti*, it is possible that either one influenced the other, or both influenced each other. Given the fact that the Code of Hammurabi contains 282 laws and the *Manusmṛti* contains thousands of laws, it is possible that the *Manusmṛti* had a greater influence.

6.11 Decline of the Indus/Haṛappan Civilisation, no More Weights and Measures

The Indus/Haṛappan Civilisation localisation era is dated approximately 3,900 years ago (1900-1300 BCE), after the earthquakes and drying-up of the river Sarasvatī. Although there was a continuation of some culture, there is no more evidence of writing nor the use of standardised weights. There also seems to have been a breakdown of international trade.[25] Before the earthquake (and apparently the drying up of the river Sarasvatī), weights and measures were made of chert, agate and shell; varying series were made with all sides beautifully polished. Such weights and measures have never been found later; the precision, accuracy and refinement were lost.[26]

25. See Subhash Kak, "The Mahābhārata and the Sindhu-Sarasvatī Tradition", in Agrawal (ed.), *In Search of Vedic-Haṛappan Relationship*, Aryan Books International, 2005, p. 82.

26. See H.D. Sankalia, *Pre-Historic Art in India*, Carolina Academic Press, 1978, p. 68.

This seems similar to the *Manusmṛti*; weights were in existence and even codified into law — certainly the *Manusmṛti* seems to reflect weights and measures as a serious matter.

The fact is that after the decline of the Indus/Haṛappan Civilisation, the loss of the making of weights occurred and the use of weights went out of fashion. This period after the decline of the Indus/Haṛappan Civilisation certainly does not seem like the time of the *Manusmṛti*, when the laws were such that very exacting weights and measures were mandated, and, apparently, very much in use. The *Manusmṛti* seems much more like the middle of the Indus/Haṛappan Civilisation: the time when local trade and international trade flourished and weights and measures were in great use and high demand.

6.12 Conclusion

The Indus/Haṛappan Civilisation covered an area considerably larger than those covered by either ancient Egypt or Mesopotamia. Evidence of an earthquake in Dholavīra has been dated to about 4,200 years ago (2200 BCE), which probably resulted in the diversion of the drainage system; the Sarasvatī River became shallower, probably resulting in the beginning of a large scale trade disaster. Mesopotamia tablets from about 4,100 years ago (2100 BCE) mention the stoppage of trade from Meluhha (the Indus/Haṛappan Civilisation) for unknown reasons.[27]

There is evidence that points to strong trading ties, i.e. transfer of goods (pre-Hammurabi Dynasty) between Mesopotamia and Meluhha (most probably the ancient Indian Haṛappā Civilisation). There was, most likely, also trading of information and philosophy between Mesopotamia and Meluhha. If the *Manusmṛti* was in existence at the time, it could have influenced the Code of Hammurabi or the other way around.

27. See Aniruddh Singh Gaur, *Harappan Maritime Legacies of Gujarat*, Asian Publishing Services, 2000, p. 160.

There is much similarity between the weights and measures of the Indus/Haṛappan Civilisation and the *Manusmṛti*. The decline in the use of weights and measures by most of the Indus/ Haṛappan Civilisation 3,900 years ago (1900 BCE) certainly makes it possible that the *Manusmṛti* society existed in that urban setting with international trade, at that same time.

It seems that the combination of earthquakes and probable drying up of river Sarasvatī, along with the overuse of the natural resources, was just too much of a strain to sustain the complexities of the Indus/Haṛappan Civilisation.

7

Comparative Law

7.1 Ancient Legal Codes / which Ones are Extant or have Survived?

THE word "extant" is usually defined as still existing, not destroyed or lost. When discussing various ancient law codes, some originals and copies have been lost, but have been referred to in commentaries.

Most of the ancient law codes were very short, even though they were intended to govern all aspects of society. Many also were accompanied by a statement that these laws were given to the lawgiver by God.

Next will follow a brief description of ancient law codes and their comparisons with the *Manusmṛti*.

7.2 4,300 Years Ago (2350 BCE): Urukagina's Code (Sumeria)

This code is Not Extant, meaning that an original or copy of it has never been found. It is simply mentioned in other documents. It is now considered short and harsh by modern norms.

7.3 4,200 Years Ago (2050 BCE): Ur-Nammu's Code (Mesopotamia)

This code is close to Not Extant, since only five articles can be read, and even the five articles have words missing. Other evidence seems to indicate a legal system with judges and sworn testimony.

7.4 3,900 Years Ago (Pre-1900 BCE): The Manusmṛti (India)

This is the theory advanced in this book that, although undated, the *Manusmṛti*, in some form or another, was composed prior to 3,900 years ago (1900 BCE). As described above, it is a Law Code containing more than 2,500 laws, about 1,000 of which are what we today would classify as civil or criminal law, the rest about philosophy, "sacred" and otherwise. Most scholars believe that it is extant, even though it has been passed down by oral tradition and not preserved in writing until much later, perhaps 2,400 years ago (400 BCE).

7.5 3,700 Years Ago (1700 BCE): Hammurabi's Code (Babylonia)

The Code of Hammurabi is very interesting. Not only have many copies (in stone and clay) survived, more of the actual text survived. The Code of Hammurabi is, arguably, the best existing evidence of a law code that was widespread at its time. Its most famous form is one giant slab of stone, carved in cuneiform script, currently housed in Paris, at the Louvre Museum.[1]

The Code of Hammurabi also appeared to be used throughout an entire civilisation, not just in a smaller kingship, as seems to be the case with slightly older codes, the *2350 BCE: Urukagina's Code*, and the *2050 BCE: Ur-Nammu's Code*. King Urnammu of Ur wrote a legal code about 400 years before Hammurabi, so did King Bilalama of Eshunna. Urnammu's and Bilalama's codes were short lists of laws, only obeyed in one city-state. Hammurabi's Code was meant to help govern a vast empire. Copies of his code, written in clay and stone, have been found all over Babylon (modern day Iraq).

7.6 3,600 Years Ago (1600 BCE): Hittite Code (Assyria)

The Middle Assyrian law was called the Hittite legal code. It has

1. See L.W. King, *The Code of Hammurabi*, Kessinger Publishing, 2004.

no preamble or epilogue. It does not mention any god, but deals with some crimes, like assault and murder. It also deals with inheritance, marriage, slave law and incest. More than 13,000 clay tablets have been found representing mostly business receipts and some laws written front and back in cuneiform characters.[2]

7.7 3,300 Years Ago (1300 BCE): The Ten Commandments (Judea)

Moses was said to have received the Ten Commandments directly from God, according to Jewish, Christian and Islamic history and passed down orally. Later, these laws were written down. Many Christian legal scholars believe that the Ten Commandments were the most influential of all ancient legal codes for modern law. Other legal scholars disagree with this thought.

Many of the Ten Commandments were similar to the codes before and after, including "thou shalt not kill," "thou shalt not commit adultery," and "thou shalt not steal." The Chapter of the Bible, Exodus, has other legal rules, some very similar to Hammurabi's Code, such as "an eye for an eye, tooth for a tooth" legal philosophy.[3]

7.8 2,600 Years Ago (621 BCE): Draco's Law (Athens)

In the ancient city-state of Athens, in what is now Greece, a citizen named Draco was chosen to write a code of law. He thought that the death penalty should be used for many crimes, even relatively small ones. His name, Draco, therefore became synonymous with unreasonably harsh laws. His name is the origin of one English word meaning harsh, "draconian."[4] Draco's

---

2. See Harry Hoffner, *The Laws of the Hittites*, Brill, 1997.
3. Exodus: Thou shalt give life for life, eye for eye, tooth for tooth, hand for hand, foot for foot, burning for burning, wound for wound, stripe for stripe.
4. See Edwin Carawan, *Rhetoric and the Law of Draco*, Oxford University Press, 1998.

legal code seems harsh by modern standards. But it did create a uniform set of laws for the citizens of Athens.

7.9 2,600 Years Ago (600 BCE): Lycurgus' Law (Sparta)

In another ancient city-state of Greece, Sparta, King Lycurgus became the renowned lawgiver. His laws were transmitted orally and were designed to support the military calling of all Sparta men. Women had a duty to produce children; boys became wards of Sparta at the age of seven to prepare them for military duty.[5]

7.10 2,500 Years Ago (550 BC): Solon's Laws (Athens)

In Athens, following Draco, was Solon. Solon refined Draco's laws and made courts more accessible to citizens of Athens. One common practice that was outlawed by the laws of Solon was *mortgages* on human beings. Formerly, creditors could enslave a debtor and his entire family. A type of trial by jury was developed by Solon as well as modifying the government.[6]

7.11 2,500 Years Ago (536 BCE): The Book of Punishments and Confucius (China)

Castration, feet amputation and death were mentioned as means to punish a lawbreaker in the Book of Punishments (536 BCE) in China. Confucius (Kong Fuzi) (551–479 BCE) was a great philosopher of China, whose teachings greatly influenced East Asia for more than 2,000 years. Confucius wanted everyone to strive to become a "perfect man," that is, one who is combined with qualities of a saint, scholar and gentleman.[7]

---

5. See Charles Rollin, *The Ancient History of the Egyptians*, Harper, 1839.
6. See Terry Buckley, *Aspects of Greek History 750-323 BCE*, Routledge, 1996.
7. See Edward H. Parker, *China and Religion*, J. Murray, 1905.

7.12 2,400 Years Ago (450 BCE): The Twelve Tables (Rome)

Although the twelve tables were considered very famous at the time of their development, and mentioned in many historical accounts, no evidence of them exists today. All copies of the twelve tables were destroyed. From what we can decipher from the commentaries, these laws are considered to be the foundation of most of modern public and private laws. Public prosecution of crimes and a way for injured parties to seek compensation were included in these laws.

7.13 1,500 Years Ago (529 CE): Justinian's Code (Roman Empire)

The relatively non-ancient, "super-sophisticated" Code, called Corpus Juris Civilis, was ordered by the Emperor Justinian to be comprised of all of the known existing codes and legal theories of the time. It formed the basis of the Napoleonic Code and other modern-day civil law codes.[8]

7.14 Hammurabi's Code Influenced Many Other Legal Codes

There is no doubt that Hammurabi's Code influenced many of the legal codes that followed it, especially throughout the Middle East. Much of Mosaic Law seemed to come directly from the Code of Hammurabi. The Code of Hammurabi is definitely the most sophisticated extant ancient legal code, except for the possibility that the *Manusmṛti* was older and influenced the Code of Hammurabi.

7.15 The Law Code of Manu may have Influenced the Code of Hammurabi

The *Manusmṛti* may have influenced the Code of Hammurabi. From the analysis presented above, it appears that the *Manusmṛti* could

---

8. See John B. Bury, *The Cambridge Medieval History*, Macmillan, 1913.

be older than Hammurabi's Code. As detailed above, the *Manusmṛti*'s predecessor, the *Ṛgveda*, mentions the river Sarasvatī as being a mighty and wide river that flows to the ocean. The *Manusmṛti* cites the river Sarasvatī as a still flowing natural boundary. Within the last 30-40 years, since space satellites have taken pictures of the earth, the "now dried-up path" of a great river, probably river Sarasvatī, has been photographed from space. Scientists have dated that "drying up" at about 3,900 years ago (1900 BCE). If that is correct, then both the *Ṛgveda* and the *Manusmṛti* are older than 1900 BCE, making the *Manusmṛti* older than the Code of Hammurabi, which is commonly dated to around 1700 BCE.

International trade between India and contemporaneous civilisations in the Middle East seems to have taken place, based on evidence of the sea voyages of the Indian and Arab traders and goods from ancient India having been discovered in the Middle East. There is also a striking similarity between some of the specific laws of the *Manusmṛti* and the Code of Hammurabi.

7.16 Trial by Ordeal in Both Codes

The *Manusmṛti* had some instances of trial by ordeal, when there was no other way to decide a case. In the Code of Hammurabi trial by ordeal was quite common. Apparently, learning to swim in a river was not common at the time of the Code of Hammurabi; therefore, to drop an accused man into a river and to observe if his "innocence" allowed him to survive (or spontaneously to learn how to swim) was a means of determining guilt or innocence.

Code of Hammurabi Law 2: If anyone brings an accusation against a man, and the accused goes to the river and leaps into the river, if he sinks in the river his accuser shall take possession of his house. But if the river proved that the accused was not guilty, and he escaped unhurt, then he who had brought the accusation shall be put to death, while he who leaped into the river shall take possession of the house that had belonged to his accuser.

7.17 Judicial Misconduct in Both Codes

The *Manusmṛti* seemed to expect judicial misconduct if the judge came from the lowest class, the śūdras. In the Code of Hammurabi judicial misconduct and judicial mistake may have been much more common for any class of judges.

Code of Hammurabi Law 5: If a judge should try a case, reach a decision, and present his judgement in writing; if later error shall appear in his decision, and it be through his own fault, then he shall pay twelve times the fine set by him in the case, and he shall be publicly removed from the judge's bench, and never again shall he sit there to render judgement.

7.18 Curse if One does not Respect the Law in Both Codes

The *Manusmṛti* said that harsh punishment both during this life and especially in the life after death awaited one who did not follow the law. In the Code of Hammurabi, one long curse, in which Hammurabi describes what will happen to anybody who does not respect his laws. "May the mighty gods in heaven and earth curse him," says the king, "and his children, and his land, his people. . . ."

7.19 Punishment based on Class in Both Codes

The *Manusmṛti* had different punishments depending on the class or caste of the perpetrator of the crime. Generally, the lower the caste, the harsher the punishment. In the Code of Hammurabi a different kind of thinking applied, for instance, the higher the societal status of the victim, the harsher the punishment, unless he had no money to pay the fine and then he would be put to death.

Code of Hammurabi Law 8: If anyone steals cattle or sheep, or an ass, or a pig or a goat, if it belongs to a god or to the court, the thief shall pay thirtyfold; if they belonged to a freed man of the king he shall pay tenfold; if the thief has nothing with which to pay he shall be put to death.

7.20 Negligence in Both Codes

The *Manusmṛti* had punishment for negligence. The Code of Hammurabi also had punishment for negligence.

Code of Hammurabi Law 53. If anyone be too lazy to keep his dam in proper condition, and does not so keep it; if then the dam breaks and all the fields be flooded, then shall he in whose dam the break occurred be sold for money, and the money shall replace the corn which he has caused to be ruined.

7.21 Ferry Boat Negligence in Both Codes

The *Manusmṛti* had punishment for ferry negligence. The Code of Hammurabi also had punishment for ferry negligence.

Code of Hammurabi Law 240: If a merchantman runs against a ferryboat, and wreck it, the master of the ship that was wrecked shall seek justice before God; the master of the merchantman, which wrecked the ferryboat, must compensate the owner for the boat and all that he ruined.

7.22 Influence of the Ten Commandments 3,300 Years Ago (1300 BCE) on Modern Law

Many Christian legal-historical writers look to their most ancient religious law to see if they can find a link between their religious law and their modern law. Those Christian writers start with the supposition that the Hebrew or Mosaic (Moses) Ten Commandments are the most important ancient law to influence modern Western nation-states, which at least at the time of their nation-state beginnings, had a population that was majority Christian.

7.23 Possible Manusmṛti Influence on the Ten Commandments

In order for the possibility to even exist that the *Manusmṛti* influenced the Ten Commandments, the following conditions need to apply:

1. The date of codification of the *Manusmṛti*; that is, the *Manusmṛti* must pre-date the Ten Commandments;
2. There must have been sufficient international trade or other contact at the time between ancient India and either the Hebrews themselves, or one of their trading partners; and
3. The *Manusmṛti* must have contained content similar to the Ten Commandments.

We shall start with the last point first. The *Manusmṛti* contains many similarities to the Mosaic Ten Commandments. In the 12th chapter of the *Manusmṛti*, verses 5, 6, and 7 contain many of the Ten Commandments concepts, although in a different order and slightly different language:

The *Manusmṛti*, chapter 12.5. Coveting the property of others, thinking in one's heart of what is undesirable, and adherence to false (doctrines), are the three kinds of (sinful) mental action.

The *Manusmṛti*, chapter 12.6. Abusing (others, speaking) untruth, detracting from the merits of all men, and talking idly, shall be the four kinds of (evil) verbal action.

The *Manusmṛti*, chapter 12.7. Taking what has not been given, injuring (creatures) without the sanction of the law, and holding criminal intercourse with another man's wife, are declared to be the three kinds of (wicked) bodily action.[9]

7.24 The Ten Commandments: Similarity to the Manusmṛti

In Exodus, chapter 20, verses 12-17, six of the Ten Commandments bear an amazing similarity to that section of the *Manusmṛti* described above:

---

9. See G. Buehler, *Laws of Manu*, Oxford (Sacred Books of the East, vol. XXV), 1896.

20:13. Thou shalt not *kill.*

20:14. Thou shalt not commit *adultery.*

20:15. Thou shalt not *steal.*

20:16. Thou shalt not *bear false witness* against thy neighbour.

20:17. Thou shalt not *covet* thy neighbour's house; neither shalt thou *desire* his wife, nor his servant, nor his handmaid, nor his ox, nor his ass, nor any *thing* that is his.

7.24 No Keeping Seventh Day Holy

There is no law exactly the same in the *Manusmṛti* about keeping the Seventh Day holy, but there are multiple prescriptions for days of worship.

7.26 Not Exactly Honouring Thy Father and Mother

There is no law about honouring both father and mother in the *Manusmṛti*. Instead, there are laws that state that a father has control over his household and that one should take care of one's mother.

7.27 The Manusmṛti pre-dates the Ten Commandments

There appears to be evidence to suggest the possibility that the *Manusmṛti* may pre-date the Ten Commandments. As detailed above, the predecessor to the *Manusmṛti*, the *Ṛgveda*, mentions the river Sarasvatī as being a mighty and wide river that flows to the ocean. And the *Manusmṛti* mentions the river Sarasvatī as a geographical marker. Within the last 40 years, since space satellites have been taking pictures of the earth, the "now dried-up path" of a great river, probably the Sarasvatī, has been photographed from space. Scientists have dated that occurrence at about 3,900 years ago (1900 BCE). If that is correct, then both the *Ṛgveda* and the *Manusmṛti* are older than 1900 BCE, making the *Manusmṛti* at least 600 years older than the Ten Commandments, which is commonly dated at 3,300 years ago (1300 BCE).

There appears to be ample evidence that there was international trade between ancient India and Hebrew trading partners. As was discussed in chapters above, strong archaeological evidence exists that there was international trading between ancient India and both Mesopotamia and Egypt. According to the Bible, Moses was given the Ten Commandments by God. Moses was raised in the house of the Pharaoh of Egypt. He must have known about the Code of Hammurabi and possibly the *Manusmṛti*.

7.28 Assura Code 3,100 Years Ago (1075 BCE) vs. the Manusmṛti

The Assura Code, also known as the Code of the Assyrians, seems much harsher than the *Manusmṛti*. The author would conclude that the Assura Code, therefore, does not seem to have been influenced by the *Manusmṛti*.

Women were criticised but also honoured in the *Manusmṛti*. The *Manusmṛti*, chapter 9, verse 17, states: "(When creating them) Manu allotted to women (a love of their) bed, (of their) seat and (of) ornament, impure desires, wrath, dishonesty, malice, and bad conduct."[10] But in other places in the text, the *Manusmṛti* says to honour women: "Women must be honoured and adorned by their fathers, brothers, husbands, and brothers-in-law, who desire (their own) welfare."[11] And in the next verse, even a spiritual angle is invoked to honour women. "Where women are honoured, there the gods are pleased; but where they are not honoured, no sacred rite yields rewards."[12]

Women got harsher punishments than men in the Assura Code. Also, in the Assura Code, a woman could not even strike a man. Assura Code I.7: If a woman brings her hand against a

10. See G. Buehler, *Laws of Manu*, Oxford (Sacred Books of the East, vol. XXV), 1896, p. 230.
11. Ibid., p. 58.
12. Ibid.

man, they shall prosecute her; 30 *manas* of lead shall she pay, 20 blows shall they inflict on her.[13] And a husband could even beat his wife without punishment. Assura Code I.58: Unless it is forbidden in the tablets, a man may strike his wife, pull her hair, her ear he may bruise or pierce. He commits no misdeed thereby.[14]

In the case of divorce, there was no payment to women in the Assura Code. In the *Manusmṛti*, a divorced wife received some money. In the Assura Code, it is entirely up to the husband. He could give her nothing.

Negligent or intentional "meddling" with a neighbour's field was more harshly punished in the Assura Code. In the *Manusmṛti*, a man who meddles with his neighbour's field must pay back for his damage. In the Assura Code, not only must the lawbreaker pay three times the damage, he gets one finger cut-off, receives 100 blows and has to do volunteer work for the king.

Assura Code II.8: If a man meddles with the field of his neighbour, they shall convict him. Threefold shall he restore. One of his fingers they shall cut-off, 100 blows they shall inflict upon him, one month of days he shall do the king's work.[15]

7.29 Hittite (Nesilim) Code 3,600 Years Ago (1600 BCE) vs. Manusmṛti

The Hittite (Nesilim) Code seems much harsher than the *Manusmṛti*. The author would conclude that the Hittite (Nesilim) Code, therefore, does not seem to have been influenced by the *Manusmṛti*.

There was no right to appeal in the Hittite (Nesilim) Code, whereas there was a right to appeal in the *Manusmṛti*. The *Manusmṛti* allowed an appeal from the King's judgement, or from

13. See J.M. Powis Smith, *The Origin and History of Hebrew Law*, Lawbook Ex., 2005, p. 224.
14. Ibid., p. 236.
15. Ibid., p. 239.

a judgement made by a judge appointed by the king. The losing party had to pay double the amount of the judgement to start the appeal.[16] In the Hittite (Nesilim) Code, harsh punishment was the rule for someone who was foolish enough to challenge a judgment.

Hittite (Nesilim) Code, 173: If anyone opposes the judgement of the king, his house shall become a ruin. If anyone opposes the judgement of a lord, his head shall be cut-off. If a slave rises against his master, he shall go into the pit.[17]

7.30 Solon's Code 2,600 Years Ago (600 BCE) vs. Manusmr̥ti

Solon's Code provided reforms that seem in part to be modelled after the *Manusmr̥ti*. Solon's Code may have been influenced by the *Manusmr̥ti*. Athens before the time of Solon was apparently controlled by a small percentage of people in power. Solon came and introduced reforms, some of which seemed similar to the *Manusmr̥ti*.[18]

7.31 Twelve Tables (450 BCE) vs. Manusmr̥ti

The Twelve Tables influenced the Justinian Code (CE 529). The compilers of the super-sophisticated, non-ancient, Justinian's Code (Corpus Juris Civilis) said that they were influenced by the Twelve Tables. No original text survived, so the Twelve Tables are considered partially extant by many legal historical scholars, for many "laws" survived through commentaries.[19] *Manusmr̥ti*

---

16. See Ganganath Jha, *Manusmr̥ti with the Manubhāṣya of Medhātithi*, Motilal Banarsidass, vol. 6 (1st edn. 1920; 2nd 1999), p. 7.
17. Oliver J. Thatcher (ed.), *The Library of Original Sources* (Milwaukee: University Research Extension Co., 1901), vol. III: *The Roman World*, pp. 9-11.
18. See Aristotle (tr. Kenyon) *The Athenian Constitution* (350 BCE, 1891, rpt. 2004).
19. See S.P. Scott, *The Civil Law I: Including the Twelve Tables, etc.*, AMS, 1932.

may have influenced the Twelve Tables. The Twelve Tables are harsher than the *Manusmṛti*, but, as discussed above, the *Manusmṛti* is most probably older, international trade existed between the regions, and there is some similarity between some of the laws of the *Manusmṛti* and the Twelve Tables.

7.32 Treason in Both Codes

The *Manusmṛti*, as we discussed above, had some beginning notions of treason, although the activity specifically was turning against a village or city. In the Twelve Tables, Table IX: Public law said that if anyone should stir up war against his country, or delivers a Roman citizen into the hands of the enemy, he shall be punished with death.

7.33 No Marriage between Classes in Both Codes

The *Manusmṛti* had more classes than the Twelve Tables, but both tried to forbid intermarriage. In the Twelve Tables, Table XI said that those who belong to the Senatorial Order and are styled Fathers, shall not contract marriage with plebeians.

7.34 Debt Punishment in Both Codes

The *Manusmṛti* had less severe punishments than the Twelve Tables for someone who did not pay his debts, but both tried to prevent such occurrences.

In the Twelve Tables, Table III: Debt: Where anyone, having acknowledged a debt, has a judgement rendered against him requiring payment, thirty days shall be given to him in which to pay the money and satisfy the judgement. If he does not satisfy the debt, within 60 days, he can be sold into slavery. After he has been kept in chains for 60 days, and the sum for which he is liable has been three times publicly proclaimed in the Forum, he shall be condemned to be reduced to slavery by him to whom he was delivered up; or, if the latter prefers, he can be sold beyond the Tiber.

7.35 Usury Comparing Two Ancient Legal Codes

The following is a simple example to give a more complete picture of ancient legal thought. We shall compare and contrast one narrow topic, usury, within the proven ancient extant legal code, the Code of Hammurabi and the *Manusmṛti*.

7.36 Classes of People

A. MANUSMṚTI

In the *Manusmṛti*, as we have seen, all human beings were divided up into four classes or castes (assigned at birth by the class of one's father and mother, but the commentaries seem to suggest that some small movement was possible). Those four castes, as were discussed above, were the brāhmaṇa (the literate class, who memorised sacred and other books and used that knowledge for sacerdotal, educational and judicial functions); the kṣatriya (the kings, warriors and protectors of the people); the vaiśya (the landowners, traders, farmers and shopkeepers); and the śūdra (the lifelong servant class). Women were part of the four castes, but were also in a "lesser" category themselves.

B. CODE OF HAMMURABI

In the Code of Hammurabi, the classes were the *amelu* (landowners), the *muskinu* (non-landowner) and the *ardu* (the slave).

7.37 Usury: The Amount of Interest that One Could Legally Charge

A. MANUSMṚTI

In order to understand the *Manusmṛti* regarding usury, annual percentage rate interest must be examined. With regard to the monthly and annual percentage rate *Manusmṛti* says that a moneylender may charge, one section starts out at 1.25 per cent per month (the eightieth part of a hundred) or 15 per cent per year (annual percentage rate):

"A moneylender may stipulate as an increase of his capital, for the interest, allowed by Vasiṣṭha and take monthly the eightieth part of a hundred." (Vasiṣṭha was another learned sage, author of the seventh *maṇḍala* of *Ṛgveda*, which pre-dates the time that the *Manusmṛti* was handed down).[20]

Such was sufficient interest for moneylenders during the time of Vasiṣṭha (pre-Manu), but probably over time, the money lenders governed by the *Manusmṛti* wanted to charge a little more. Could it be done and still be within the law? The first answer was yes, up to 2 per cent (2 per cent) per month or 24 per cent (24 per cent) annual percentage rate yield. "Or, remembering the duty of good men, he may take two in the hundred (by the month), for he who takes two in the hundred becomes not a sinner for gain."[21] The next verse differs dramatically from the above and brings us to one of the most interesting parts of ancient society in India, the different treatment that is accorded to the different classes or castes:

> Just two in the hundred, three, four, and five (and not more), he may take as monthly interest according to the order of the castes (*varṇa*).[22]

That is to say that the higher up in the caste of society one was, the more interest one was allowed to charge (24 per cent annual percentage rate for the lowest caste, the śūdra; 36 per cent annual percentage rate for the next higher caste, the vaiśya; 48 per cent annual percentage rate for the next higher caste, the kṣatriya; and 60 per cent annual percentage rate for the highest caste, the brāhmaṇa).[23] Two things are of note here: one, that the interest rate must be fixed or stipulated. The other, involving liquor,

20. See G. Buehler, *Laws of Manu*, Oxford (Sacred Books of the East, vol. XXV), 1896, p. 194.
21. Ibid.
22. Ibid.
23. See G. Jha, *Manusmṛti with the Manubhāṣya of Medhātithi*, Motilal Banarsidass, vol. 6 (1st edn. 1920; 2nd 1999), p. 164.

that the rate of interest is eight times the principal, which, apparently, is 800 per cent.

B. IN THE CODE OF HAMMURABI

Merchants (and even temples in some cases) made ordinary business loans, charging from 20 to 30 per cent.

7.38 Conclusion

The *Manusmṛti*, if it existed at the time of Indus/Haṛappan Civilisation, probably did influence other legal codes of the time, especially the Code of Hammurabi and the Mosaic Code. If the *Manusmṛti* was not the code used by the Indus/Haṛappan Civilisation, then the amount of influence may have been very small or none at all.

8

Conclusion

8.1 The Original Manusmṛti may Possibly have been Composed During the Indus/Haṛappan Civilisation 4,000 to 5,000 Years Ago (2000-3000 BCE)

AN analysis of the *Manusmṛti* reveals a possible original composition date during the height of the ancient Indian Indus/ Haṛappan Civilisation, approximately 4,000 to 5,000 years ago (2000-3000 BCE) and survived, probably with alterations, first by oral tradition and then in writing. Even though some scholars today date the *Manusmṛti* to 2,100 years ago (100 BCE), the original British judge who translated the *Manusmṛti* from Sanskrit to English, William Jones, in 1790, first dated it 3,500 years ago (1500 BCE) and upon further research dated it 4,000 years ago (2000 BCE). Archaeological evidence from the Indus/Haṛappan Civilisation seems to supply many clues which may allow the possibility of a new Time Line dating of the *Manusmṛti* of 4,000 to 5,000 years ago (2000 to 3000 BCE).

8.2 Manusmṛti Composed after Ṛgveda, Before 250 BCE

The *Manusmṛti* seems to have been originally composed after the oldest surviving composition of India, *Ṛgveda*, because *Ṛgveda* is mentioned as the major "cornerstone" of the *Manusmṛti*, but the *Manusmṛti* is not mentioned at all in *Ṛgveda*. Since the king who ruled India about 2,200 years ago (250 BCE) was Aśoka, who converted to Buddhism, the Vedic-oriented *Manusmṛti* was most likely composed prior to his reign.

8.3 Oral Preservation of Ṛgveda and the Manusmṛti

Many compositions from ancient India, such as *Ṛgveda* and the *Manusmṛti* were preserved orally for perhaps thousands of years by means of creating a class of human beings called brāhmaṇas that the author refers to as "mouths of the Creator" or "human library books" or "human computers." It was correctly predicted in ancient India that most ancient writing would be or could be destroyed over time and that a strong oral tradition was an effective means of preserving knowledge.

Ṛgveda was considered Śruti or the "song of the divine" and therefore survives, apparently almost unchanged, even today after thousands of years. The *Manusmṛti* was Smṛti or "that which was remembered" and was apparently modified over time.

8.4 River Sarasvatī dates Ṛgveda and Manusmṛti

Many scholars now believe that the river Sarasvatī is shown by modern space satellite images to be a once large river now dried up in north-west India and Pakistan. Many scientists believe earthquakes dried up the river 3,900 years ago (1900 BCE). *Ṛgveda* mentions river Sarasvatī in glowing terms, praising the river as a "great and mighty river" flowing all the way from "the mountains to the sea" and the *Manusmṛti* mentions the river Sarasvatī as an important geographical boundary. In the light of the above, many scholars have concluded that the *Ṛgveda* has an extremely strong possibility of being composed prior to 1900 BCE and little possibility of being composed after 1900 BCE. That same argument can be advanced for the *Manusmṛti*, probably originally composed prior to the earthquakes, prior to the river Sarasvatī drying up and therefore prior to 1900 BCE.

8.5 Urban Civilisation Similarities

The *Manusmṛti* seems to have been originally composed during an urban civilisation period because of all of its urban civilisation references. Urbanisation was quite developed during the height of the Indus/Haṛappan Civilisation, 4,000 to 5,000 years ago (2000-3000 BCE) and fell off after the collapse of the Indus/Haṛappan Civilisation, probably triggered in part by earthquakes that dried up the river Sarasvatī 3,900 years ago (1900 BCE). Urbanisation did not begin to come back to India until the time of the Buddhist King Aśoka in about 250 BCE, and even then, not in the orderly, Ṛgvedic-worshipping-way that may have been present in the Indus/Haṛappan Civilisation.

8.6 "Water Luxury" Similarities

The *Manusmṛti* seems to have been originally composed during a time when water and bathing were very important and prevalent because of all of its water references and frequent ritual bathing requirements. One of the major archaeological discoveries of the Indus/Haṛappan Civilisation was "water luxury," its emphasis on apparent ritual bathing, urban pools, indoor plumbing and unparalleled drainage. Such "water luxury" fell off in India after the decline of the Indus/Haṛappan Civilisation about 3,900 years ago (1900 BCE) for several thousand years.

8.7 Technological Similarities

The *Manusmṛti* seems to have been originally composed when technology was great because of many technological references. One of the archaeological discoveries of the Indus/Haṛappan Civilisation was its emphasis on technologies such as high-fired jewellery and civil engineering, which fell off in India after the decline of the Indus/Haṛappan Civilisation 3,900 years ago (1900 BCE) for several thousand years.

8.8 Craft Guild Similarities

The *Manusmṛti* seems to have been originally composed when craft guilds were strong because of many such references. Breach of a guild contract was especially punished harshly. One of the archaeological discoveries of the Indus/Haṛappan Civilisation was its emphasis on technology, including high-fired jewellery and civil engineering, which many scholars believe was only possible with well-organised craft guilds, which apparently fell off in India after the decline of the Indus/Haṛappan Civilisation 3,900 years ago (1900 BCE) for several thousand years.

8.9 International Trade Similarities

The *Manusmṛti* seems to have been originally composed when international trade was thriving because of all of its trade references. One of the archaeological discoveries of the Indus/ Haṛappan Civilisation was its apparently vigorous international trade, which fell off in India after the decline of the Indus/ Haṛappan Civilisation 3,900 years ago (1900 BCE) for several thousand years.

8.10 Sophisticated Government Similarities

The *Manusmṛti* seems to have been originally composed when a sophisticated government was in control because of all governmental references including its sophisticated code of law, the *Manusmṛti* itself. Although the word *rāja* means to reign, or be king or chief, the *Manusmṛti* instructed kings and chiefs of their main role: to protect the people.

One of the archaeological discoveries of the Indus/Haṛappan Civilisation was its well laid-out cities and towns that protected the people and no lavish palaces such as those that existed in contemporaneous cultures. Evidence also exists of vigorous Indus/Haṛappan Civilisation international trade, which was probably only possible with a sophisticated government, all of which fell off in India after the decline of the Indus/Haṛappan Civilisation 3,900 years ago (1900 BCE) for several thousand years.

8.11 Weights and Measures Similarities

The *Manusmṛti* seems to have been originally composed when standardised weights and measures were used extensively, especially since the Indus/Haṛappan Civilisation weights and measures are similar to the *Manusmṛti* weights and measures. The production and use of weights and measures fell off in India after the decline of the Indus/Haṛappan Civilisation 3,900 years ago (1900 BCE) for several thousand years.

8.12 Prior to Greek Mathematics and Astronomy: Manusmṛti

The *Manusmṛti* seems to have been originally composed prior to Greek mathematics and Greek astronomy according to Greek historians, who described concepts that were included in *Ṛgveda* and also present in the *Manusmṛti*. The Greek historians, Pliny and Arrian, say that the earliest calendar in India had a cycle of 2,700 years, called the *saptaṛṣi* calendar; Pliny suggested that the very same *saptaṛṣi* calendar was the one that the people of India began to use in 6676 BCE. Vedic people, as described by Greek historians, discovered sidereal time (telling time based on the stars), in addition to the regular solar time that most of us use today in order to determine the time of day.

8.13 Manusmṛti Similarities to Other Ancient Law Codes

The *Manusmṛti* seems to have been originally composed either before or somewhat contemporaneously to the abbreviated, but somewhat similar laws in Mesopotamia, Babylonia, Ur, and Sumeria, such as the Law Code of Hammurabi and the Jewish Torah or Christian Bible Old Testament. One of the archaeological discoveries of the Indus/Haṛappan Civilisation was its international trade, which would have been necessary for such international philosophical interactions, which fell off in India after the decline of the Indus/Haṛappan Civilisation 3,900 years ago (1900 BCE) for several thousand years.

8.14 Conclusion

The *Manusmṛti*, possibly in an earlier shorter form, seems to have been composed prior to 3,900 years ago (1900 BCE), given the aforementioned evidence. The geographical boundary descriptions in the *Manusmṛti* seem very similar to some of the locations of archaeological remains of cities and towns of the Indus/Haṛappan Civilisation. Other similarities between the *Manusmṛti* society and the Indus/Haṛappan Civilisation such as sophisticated urban thinking, sophisticated governmental thinking, sophisticated weights and measures, sophisticated mathematical, astronomical and engineering thinking and international trade perhaps may allow scholars to rethink a possible relationship between the Indus/Haṛappan Civilisation and the *Manusmṛti*.

Appendix A
Indus/Haṛappan Civilisation Script

Guarding Knowledge Through Memorisation, Not Writing

THE skill of memorisation seemed to have been widely practised by the *Manusmṛti* society and very possibly the Indus/Haṛappan Civilisation, and the art of writing, whether or not it was available or whether or not it was known to many people, seemed to be hardly practised at all in ancient India prior to about 300 BCE, evidenced by the Brāhmī-script engraved rock edicts of the Buddhist king, Aśoka. The Indus/Haṛappan Civilisation "script" has not yet been translated to the satisfaction of a majority of scholars and a minority of scholars label it "graffiti."

Since the evidence points to much international trade in the Indus/Haṛappan Civilisation, the chances of the traders being able to read "foreign writing" is quite high. This seems to be especially likely in the light of the high intelligence levels that the people of the Indus/Haṛappan Civilisation must have possessed to have invented and perfected the engineering, art and science that is clearly apparent in the archaeological remains. (For example, without writing, all of these engineering calculations had to be done in one's head, without the aid of pen or paper.) The chances of Indus/Haṛappan Civilisation international traders "borrowing" some "foreign characters" to make up at least a rudimentary Indus/Haṛappan Civilisation alphabet also seems to be fairly high. This theory, championed by S.R. Rao in 1982, and most of the other major theories on decipherment are summarised in a recent work, *The Decipherment of the Indus-Saraswati Script* by Karuna S. Shukla.[1]

Even the Greek philosopher, Plato, was a champion of memorisation and not writing. Plato wrote, concerning students and their trust in the written word, that external characters had no part of them and would discourage their memories.[2]

The Minority Theory of Graffiti

There is a minority of scholars who advance the theory that all of the Indus/Haṛappan Civilisation "script" is really "graffiti." The word "graffiti" originally meant scratched, and modernly is used to describe worldwide, spray-paint vandalism usually consisting of letters, numbers and other designs, as well as random marks.

The author has had the opportunity of personally viewing Indus/Haṛappan Civilisation seals at three museums in India, in Delhi, Mumbai and Lothal, and has formed the opinion that if the "graffiti scholars" are correct and the "marks" on those seals are "graffiti," then those "graffiti-artists" were among the best in the ancient world, and must have travelled extensively over the entire Indus/Haṛappan Civilisation realm, repeating similar-looking "graffiti" again and again over a 1,000 year period.

Indus/Haṛappan Civilisation Character Script

S.R. Rao, in his book, *New Frontiers of Archaeology*, theorises that in the early Indus/Haṛappan Civilisation script of about 4,000 to 4,500 years ago (2500-1900 BCE), the number of basic signs is 64 including 22 pictures and in late Haṛappan script 3,700 to 3,900 years ago (1900-1700 BCE), the number of basic signs gets reduced to 24.[3] In comparison with other languages, S.R. Rao compared

1. See Karuna S. Shukla, *The Decipherment of the Indus-Saraswati Script*, B.R. Publisher, 2007
2. See Jürgen Pieters, *Speaking with the Dead: Exploration in Literature and History*, Edinburgh University Press, 2005, p. 50.
3. See S.R. Rao, *New Frontiers of Archaeology*, Popular Prakashan, 1994, p. 32.

the basic cursive signs of the Indus script with those of a known phonetic script of 23 consonantal signs used about 3,300 to 3,600 years ago (fifteenth-eleventh century BCE) by the people speaking Phoenician, Hebrew, Aramaic and South Arabian languages. The result was that 17 signs in the two scripts are identical and he theorised that it was, therefore, reasonable to assign the phonetic value of the Semitic signs to the analogous basic cursive sign of the Late Haṛappan script and that the Indus/Haṛappan Civilisation language was close to Vedic Sanskrit.[4]

S.R. Rao's theory is actually very well explained, presented and mostly agreed with in a book called *A New Theory on the Origin and Evolution of Brahmi Alphabet* by A. Banerjee.[5] Other books which agree in part and disagree in part with S.R. Rao's theory include *Vedic Glossary on Indus Seals* by N. Jha,[6] *The Deciphered Indus Script* by N. Jha and N.S. Rajaram,[7] *Decipherment of the Indus-Brahmi Inscriptions of Chandraketugarh (Gangahrada): The Mohenjodaro of East India* by Sambhu Nath Mondal,[8] and *The Decipherment of the Indus-Saraswati Script* by Karuna S. Shukla.[9]

No Writing for "Social Control" Theory

For the *Manusmṛti* society, perhaps the emphasis on memorisation instead of writing was a means of "social control." Since the *Manusmṛti* seemed to codify the change from the *Ṛgveda* "non-fixed caste" to a "fixed caste" system, perhaps it was easier to

4. See S.R. Rao, *New Frontiers of Archaeology*, Popular Prakashan, 1994, p. 36.
5. See A. Banerjee, *A New Theory on the Origin and Evolution of Brahmi Alphabet*, Black and White, 2006.
6. See N. Jha, *Vedic Glossary on Indus Seals*, Ganga Kaveri, 1996.
7. See N. Jha and N.S. Rajaram, *The Deciphered Indus Script*, Aditya Prakashan, 2000.
8. See Sambhu Nath Mondal, *Decipherment of the Indus-Brahmi Inscriptions of Chandraketugarh (Gangahrada): The Mohenjodaro of East India*, S.P. Saha, 2006.
9. See Karuna S. Shukla, *The Decipherment of the Indus-Saraswati Script*, B.R. Publisher, 2007.

"keep people in line" by discouraging them to learn to read and write and possibly discovering for themselves what *R̥gveda* really said on the subject.

Since the Veda was considered to contain important and "magical" information, the "guarding" of such information was codified by the *Manusmr̥ti*, in chapter 2, verse 116, "But he who acquires without permission the Veda from one who recites it, incurs the guilt of stealing the Veda, and shall sink into hell."[10] The operative phrase here, in the opinion of the author, is "from one who recites it." Obviously, there did not exist the possibility of "stealing the Veda" from one who possessed a written copy, because there was no mention of writing.

There were no printing presses at the time of the *Manusmr̥ti* society, but if there were, the Veda would probably be the last thing that those "in control" would have wanted printed. Those "in control" at the time of the *Manusmr̥ti* society must have believed that knowledge was power and that it was better to keep the knowledge and power in the hands of the privileged few. The course of study to memorise the Vedas was very long. The *Manusmr̥ti* prescribed intense study, not to learn to write, but to learn to memorise, in chapter 3 verse 1, "The vow (of studying) the three Vedas under a teacher must be kept for 36 years, or for half that time, or for a quarter, or until the student has perfectly learnt them."[11] If one studies for 36 years, that is a long time, even if one begins in early childhood.

No Writing for Strengthening the Mind

Perhaps the *Manusmr̥ti* and Indus/Haṛappan Civilisation societies believed that memorisation kept the human mind strong and that learning to write would weaken the mind. This theory was later put forward by the Greek philosopher, Plato, when he said

10. See G. Buehler, *Laws of Manu*, Oxford (Sacred Books of the East, vol. XXV), 1896, p. 34.

11. Ibid., p. 51.

that trusting writing would discourage the use of a student's memory.[12]

"Bull" Connection of Ṛgveda, Manusmrti and Indus/Haṛappan Civilisation

Many of the drawings and carvings of the Indus/Haṛappan Civilisation were of bulls and there are references to the importance of bulls in *Ṛgveda* and in the *Manusmṛti.*

There are many references to the gods in *Ṛgveda* as bulls. This is one of the "links" that some scholars look to in order to theorise the connection between *Ṛgveda* and the Indus/Haṛappan Civilisation. In *Ṛgveda,* the god Agni, the god of fire, etc. to whom the largest number of Ṛgvedic hymns are addressed is sometimes referred to as a bull.[13] Female figures seem to be missing from the seals, for instance, it is the bull, not the cow which is depicted on the seals.[14] (This is in spite of the fact that the Indus/Haṛappan Civilisation was very dependent on dairy products.) These facts will be brought up again below when discussing the script of the Indus/Haṛappan Civilisation.

In the *Manusmṛti,* "justice" is personified as a bull in chapter 8, verse 16, "For divine justice (is said to be) a bull (*vṛṣa*). . . ."[15] Many animals are represented on Haṛappan seals; the unicorn seems to stand for the deified composite figure of the bull and the horse. The basic concepts about cosmology, society and state seem to be almost identical between the Indus people and the Ṛgvedic people.[16] This is a very interesting conclusion regarding the Indus/Haṛappan Civilisation.

12. See Jüergen Pieters, *Speaking with the Dead: Explorations in Literature and History,* Edinburgh University, 2005, p. 50.
13. See K.D. Sethna, *Karpasa in Prehistoric India,* Biblia Impex, 1981, p. 33.
14. See Bhagwan Singh, *The Vedic Harappans,* Aditya Prakashan, 1996, p. x.
15. See G. Buehler, *Laws of Manu,* Oxford (Sacred Books of the East, vol. XXV), 1896, p. 178.
16. See S.R. Rao, *New Frontiers of Archaeology,* Popular Prakashan, 1994, pp. 46-47.

Conclusion

The Indus/Haṛappan Civilisation carvings on seals may indicate *R̥gveda* representations of gods as bulls and/or the *Manusmr̥ti* representation of Justice as a bull. The language of *R̥gveda* is in a form of ancient Sanskrit and the *Manusmr̥ti* is in a more modern form of Sanskrit. The Indus/Haṛappan Civilisation written script could be ancient Sanskrit or related to ancient Sanskrit.

Appendix B
Theories Regarding Indus/Haṛappan Civilisation Script

SEVERAL Sanskrit-based theories regarding the Indus/Haṛappan Civilisation Script will now be examined using the definitions for Sanskrit characters and the shapes of Brāhmī, Devanāgarī, some Phoenician letters and some of the similar Indus/Haṛappan Civilisation "characters."

Yoga and Cakra Theory of Indus/Haṛappan Civilisation Script

Terracotta figures from the Indus/Haṛappan Civilisation in what we call today physical "*haṭha-yoga* postures" seem to give strong evidence that the Indus/Haṛappan Civilisation people practised *haṭha-yoga*.

Some modern philosophers in India believe that one corollary to *haṭha-yoga* practice is the *cakra* theory. There seems to exist some evidence that there were individuals in the Indus/Haṛappan Civilisation that also believed in *cakra* theory and perhaps also believed that *haṭha-yoga* enhanced the correct functioning of *cakra*s. The *cakra* theory is a theory that there are many invisible "wheels" in the human body (especially six major ones along the spine) that influence health. There is a different, yet related theory that the belief in *cakra* theory influenced the Sanskrit Devanāgarī script; this theory is presented in a book called *Unfolding the Petals*.[1]

The validity of *cakra* theory will not be examined here. Rather,

1. See David Teplitz, *Unfolding the Petals*, Humanities Press, 1982.

whether or not belief in this theory influenced modern Sanskrit Devanāgarī script, possibly its precursor, Sanskrit Brāhmī script, and possibly the script of the Indus/Harappan Civilisation. *Cakras* are defined by Monier-Williams as: a circle or depression of the body for mystical or chiromantic purposes; six in number, one above the other, viz.

1. *mūlādhāra*, the parts about the pubis;
2. *svādhiṣṭhāna*, the umbilical region;
3. *maṇi-pūra*, the *pitta* of the stomach or epigastrium;
4. *anāhata*, the root of the nose;
5. *viśuddha*, the hollow between the frontal sinuses;
6. *ājñākhya*, the fontanelle or union of the coronal and sagittal sutures;

various faculties and divinities are supposed to be present in these hollows.[2]

Once again, the point here is not to debate in this context whether or not *cakra* theory is correct or whether or not there are invisible energy "wheels" that influence human health. There is a chance that those responsible for the Indus script believed in *cakra* theory and that such theory influenced at least some of the Indus script characters, particularly semi-vowels.

According to John Woodroffe's translation of *Ṣaṭ-Cakra-Narūpaṇa*, certain *haṭha-yoga* positions may be able to take "energy," which is described as the *vajra* or thunderbolt from that first *cakra* and reach to the head.[3] The clearest example one can give is the well-known Indus/Haṛappan Civilisation engraving that many Westerners call "a horned-god." The engraving shows a man (or god) sitting on his heels with horns in the shape of a horizontal "3" "sprouting" out of his head.

---

2. See Monier-Williams, *A Sanskrit-English Dictionary*, Oxford, 1899.
3. See Arthur Avalon (Sir John Woodroffe), *Serpent Power*, Courier Dover, 1974, p. 1.

For those who believe in the combination of *haṭha-yoga* and *cakra* theory, sitting on one's heels, in addition to physical health benefits, aids in the correct functioning of the first *cakra* or "wheel" at the base of the spine. According to this theory, two other things will happen. One, the positively-influenced first *cakra* or "wheel" will make the physical organs nearby function better. Second, the positively-influenced first *cakra* or "wheel" will make more "energy" available to the body, especially to bring to the head far more advanced spiritual experiences. The proponents of this theory agree with John Woodroffe's translation of *Ṣaṭ-Cakra-Narūpaṇa*, describing that the *vajra* or thunderbolt from that first *cakra* can be encouraged to reach to the head. And once reaching the head, the individual's spiritual experience is like sprouting energy that could be depicted as horns "sprouting" from one's head.

Perhaps one of the messages from the Indus/Haṛappan Civilisation is that if one practises the *haṭha-yoga* position of sitting on one's heels, one may have a "spiritual experience" in one's head.

Sanskrit–Devanāgarī–Brāhmī Indus/Haṛappan Civilisation Script

All scholars now accept that the Sanskrit Brāhmī script is the precursor of the modern Sanskrit, called Devanāgarī or Nāgarī. The debate that is now going on among scholars is whether or not the script of the Indus/Haṛappan Civilisation and the later Brāhmī script are related.

The Sanskrit to English dictionary by Monier-Williams has definitions not only for words but also syllables.[4] If one accepts that the *Ṛgveda* with its river Sarasvatī flowing from the "mountains to the ocean" must have been present before the great earthquakes in 1900 BCE, then it is likely that the language of the Indus/Haṛappan Civilisation was related to some sort of

4. See Monier-Williams, *A Sanskrit-English Dictionary*, Oxford, 1899.

ancient Sanskrit. If that is so, then perhaps some insight can be gained by examining closely the definitions of each Sanskrit letter.

Cakra Theory and Semi-Vowels

The *cakra* theory, as described above, may relate to Sanskrit semi-vowels. The sounds of the *cakra*s are from the book, *Unfolding the Petals*.[5] The Devanāgarī alphabet is from the Monier-Williams dictionary.

The sound of the first *cakra* is *la* or *lam*. The Sanskrit semi-vowel *la* is defined by Monier-Williams as "Indra (lord of rain, sky) cutting," for instance, the "cutting" of one mountain to make two mountains. The Devanāgarī *la* looks like one mountain (from a distance) cut into two and looks like a handwriting *m*. The Phoenician *l* looks like a vertical line with either a rounded or angled hook on the end and apparently comes from lamd, or lamedh, a word for goad or hook, a good representation of which is in a book that shows alphabetic development, *Groundbreaking Scientific Experiments, Inventions, and Discoveries of the Ancient World* by Robert and Carolyn Krebs.[6] (The following Phoenician examples will be taken from that book.) The Brāhmī *la* is very similar to the Phoenician rounded hook.[7] (The following Brāhmī examples will be taken from Banerjee's book, *A New Theory on the Origin and Evolution of Brāhmī Alphabet*.) The angled Phoenician *l* is very similar to one Indus/Haṛappan Civilisation character and may represent *la* because it looked like a thunderbolt of Indra.

The sound of the second *cakra* is *va* or *vam*. The Sanskrit semi-vowel *va* is defined by Monier-Williams as "air, wind, Varuṇa

5. See David Teplitz, *Unfolding the Petals*, Humanities Press, 1982.

6. See Robert Krebs and Carolyn, *Groundbreaking Scientific Experiments, Inventions, and Discoveries of the Ancient World*, Greenwood, 2003, p. 94.

7. See A. Banerjee, *A New Theory on the Origin and Evolution of Brahmi Alphabet*, Black and White, 2006, p. 106.

(king of the gods and the ocean), water, to blow upon." The Devanāgarī *va* looks like circle on a vertical line, a hole one can blow through, and the Devanāgarī *ba* is the same with a diagonal line through the circle. (In some Latin American countries, there is little difference between Spanish *va* and *ba* sounds, just like similarities between the Devanāgarī *va* and *ba*.) The Brāhmī *va* looks like circle attached to a vertical line, the Brāhmī *ba* looks like a square and the Brāhmī *bha* looks like a square, open on the bottom, attached to a vertical line on top. There are some Indus/ Haṛappan Civilisation characters that look quite similar, circles and squares (open and closed, some divided with a line), some attached to a vertical line. The Phoenician "b" looks like a circle or triangle (open or closed) with a curved line attached and apparently comes from "bet," a word for house or tent, as in an architectural drawing.

The sound of the third *cakra* is *ra* or *ram*. The Sanskrit semi-vowel *ra* is defined by Monier-Williams as "acquiring, possessing, giving, effecting, fire, heat, love, brightness, splendour." The Devanāgarī character looks like an English capital "R" without the vertical line, which is similar to a flipped, squiggled, modified Brāhmī *ra*. The Phoenician "r" looks like a triangle with a vertical line attached, apparently coming from the word "resh, rush or res" for head. A rounded Phoenician *ra* is very similar to one Indus/ Haṛappan Civilisation character and may represent *ra* because it may have also looked like a stomach. The idea suggested by S.R. Rao that a human "stick figure" also represents *ra* is not clear.

The sound of the fourth *cakra* is *ya* or *yam*. The Sanskrit semi-vowel *ya* is defined by Monier-Williams as "goer or mover, wind, joining, restraining . . . meditation, of Lakṣmī (goddess of fortune and beauty)" perhaps influencing the English words "yoke" and "union." The Devanāgarī *ya* looks like a kind of yoke or heart. The Brāhmī character *ya* looks like a downward-facing arrow with a curved head. The Phoenician "y" looks similar to a rotated Devanāgarī *ya*. There are some Indus/Haṛappan Civilisation characters that look quite similar to the Brāhmī character *ya* and the Phoenician *ya*.

The sound of the fifth *cakra* is *ha* or *ham*. The Sanskrit sibilant *ha* is defined by Monier-Williams as "meditation, auspiciousness, sky, heaven, pleasure, delight, killing, destroying, removing, abandoning, deserting, avoiding." The Brāhṃī *ha* character is a vertical line with a type of "fish-hook" at the bottom (perhaps representing a throat), and the Devanāgarī *ha* character is somewhat similar, just much more ornate. The Phoenician "h" either looks like a type of "fence" with three lines, or a mirror-image, rotated English capital "E". There are some Indus/Haṛappan Civilisation characters that look quite similar to the Phoenician *ha*, although some are rotated upwards, like a representation of a "rake," some with more than the three "fingers."

The sound of the sixth *cakra* is *oṁ* or *auṁ*. Here the analysis could be similar or could be different. Is the "3" rotated horizontally on Indus/Haṛappan Civilisation figure the same as the "3" figure that is recognised as the Devanāgarī *oṁ*?

Vowel Character "A" Analysis

The Sanskrit vowel *a* is defined by Monier-Williams as "a prefix having a negative or contrary sense, occasionally comparison and sometimes disparagement, sometimes diminutiveness" and the Sanskrit vowel *A* as "a particle of reminiscence, also of compassion or pain, a prefix of verbs, near, near to, towards, with some verb-roots reverses the action, out of, from among, towards, to, as far as, from, in, at, on." The Devanāgarī character is a "3" attached to a vertical line. The Phoenician *a* looks like a rotated English "v" with a line across the top, a stylised version of the head of an ox which apparently was its origin. The Brāhmī *ha* character is similar. There are many Indus/Haṛappan Civilisation characters that look quite similar to the Phoenician "a," although most are rotated with the middle of the "v" empty, in the famous "jar" shape.

Other vowels are more difficult to decipher, although the three dots of the Brāhmī *i* character are similar to many Indus/ Haṛappan Civilisation characters.

Consonant Character Analysis

The Sanskrit guttural consonant *ka* is defined by Monier-Williams as "splendour, light. . . ." The Brāhmī *ka* character is just a cross, and the Devanāgarī character is a cross with two almost-completed circles for arms. The phoenician "k" looks like a mirror-image, rotated English "k," with the ends pointing either to the left or upwards. There are similar Indus/Haṛappan Civilisation characters.

The Sanskrit guttural consonant *kha* is defined by Monier-Williams as "a cavity, hollow, cave or an aperture of the human body (of which there are nine, the mouth, the two ears, the two eyes, the two nostrils, and the organs of excretion and generation)." The Brāhmī *kha* character is a circle with a hook on top, similar to the Brāhmī *va* character. The Devanāgarī *kha* character is a combination of the *ra* and *va* characters. There are similar Indus/Haṛappan Civilisation characters.

The Sanskrit guttural consonant *ga* is defined by Monier-Williams as "going, moving." The Phoenician "g" character is an upside down "V" or outlined "V". The Brāhmī *ga* character is almost exactly the same. The Devanāgarī *ga* character is different. There are similar Indus/Haṛappan Civilisation characters.

The Sanskrit guttural consonant *gha* is defined by Monier-Williams as "(used to lay stress on a word) at least, surely, verily, indeed." The Brāhmī *gha* character is a vertical line with a double "foot" to the right. The Devanāgarī *gha* character looks like the Brāhmī *gha* character rotated 90 degrees. There are similar Indus/ Haṛappan Civilisation characters.

The Sanskrit guttural consonant *nga* (*Ga*) is defined by Monier-Williams as "an object of sense; desire for any sensual object." The Brāhmī *nga* character looks like the left half of a squarish parenthesis. The Devanāgarī *nga* character looks like an "S" with an overemphasis on the bottom circle. There are similar Indus/Haṛappan Civilisation characters.

The Sanskrit palatal consonant *ca* is defined by Monier-Williams as "and, both, also, moreover, as well as, moving to and fro." The Brāhmī *ca* character is similar, just the triangle has changed to a half-circle. The Devanāgarī *ca* character is a more stylised version of the Brāhmī. There are similar Indus/Haṛappan Civilisation characters.

The Sanskrit palatal consonant *cha* is defined by Monier-Williams as "dividing; a fragment, pure, clean; a mark, sign." The Brāhmī *cha* character is less similar, the half-circle is now on both sides of the vertical line. The Devanāgarī *cha* character is a more stylised, rotated version of the Brāhmī. There are similar Indus/Haṛappan Civilisation characters.

The Sanskrit palatal consonant *ja* is defined by Monier-Williams as "born, produced or caused by." The Brāhmī *ja* character is like a backwards "3" and the Devanāgarī *ja* character is just like one part of the "3" rotated 90 degrees. There are similar Indus/Haṛappan Civilisation characters.

The Sanskrit palatal consonant *jha* is defined by Monier-Williams as "asleep, playing a tune, beating time, a jingling, clanking." The Brāhmī *jha* character is like a mirror-image, upside down English "h" and the Devanāgarī *jha* character is a type of English "S". There are similar Indus/Haṛappan Civilisation characters.

The Sanskrit palatal nasal consonant *jña* is defined by Monier-Williams as "a singer, a jingling sound, an ox, the planet Śukra." The Brāhmī *jña* character is an upside-down version of the Brāhmī *jha* character. The Devanāgarī *jña* is a half circle attached to the left of a vertical line. There are similar Indus/Haṛappan Civilisation characters.

The Sanskrit cerebral consonant *ta* is defined by Monier-Williams as "sound, a dwarf, a quarter, 4th". The Brāhmī *ta* character is like a capital "C" and the Devanāgarī *ta* is like a small "c." There are similar Indus/Haṛappan Civilisation characters.

The Sanskrit cerebral consonant *tha* is defined by Monier-Williams as "a loud noise; the moon's disk." The Brāhmī *tha* character is a circle without a dot in the middle and the Devanāgarī *tha* is a circle, like a small "o." There are similar Indus/Haṛappan Civilisation characters.

The Sanskrit cerebral consonant *da* is defined by Monier-Williams as "a sound, a kind of drum, a basket, etc. carried by a sling." The Brāhmī *da* character is like a mirror-image square "h," missing one bottom leg. The Devanāgarī *da* is another one of those capital "S" forms. There are similar Indus/Haṛappan Civilisation characters.

The Sanskrit cerebral consonant *dha* is defined by Monier-Williams as "a large drum." The Brāhmī *dha* character looks just like a capital "D" and the Devanāgarī *dha* is a half-circle with a tiny circle at its foot, like a very small "o." It does look similar to the cerebral Phoenician "t" letter. There are similar Indus/Haṛappan Civilisation characters.

The Sanskrit cerebral nasal consonant *na* is defined by Monier-Williams as "knowledge, a water-house." The Brāhmī *na* character looks just like a capital "I" and the Devanāgarī *na* is either a *ra* with a small and larger vertical line following, or an upside-down "u" with a vertical line following. There are similar Indus/Haṛappan Civilisation characters.

The Sanskrit dental consonant *ta* is defined by Monier-Williams as "a tail, the breast, the womb, crossing." The Brāhmī *ṭa* is like an upside-down "Y". It does look similar to the Phoenician "" letter. The Devanāgarī *ṭa* is like a mirror-image, small "h." There are similar Indus/Haṛappan Civilisation characters.

The Sanskrit dental consonant *ṭha* is defined by Monier-Williams as "a mountain, sign of danger." The Brāhmī dental *ṭha* character is a circle with a dot in the middle but the Devanāgarī dental *ṭha* is a half-circle, a backwards "c" with a small "o" at the top and the whole thing connected to a vertical line. There are similar Indus/Haṛappan Civilisation characters.

The Sanskrit dental consonant *ḍa* is defined by Monier-Williams as "giving, offering, a gift, a mountain." The Phoenician "d" is a triangle that points left. The Devanāgarī *ḍa* is like a small "c" with small vertical lines coming from the beginning and end of the "c." The Brāhmī *ḍa* is almost mirror-image of the Devanāgarī. There are similar Indus/Haṛappan Civilisation characters.

The Sanskrit dental consonant *ḍha* is defined by Monier-Williams as "placing, putting, holding, having, bestowing, granting, virtue, merit, wealth, property." The Brāhmī *ḍha* character looks just like a capital "D" and the Devanāgarī dental *ḍha* is a slanted "3" with a tiny circle at its beginning, like a very small "o." There are similar Indus/Haṛappan Civilisation characters.

The Sanskrit dental nasal consonant *ṇa* is defined by Monier-Williams as "no, not, knowledge, . . . unbroken." The Brāhmī dental *ṇa* character looks just like a capital "I" without the top line and the Devanāgarī dental *ṇa* is a horizontal line going left with a tiny circle at the end. There are similar Indus/Haṛappan Civilisation characters.

The Sanskrit palatal *pa* consonant is defined by Monier-Williams as "drinking, guarding, protecting, ruling, wind." The Brāhmī palatal *pa* is an upside-down "candy cane" with its hook to the right. The Devanāgarī palatal *pa* is more like a mirror-image of the Indus *pa*, or a mirror-image, upside-down Brāhmī *pa*. There are similar Indus/Haṛappan Civilisation characters.

The Sanskrit palatal *pha* consonant is defined by Monier-

Williams as "swelling, flowing, bubbling, boiling." The Brāhmī *pha* is like the Brāhmī *pha* with a more pronounced "hook." The Devanāgarī *pha* is like the Devanāgarī *pa* with an extra hook on the right. There are similar Indus/Haṛappan Civilisation characters.

The Sanskrit palatal *ba* consonant has been covered above.

The Sanskrit palatal *bha* consonant is defined by Monier-Williams as "of the planet Venus (Śukra, which also means clear, bright, seed), light or beam of light. The Devanāgarī *bha* has little circles on two sides of the square. The Brāhmī *bha* is related to both, a square with one side open, attached to a vertical line. There are similar Indus/Haṛappan Civilisation characters.

The Sanskrit palatal *ma* is defined by Monier-Williams as "me, mother, to measure, time, the moon." The Devanāgarī *ma* looks like a stylised version of the Indus "*ma*-tweezer" character. The Brāhmī *ma* character looks like the Indus "*ma*-tweezer" character rotated 90 degrees and more rounded. There are similar Indus/Haṛappan Civilisation characters.

The semi-vowels were discussed above.

The Sanskrit sibilant *śa* is defined by Monier-Williams as *śastra*, Śiva, *śam*". The Devanāgarī *śa* looks like a large number 2" and a vertical line. The Brāhmī *śa* character looks like the head of a very large arrow (just the lines). There are similar Indus/Haṛappan Civilisation characters.

The Sanskrit sibilant *ṣa* is defined by Monier-Williams as best, excellent, wise . . . eternal happiness, final emancipation, heaven, paradise, sleep." For the Indus *ṣa* see *śa* above. The Devanāgarī *sa* character looks like an upside-down, mirror-image n" with a diagonal line through the body of the character. The Brāhmī "sa" looks like a mirror-image "J" with a left "hook." There are similar Indus/Haṛappan Civilisation characters.

The Sanskrit sibilant *ṣa* is defined by Monier-Williams as "a lake, air, wind, a bird, of Viṣṇu or Śiva, knowledge, meditation.

. . ." The Devanāgarī *ṣa* character looks like the Devanāgarī *ma* character with an extra line on the left bottom. The Brāhmī *ṣa* looks like the above mirror-image "J" with an extra small right hand horizontal line. There are similar Indus/Haṛappan Civilisation characters.

The Sanskrit sibilant *ha* was discussed above.

Appendix C
Sanskrit Character Definitions

Sanskrit to English Dictionary: Summary of Syllables Defined by Monier-Williams

EXAMINING Monier-Williams' Sanskrit syllables may shed some light on the possible relationship between Sanskrit and the script of the Indus/Haṛappan Civilisation.

a – a prefix having a negative or contrary sense, occasionally comparison and sometimes disparagement, sometimes diminutiveness.

ā – a particle of reminiscence, also of compassion or pain, a prefix of verbs, near, near to, towards, with some verb-roots reverses the action, out of, from among, towards, to, as far as, from, in, at, on.

i – an interjection of anger, calling, sorrow, distress, compassion, to go, to walk, to flow, to blow, to advance, spread, get about, to go to or towards, come, to go away, escape, pass, retire, to arise from, come from, to come back again, return, to succeed, to arrive at, reach, obtain, fall into, come to, to approach with prayers, gain by asking, to undertake anything, to be employed in, go on with, continue in any condition or relation, to go quickly or repeatedly, to come, wander, run, spread, get about, to appear, make one's appearance, to approach anyone with requests, to ask, request, to cause to go or escape.

ī – Kandarpa, the god of love, Lakṣmī, an interjection of pain or anger, a particle implying consciousness or perception, consideration, compassion.

u – an interjection of compassion, anger, a particle implying assent, calling, command, an enclitic copula used frequently in the Vedas as a particle implying restriction and antithesis, and also further, on the other hand, this very person, now, to call to, hail, to roar, bellow, of Brahmā.

ū – an interjection of calling to, of compassion, a particle implying promise to protect, helping, protecting, the moon, of Śiva.

ṛ – an interjection expressing laughter, a particle implying abuse, in heaven, to go, move, rise, tend upwards, to go towards, meet with, fall upon or into, reach, obtain, to fall to one's share, occur, befall, advance towards a foe, attack, invade, to hurt, offend, to move, excite, erect, raise, to cause to move, throw, cast, to pierce, to put in or upon, place, insert, fix into or upon, fasten, to apply, to direct or turn towards, to deliver up, surrender, offer reach over, present, give, to give back, restore, to move or go towards, with speed or zeal, to wander about, haste towards.

e – an interjection, a particle of recollection, addressing, censure, contempt, compassion, Viṣṇu, to come near or towards, go near, approach, to come back, come again to, to reach, attain, enter, come into, to submit, fall to one's share, to hasten near, to request.

ai – an interjection, a particle of addressing, summoning, remembering.

o – an interjection, a particle of addressing, calling, reminiscence, of compassion, Brahmā.

au – an interjection, a particle of addressing, calling, prohibition, ascertainment, a sound, the Setu or sacred syllable of the śūdras, of the earth.

ka – of *Brahman*, of Viṣṇu; of Yama; a particular comet; the sun; fire; splendour, light; air; a peacock; the body; time; wealth; sound; a king, n. happiness, joy, pleasure; water; the head; hair, a head of hair.

– interrog. pron., who? which? what? may express "how is it possible that?" "what power have I, you, they, etc.?" or with the potential.

kā – to seek, desire, yearn, love; to like, enjoy, be satisfied with, to please, be sought after, satisfy.

kha – a cavity, hollow, cave, cavern, aperture; an aperture of the human body (of which there are nine, viz. the mouth, the two ears, the two eyes, the two nostrils, and the organs of excretion and generation), the hole made by an arrow, wound; the hole in the nave of a wheel through which the axis runs; vacuity, empty space, air, ether, sky; *Brahman* (the Supreme Spirit); the *anusvāra* represented by a circle (*bindu*); n. of the tenth astrological mansion; a city; a field; happiness (a meaning derived from *su-kha*) action; understanding, f. a fountain, well.

ga – going, moving, going in a carriage, going quickly; having sexual intercourse with, reaching to; staying, being, abiding in; relating to or standing in connection with going, moving.

gā – to go, go towards, come, approach; to go after, pursue; to fall to one's (dat.) share, undergo, obtain; to go away; to come to an end; to walk, to be born.

gha – a rattling or gurgling or tinkling sound; a bell; f. a tinkling ornament worn by women round the waist; at least, surely, verily, indeed, especially; striking, killing.

ga – an object of sense; desire for any sensual object.

ca – and, both, also, moreover, as well as, moving to and fro; mischievous, seedless, a thief; the moon, a tortoise; Śiva; occasionally {ca} is disjunctive, "but," "on the contrary," "on the other hand," yet, "nevertheless."

cha – dividing; a fragment, pure, clean, tremulous, unsteady, covering, concealing; a mark, sign.

ja – born, produced; offspring pl. descendants; speedy, swift; victorious; eaten; speed; enjoyment; light, lustre; poison; born or descended from, produced or caused by, born or produced in or at or upon, growing in, living at; prepared from, made of or with; "belonging to, connected with, peculiar to," a son of; father; birth; f. a race tribe, a daughter, Viṣṇu, Śiva.

jha – asleep, playing a tune, beating time, a sound like the splashing of water or clashing of symbols, jingling, clanking, wind accompanied by rain, anything lost or mislaid, Bṛhaspati, a waterfall.

jña – a singer, a jingling sound, a heretic, an ox, the planet Śukra".

ta – sound, a dwarf, a quarter, 4th, the earth, an oath, confirming an assertion by ordeal.

tha – a loud noise (an imitative sound as of a golden pitcher rolling down steps); the moon's disk; a disk; a cypher; a place frequented by all; Śiva.

da – a sound, a kind of drum, submarine fire, Śiva, a Ḍākinī, a basket, etc. carried by a sling.

dha – an imitative sound, a large drum, a dog, a dog's tail, a serpent.

na – knowledge, certainty, ascertainment, ornament, a water-house, a bad man, of Śiva or of Buddha, the sound of negation, gift.

ṭa – a tail (esp. of a jackal), the breast, the womb, the hip, a warrior, a thief, a wicked man, a *mleccha*, a Buddha, a jewel, nectar, crossing, virtue, Lakṣmī.

ṭā – impassableness, insurmountableness, inaccessibility; inviolability, indisposition, sickness.

ṭha – a mountain, a protector, sign of danger, a disease, eating, preservation, fear, an auspicious prayer.

ḍa – giving, granting, offering, effecting, producing, a gift, a wife, heat, pain.

ḍā – to give, bestow, grant, yield, impart, present, offer to (to give (a daughter) in marriage; to hand over; to give back, to pay (*daṇḍam*), a fine, a debt, to give up, cede (*āsanam*) "one's seat" (to give up the road, allow to pass); to sell (with instr. of the price); to sacrifice {*ātmānam*} "one's self," to give one's self up to grief; to offer (an oblation, etc.); to communicate, teach, utter (blessings, give (answer (*prativacas*), speak (*satyaṁvacas*) the truth, to address a speech to; to permit, allow; to permit sexual intercourse; to place, put, apply; to add, to grant a boon, to cause grief, to give room or space, allow to enter, "to spare anyone's life," to slap with the palms of the hands, to strike with the palm, to beat time with the hands, to make a sign; to make an appointment, to propose an agreement, to compare with, to proclaim with the drum, to make a noise, call out, to utter a curse, to embrace, to jump, to accomplish, to give battle, fight with, to give an order, command, (*darśanam*), to show one's self, to fix the eyes on, listen, to set on fire (*agni*), to consume by fire, to draw a bolt, to cause to give or be given, cause to bestow or present or give up, oblige to pay, make, restore, to cause to be made known, to wish to give in marriage.

ḍha – placing, putting, holding, possessing, having, bestowing, granting, causing, of Brahmā or Kubera, virtue, merit, wealth, property.

ḍhā – to put, place, set, lay in or on, to inflict punishment on, to put one's foot in another's footstep, i.e. imitate, to take or bring or help to, fix or resolve upon; to destine for, bestow on, present or impart to, to be given or granted, fall to one's lot or share; to make, produce, generate, create, cause, effect, perform, execute; to seize, take hold of, hold, bear, support, wear, put on (clothes), to accept, obtain, conceive (esp. in the womb), get, take, to take pleasure or delight in; to assume, have, possess, show, exhibit, incur, undergo, to wish to put in or lay on; Old Sax. (duan), Angl. Sax. (don), Engl. (do); Germ. (tuan); (tuon), (thun).

ṇa – not, no, nor, neither, it is not so; thin, spare; vacant, empty; identical; unvexed, unbroken; m. band, fetter; jewel, pearl; war; gift; welfare; name of Buddha; name of Gaṇeśa; f. the navel; a musical instrument; knowledge.

pa – drinking, guarding, protecting, ruling, wind, a leaf.

pā – to drink, quaff, suck, sip, swallow; to imbibe, draw in, appropriate, enjoy, feast upon (with the eyes, ears, etc.), to drink up, exhaust, absorb; to drink intoxicating liquors, to cause to drink, give to drink, to drink greedily or repeatedly, to watch, keep, preserve; to protect from, defend against; to protect (a country) i.e. rule, govern; to observe, notice, attend to, follow; keeping, protecting, guarding, etc.

pha – manifest, a gale, swelling, gaping, gain, flowing, bubbling, boiling, angry or idle speech.

phā – heat; idle talk.

ba – Varuṇa, Sindhu, *bhaga, gandana, vapana*.

bha – of the planet Venus, delusion, error, light or beam of light, lustre, appearance, resemblance, likeness, a star, planet, lunar mansion.

bhā – to shine, be bright or luminous; to shine forth, appear, show one's self; to be splendid or beautiful or eminent, to appear as, seem, look like, pass for, to show, exhibit, manifest, light, brightness, splendour.

ma – 1,000 names of Rāma, a metre, 1st personal pronoun, time, poison, a magic formula, the moon, of various gods, a mother, measure, authority, light, knowledge, binding, fettering, death, a woman's waist, happiness, welfare, water.

mā – to sound, bellow, roar, bleat (esp. said of cows, calves, goats, etc.) . . . to measure, mete out, mark off; to measure across = traverse; compare with "to be large or long enough for," to find room or be contained in; to measure out, apportion, grant; to help anyone to anything; to prepare, arrange, fashion, form, build, make; to show, display, exhibit, he displayed or developed himself, to infer, conclude; to pray, to cause to be measured or built, measure, build, erect; Lat. (metior), (mensus), (mensura);

ya – who or which, in which of many ways, goer or mover, wind, joining, restraining, fame, barley, light, abandoning, going, a car, restraining, meditation, attaining, pudendum muliebre, of Lakīmīra.

ra – acquiring, possessing, giving, effecting, fire, heat, love, desire, speed, amorous play, giving, gold, going, motion, brightness, splendour.

rā – to grant, give, bestow, impart, yield, surrender.

la – name of Indra, cutting.

lā – to take, receive, obtain; to undertake, begin; the act of taking or beginning.

va – air, wind, the arm, name of Varuṇa, the ocean, water, addressing, reverence, conciliation, auspiciousness, a dwelling, a tiger, cloth, the esculent root of the waterlily, going, hurting, an arrow, weaving, a weaver, a Varuṇa strong, powerful.

vā – to blow (as the wind); to procure or bestow anything by blowing; to blow towards or upon; to emit an odour, be diffused (as perfume); to smell; to hurt, injure; Lat. (ventus); Eng. (wind).

śa – *śastra*, Śiva, Śam.

ṣa – best, excellent, wise, learned, loss, destruction, loss of knowledge, end, term, rest, remainder, eternal happiness, final emancipation, heaven, paradise, sleep, a learned man, teacher, a nipple, the embryo, patience, endurance.

sa – a snake, air, wind, a bird, of Viṣṇu or Śiva, of Lakṣmī or Gaurī, knowledge, meditation, a carriage road, a fence, an inseparable prefix expressing "junction," "conjunction," "possession," "similarity," "equality"; and when compounded with nouns to form adjectives and adverbs it may be translated by "with," "together or along with," "accompanied by," "added to," "having," "possessing," "containing," "having the same"; "angrily," "fraudulently"; Lat. (sim) in (simplex); (simper) Eng. (same).

sā – giving, bestowing, granting.

ha – a form of Śiva or Bhairava, water, a cipher, meditation, auspiciousness, sky, heaven, paradise, blood, dying, fear, knowledge, the moon, Viṣṇu, war, battle, a horse, pride, a physician, cause, motive, laughter, coition, a lute, Supreme Spirit, pleasure, delight, a weapon, the sparkling of a gem, calling, the sound of a lute, mad, drunk, indeed, assuredly, verily, of course, then, killing, destroying, removing, abandoning, deserting, avoiding.

hā – an exclamation expressive of pain, anger, astonishment, satisfaction, etc.; to start or spring forward, bound away, give way to, to leave, abandon, desert, quit, forsake, relinquish "to die"; to discharge, emit; to put away, take off, remove, lay aside, give up, renounce, resign, avoid, shun, abstain or refrain from; to disregard, neglect; to lose, be deprived of; to get rid of, escape from; to cause to emit, "to cause to break wind," to be left or abandoned or deserted, etc.; to be left behind, fall short of; to be excluded from or bereft of "to die"; to be overtaken by; to be deficient or wanting, suffer loss or injury, fail (also in a lawsuit), decrease, wane, decline, come to an end; to weigh less; to omit, neglect; to fall short of, be wanting in; to give up "life"; to lose "time"; to abandon "a thesis."

Bibliography

Agrawal (ed.), *In Search of Vedic-Harappan Relationship*, Aryan Books International, 2005.

Bisht, R.S., *Dholavira*, in N. Lahiri (ed.), *The Decline and Fall of the Indus Civilization*, Permanent Black, 2000.

Bryant, T. Edwin, *The Quest for the Origins of Vedic Culture: The Indo-Aryan Migration Debate*, 2001.

Buehler, G., *Laws of Manu*, Oxford (Sacred Books of the East, vol. xxv), 1896.

Cannon, Garland (ed.), *The Letters of Sir William Jones*, vol. II, 794-800, 821, Oxford, 1970.

Chakrabarti, D.K., *The External Trade of the Indus Civilization*, Munshiram Manoharlal, 1990.

Dhavalikar, M.K., *The Aryans: Myth and Archaeology*, Munshiram Manoharlal, 2007.

Doniger, Wendy and Brian K. Smith, *The Laws of Manu*, Penguin Classics, 1991.

Dube, Sita Ram (ed.), *Vedic Culture and Its Continuity*, Pratibha Prakashan, 2006.

Dutt, M.N., *Manusmṛti*, 1895, Chaukhamba Sanskrit Pratishthan, 1998.

Ghosal, Pranati, *Lifestyle of the Vedic People*, D.K. Printworld, 2006.

Feuerstein, Georg, Subhash Kak, and David Frawley, *In Search of the Cradle of Civilization*, Delhi: Motilal Banarsidass, 1999.

Frawley, David and Vasant Lad, *The Yoga of Herbs*, Lotus Press, 1986.

Gaur, Aniruddh Singh, *Harappan Maritime Legacies of Gujarat*, Asian Publication Services, 2000.

Griffith, Ralph, *Hymns of the Rig Veda*, 1889, Munshiram Manoharlal, 1999.

Head, John W. and Yanping Wang, *Law Codes in Dynastic China: A Synopsis of Chinese Legal History in the Thirty Centuries From Zhou to Qing*, Durham, North Carolina: Carolina Academic Press, 2005.

Hopkins, Edward Washburn, *The Religions of India*, Ginn and Co., 1895.

Huxley, Andrew, *Buddhist Case Law on Theft: The Vinītavatthu on the Second Pārājika*, Law Department, School of Oriental and African Studies, University of London, 1999.

Jha, Ganganath, *Manusmṛti with the Manubhāṣya of Medhātithi*, Motilal Banarsidass, 1st edn. 1920-39; 2nd, 1999.

Jha, N.S. and N.S. Rajaram, *Deciphered Indus Script*, Aditya Prakashan, 2000.

Jones, William, *The Works of Sir William Jones* (The Institutes of Hindu Law or The Ordinances of Manu According to the Closs of Caluuca), G.G. and J. Robinson, 1794.

See Joseph, Gorge Gheverghese, *The Crest of the Peacock, The Non-European Roots of Mathematics*, Princeton University Press, 2000.

Kak, Subhash, "Birth and Early Development of Indian Astronomy", in H. Selin (ed.), *Astronomy across Cultures, The History of Non-Western Astronomy*, Kluwer Academic Publisher, 2000.

Kenoyer, Jonathan Mark, *Ancient Cities of the Indus Valley Civilization*, Oxford University Press, 1998.

Kramer, Samuel Noah, *History Begins at Sumer*, University of Pennsylvania Press, 1956, 1981.

———, *Sumerian Mythology: A Study of Spiritual and Literary Achievement in the Third Millennium* BCE, University of Pennsylvania Press Philadelphia, 1944, revised 1961.

Kutty, E.T. Sankaran, *A Glimpse on Sruti*, Bharatiya Vidya Bhavan, 2006.

———, *A Glimpse on Smriti*, Bharatiya Vidya Bhavan, 2006.

Lad, Vasant Dattatray, *Textbook of Ayurveda*, Ayurveda Press, 2002.

Lahiri, Nayanjot (ed.), *The Decline and Fall of the Indus Civilization*, Permanent Black, 2000.

Lal, B.B., "Search for Vedic-Harappan Relationship — New Perspectives" in Agrawal (ed.), *In Search of Vedic-Harappan Relationship*, Aryan Books International, 2005.

———, *The Homeland of the Aryans, Evidence of Rigvedic Flora and Fauna and Archaeology*, Aryan Books International, 2005.

———, *The Sarasvatī Flows On*, Aryan, 2002.

Mondal, Sambhu Nath, *Decipherment of the Indus-Brahmi Inscriptions of Chandraketugarh (Gangahrada): The Mohenjodaro of East India*, S.P. Saha, 2006.

McCrindle, J.W., *Ancient India as Described by Megasthenes and Arrian*, Thacker, Spink, and Co., 1877.

McIntosh, Jane, *A Peaceful Realm, The Rise and Fall of the Indus Civilization*, Westview Press, 2002.

Monier-Williams, *A Sanskrit-English Dictionary*, Oxford, 1899.

———, *An English-Sanskrit Dictionary*, Oxford, 1899.

Muss-Arnolt, William, "Some Babylonian Laws", in *Assyrian and Babylonian Literature: Selected Transactions*, with a Critical Introduction by Robert Francis Harper (New York: D. Appleton and Company, 1904).

Olivelle, Patrick, *Manu's Code of Law: A Critical Edition and Translation of the Mānava-Dharmaśāstra*, South Asia Research, 2005.

Pandit, M.D., *Mathematics as Known to the Vedic Samhitas*, Sri Satguru Publications, 1993.

Possehl, Gregory L., *The Indus Civilization*, Rowman Altamira, 2002.

Ragozin, Zenaide A., *History of Vedic India*, 1984, rept. 2003.

Rajaram, N.S., *Sarasvati River and the Vedic Civilization: History, Science and Politics*, 2006.

Rao, S.R., *New Frontiers of Archaeology*, Popular Prakashan, 1994.

Ratnagar, Shereen, *Trading Encounters from the Euphrates to the Indus in the Bronze Age*, Oxford University Press, 2006.

Ray, Himanshu Prabha, *The Archaeology of Seafaring in Ancient South Asia*, pp. 80-81, Cambridge University Press, 2003.

Sankalia, H.D., *Pre-Historic Art in India*, Carolina Academic Press, 1978.

Sarup, Lakshman (ed.), *The Nighantu and The Nirukta: The Oldest Indian Treatise on Etymology, Philology and Semantics*, Motilal Banarsidass, 2002.

Selin, Helaine (ed.), *Astronomy across Cultures: The History of Non-Western Astronomy*, Kluwer Academic Publishers, 2000.

Sethna, K.D., *Karpasa in Prehistoric India*, Biblia Impex, 1981.

———, *The Problem of Aryan Origins*, S&S Publishers, 1980.

Sharma, D.P., *Early Harappans and Indus-Sarasvatī Civilization*, vol. 1, 2006.

Sharma, D.P. and Madhuri, *Harappan Civilization*, New Delhi: Kaveri Books, 2003.

Sharma, R.S., *Looking for the Aryans*, Orient Longman, 1995.

Shendge, Malati J., *The Aryas: Facts without Fancy and Fiction*, New Delhi: Abhinav Publications, 1996.

Singh, Bhagwan, *The Vedic Harappans*, Aditya Prakashan, 1996.

Singh, Shivaji, "Vedic Culture and Its Continuity: Paradigm and Dimensions", in Sita Ram Dube (ed.), *Vedic Culture and Its Continuity*, Pratibha Prakashan, 2006.

Sucharitkul, Sompong, "Thai Law and Buddhist Law", *American Journal of Comparative Law*, vol. XLVI, 1998.

Verma, Shri Ram, *Vedas: The Source of Ultimate Science*, Nag Publishers, 2005.

Index